Interculturalism

Also by Ted Cantle

COMMUNITY COHESION: A New Framework for Race and Diversity

Interculturalism

The New Era of Cohesion and Diversity

Ted Cantle

Institute of Community Cohesion (iCoCo), UK

palgrave
macmillan

First published 2012 by
PALGRAVE MACMILLAN

Palgrave Macmillan in the UK is an imprint of Macmillan Publishers Limited, registered in England, company number 785998, of Houndmills, Basingstoke, Hampshire RG21 6XS.

Palgrave Macmillan in the US is a division of St Martin's Press LLC, 175 Fifth Avenue, New York, NY 10010.

Palgrave Macmillan is the global academic imprint of the above companies and has companies and representatives throughout the world.

Palgrave® and Macmillan® are registered trademarks in the United States, the United Kingdom, Europe and other countries.

ISBN 978–1–137–02748–1 hardback
ISBN 978–1–137–02746–7 paperback

This book is printed on paper suitable for recycling and made from fully managed and sustained forest sources. Logging, pulping and manufacturing processes are expected to conform to the environmental regulations of the country of origin.

A catalogue record for this book is available from the British Library.

A catalog record for this book is available from the Library of Congress.

10   9   8   7   6   5   4   3   2   1
21   20   19   18   17   16   15   14   13   12

Printed and bound in Great Britain by
CPI Antony Rowe, Chippenham and Eastbourne

Contents

List of Tables   vii

1 **Introduction**   1

2 **Globalisation and 'Super Diversity'**   4
   The dimensions of globalisation   6
   Cohesion and solidarity – the 'paradox of diversity'   12
   Globalisation and identity   18
   From tribal to international affinities   23

3 **Reforming the Notion of Identity**   30
   The changing national context of identity   31
   'Mixed race': the legacy of racial constructs   37
   Muslim communities and retrenchment   42
   Multiple, dynamic and choice-based identities   47

4 **The 'Failure' of Multiculturalism**   53
   Early and 'defensive' forms of multiculturalism   54
   Progressive multiculturalism   63
   'State multiculturalism'   68
   Multiculturalism and 'race'   77
   Far Right and populist appeal   82
   The transition of multiculturalism to interculturalism   88

5 **The Contribution of 'Community Cohesion'**   91
   Conceptual and practical development   92
   Cohesion and interaction   102
   Developing a commitment to cohesion and a new
      narrative of place   105

6 **Segregation and Integration – And Why They Matter**   112
   The domains of segregation and integration   113
   Spatial segregation and integration   116
   Social and cultural segregation and integration   129
   Functional segregation and integration   132
   Values and segregation and integration   136

7 **Interculturalism: Conceptualisation**   **141**
  The concept of interculturalism   141
  Interculturality and intercultural dialogue   143
  Perspectives of interculturalism   152
  Interculturalism and openness   158
  Interculturalism and difference   163
  Towards interculturalism   171

8 **Interculturalism: Policy and Practice**   **176**
  Leadership and vision   176
  The politics of identity   181
  Secularism and governance in multifaith societies   188
  Responding to segregation and integration   194
  The development of cultural navigational skills and
    intercultural competences   206

Notes   213

Bibliography   215

Index   229

Tables

2.1 Most important element of identity: UK SET 2011   19
4.1 Components of multiculturalism and interculturalism
     and characteristics of a cohesive society   89
6.1 The domains of segregation and integration   115
7.1 Migration policy index III   159
7.2 Indicators of city openness   164
7.3 Total recorded hate crime in England, Wales and
     Northern Ireland (2009)   166

1
Introduction

We cannot stop the process of globalisation: the world is more interconnected than ever before. Indeed, the pace of change will probably accelerate as political, economic and social networks become more intertwined and interdependent. But change will not be easy, and tensions and conflicts are inevitable as many cultures, faiths, value systems and global forces interact and come to terms with each other. There is, however, only one direction of travel, and our urgent need is to find ways in which we can make the transition as easy as possible and allow different peoples to learn to live with each other.

Globalisation will ensure that the world – and almost every country – will become more multicultural – that is to say, that each country will find that its population is increasingly made up of more people from different cultures, nationalities, faiths and ethnic backgrounds. The ease of travel, together with the opening up of labour and financial markets, means that this is inevitable. But this also means that the policies of multiculturalism which many governments have used (as part of a broader conceptual framework) to mediate these changes will no longer be appropriate, and these have largely already become discredited as a result of their failing to adapt to the new era. If societies are to become more cohesive and to avoid being riven by cultural and other divisions, they will need a new paradigm. It is suggested here that 'interculturalism' can fulfil that need, supported by cohesion and integration programmes expanded to help develop positive relations between communities.

To date, societies have generally been fearful, trying to hold back the tide of change rather than recognise the modern realities and shaping a more positive future for themselves. This is, of course, a challenge for communities and the way in which ordinary people live their lives and relate to 'others'. It will demand new 'cultural navigation' skills, the ability to be more open and engaged with change, and even a willingness to think of ourselves and our identities in different ways.

However, it also represents a challenge to governments, which have been slow to recognise the fluidity of population change and the impact of transnational and diaspora influences, and have hardly begun to consider the implications for the notion of national solidarity and governance. Governments have attempted to cling to the idea of national sovereignty and maintain the pretence that they still command all activities within their borders, and they see this as being fundamental to their contract with the people who vote for them. Any suggestion of the loss of sovereignty is quickly contested and, rather than reflect the inevitable process of globalisation, political leaders find it difficult to acknowledge the limits of their influence over their citizens and are still promoting varying levels and forms of 'identity politics'.

There are signs that younger people in particular are beginning to think and act beyond these traditional outlooks and confines, through the burgeoning growth of social media and virtual connectedness that threatens more traditional boundaries and identities. At the same time, however, the impact of globalisation appears to be creating more inward-looking and fractured communities as people cling to more traditional identities and 'hunker down' in the face of more global uncertainties. This has been exacerbated by political leaders, particularly on the extremes, who have seized the opportunity to pursue singular and populist campaigns, which reinforce divisions.

Indeed, the ideal of a more integrated international community, in which ideas and cultures may bridge national boundaries to create a world in which we are more at ease with each other, is seldom advanced as a desirable political objective as it undermines the power base of the separate political elites. While people are themselves increasingly crossing borders, intermarrying, building new virtual networks and creating real and tangible personal relationships at all levels, they are often fearful about the impact on their communities and collective identity. Identity politics often holds back the transition, rather than supporting and inspiring a new and interconnected world.

Interculturalism now provides the opportunity to replace multiculturalism as a conceptual and policy framework and to develop as a new positive model which will underpin cohesive communities. It will also contribute to a new vision for learning to live together in a globalised and super-diverse world. We, of course, need to recognise that cultural divisions are often reinforced by inequalities in wealth and power and, where this is the case, that they will need to be tackled at the same time, together with any other real and perceived sense of grievance. However, most of all, political will backed by strong popular support is needed for a more forward-looking period in which diverse societies recognise the new reality of interdependence in the political and social spheres, as well as within a globalised economy.

*   *   *

This book follows on from *Community Cohesion: A New Framework for Race and Cohesion* (2005, Palgrave Macmillan; revised and updated in 2008) and builds upon a number of the concepts established there. In particular, the historical perspective of race and community relations, the background and development of community cohesion, and the previous and current policy and practice in this regard, are all provided in detail in this earlier work. This book focuses on the development of new and future concepts of 'race' and all aspects of difference.

2
Globalisation and 'Super Diversity'

There is little clarity about what the term 'globalisation' means, but its origins lie in the process of creating products and developing systems of wealth and power on a worldwide basis. The term has been in regular use since the 1960s, though its origins are much older – the extent and nature of international trade has developed over centuries, gradually becoming 'globalised'. However, the technological developments in communications, together with the opening up of financial markets, have dramatically accelerated the process of change, largely as a result of deregulation and improved international communications.

Globalisation has brought many benefits, but the present political focus is undoubtedly on the negative impacts. The pace and extent of change have caused widespread concern, and globalisation is now often seen as a threat to local markets and democratic systems. The anti-globalisation movement has also recently succeeded in giving the debate much more political salience, though its opposition to the apparent continued march of globalisation has, ironically, itself generated a global movement, which Sen (2006, p. 124) describes as 'the most globalised moral movement in the world today'. He would not, of course, see the rise of the Far Right in the same terms, but its recent growth on an international basis, and particularly in Europe, is also part of a transnational negative political reaction to globalisation and especially to the diversity within nations that it entails.

It is not within the scope of this book to chart the continual and inexorable rise of globalisation in business, finance and other terms in any detail but, rather, to give some consideration to the consequent impact on societal and community relations.

First, it is clear that one of the most evident results of globalisation is that populations have become far more mobile, and willing and able to relocate in search of better employment prospects and a higher standard of living, or for other short- or longer-term considerations. In 2010 there were 214 million international migrants. If they continue to grow in number at the same pace, there will be more than 400 million by 2050 (IOM, 2010). The impact of the continuing disparity between rich and poor nations, as well as other factors – notably climate change – will drive still further levels of migration.

Second, the migrant community is also increasingly diverse and this inevitably leads to much greater differentiation within nation-states, particularly in the Western economies, which are often the target countries for migration, at least in economic terms. The extent of population movement is such that all Western economies are now characterised by some degree of 'super' or 'hyper' diversity, with cities like London, Stockholm, Toronto, New York and Amsterdam with over 300 language groups. This has redefined our notion of multiculturalism, which had previously been seen as countries coming to terms with their colonial pasts and, in particular, those overwhelmingly White nations attempting to accept and integrate Black and Asian minorities from their former colonies. Multiculturalism is now much more complex and community relations are multifaceted, no longer simply revolving around majority/minority visible distinctions.

Third, the impact of global communications and the rise and importance of diasporas mean that the homogeneity and distinctiveness of national and regional identities is under threat. Diasporas have enabled religious identities in particular to become much more salient. Global communications have also given rise to global languages, particularly across the West, facilitating and encouraging further patterns of interaction and affinity.

Fourth, globalisation challenges local and national democratic processes, with the ability to transcend national borders and regulatory mechanisms. Global companies possess more economic power than many governments and are consequently outside democratic controls, potentially disempowering and alienating national electorates. There has been little by way of political adaptation to the new global world order and a fundamental breakdown of trust and communication between the political elite and the general population (Cuperus, 2011).

Fifth, social changes within and between states have broken down class-based affinities and vertical forms of identity based on deference; collective identities based on occupational and class structures have given way to atomised and individualised familial groups, and new forms of identity have emerged into the public sphere with the overcoming of social taboos, particularly in relation to sexual orientation, age, health and faith.

The Far Right in many countries are increasingly exploiting the above concerns to build substantial popular support, but these sentiments are more widely shared by populations who are not encouraged to embrace identities beyond the confines of ethnic, faith and national boundaries. Minorities are often the visible expression of the processes inherent in globalisation and while their growth is often seen as the cause of changing social and cultural patterns, they are simply the consequence of that change. This makes them highly vulnerable, but also means that societies as a whole are vulnerable to tensions and conflict.

The dimensions of globalisation

The principal dimensions of globalisation primarily revolve around business and commerce, with companies now able to exploit the increasing openness of markets. International trade is certainly more global than ever before, with multinational companies not only trading across the globe, but establishing themselves as employers with supply chains in many countries. There is now a wide range of global brands, which are instantly recognisable in hundreds of countries and which are more distinctive – and economically larger – than many nation-states. As markets have become global so too has the movement of financial capital, and the interdependence of economies is undeniable, as the recent banking and financial crisis has shown.

Technological change has dramatically reduced the cost of all forms of international communication. The use and availability of the internet, satellite-based news and information services and telephony have aided the development of international trade and the growth of companies across national boundaries. Together with the more recent development of social media, the new communication networks have begun to enable people to develop new frames of reference which can transcend national boundaries to create new affinities, or reaffirm heritage and diaspora linkages.

Virtual connections have as yet, however, had far less impact than the real movement of people across boundaries. The reduced cost of international travel has made possible the flow of migrants on a mass scale, following business decisions to invest (and disinvest) in particular industries, or following more general patterns of economic growth which often reflect the disparity between rich and poor nations. Economic interests have increasingly determined the mobility of labour and population settlement patterns.

The ease of travel and communications has also led to the development of international education on a new scale – now a global business with millions of students crossing national boundaries each year for the purposes of study. The opportunities to study in a foreign country may well lead to temporary periods of employment in that country or permanent positions in that labour market, once the study is completed. In addition, Western universities are setting up subsidiary centres in many other countries, enabling greater access and two-way study opportunities. International education centres and courses also contribute to the exchange of ideas across national boundaries, with nation-states having far less control over the form and content.

Similarly, tourism has become much more extensive, both in scale and in terms of the nature of the experience. For example, there are around 25 million tourists visiting the UK each year and around 70 million tourist visits from the UK to other countries. Some of these are simply for a short break, with little interaction with the people and cultures of the host country. However, even in these cases it is inevitable that social and cultural bonds develop. At the other end of the scale, tourism becomes life-changing. For example, around 700,000 UK residents are now permanent 'tourists' in Spain with many more in other countries. Some 3.5 million British people have a second home in another country. There are also many other forms of tourism which promote deeper experiences, perhaps as part of a language study course or to learn about the wildlife or other educational purpose. Again, it is inevitable that some of these 'exchanges' lead to more permanent relationships and transnational connections.

Prophetic views about the profound nature of change wrought by globalisation have been debated over a number of decades. Marshall McLuhan (1962) caught everyone's imagination with the concept of the 'global village' based upon the impact of new communication technologies. The rise of corporate power, or 'when corporations rule the world' (Korten, 1995), has especially been seen as a challenge to political systems. Even more profoundly, the 'end of the nation-state' (Kenichi, 1995) has also been predicted, with states losing much of their power and national sovereignty, and with states being too small to deal with the big challenges that face the world and too big to deal with the small and local concerns (Bell, 1987).

These texts might have been expressed in more strident terms if written today, given the huge advances in technology over the last ten years
or so – in particular, that the global economy is now truly electronic,
'with no parallels in earlier times . . . fund managers, banks, corporations,
as well as millions of individual investors can transfer vast amounts of
capital from one side of the world to another at the click of a mouse'
(Giddens, 2002, p. 9). The information and communication technological changes have 'rendered the distance between countries irrelevant'
(Castells, 2006) and created the opportunity for economies to be desta-
bilised almost instantly and without any real possibility of defence by
national institutions – as demonstrated by the recent financial crises.

Globalisation is, perhaps, an even bigger challenge to countries that
are less advanced in democratic terms. Hitherto, they have been able
to control the media and information flow to their citizens and to prevent oppositional movements from growing. Oppressive regimes have
tried in vain to stop their citizens from accessing alternative viewpoints,
although – as China's action against Google has shown – this is far from
a settled matter. Activists in the Middle East have found that they are
able to access the internet and to use mobile communications to challenge their leaders with great effect – most recently in the Arab Spring.
Despots are also having to recognise that their actions are now able to be
scrutinised for the first time, with the oppression in Syria, Bahrain and
other countries now being recorded on mobile devices and instantly
beamed around the world and potentially, at least, becoming the subject of the International Criminal Court (itself a relatively new product
of global agreement, established in 2002).

Not all international networks are a force for good, however. International criminal gangs can now co-ordinate their activities on a grand
scale, using technology to commit fraud by electronic means, set up
human trafficking rings and mastermind cyber attacks, without any real
fear of detection. Further, international terrorism represents the 'dark
side of globalisation' (Giddens, 2002) and international crime, in common with all other aspects of globalisation, can only be responded to by
supra-national agencies.

Political systems have adjusted to globalisation to the extent that
there is some agreement on the need to develop regulatory systems
that transcend national boundaries and a number of institutions have
been established to facilitate this. Many of these are of an economic
nature, such as the International Monetary Fund, or have an indirect
economic purpose, for example, to establish common standards in order
to facilitate trade across boundaries. Supra-national bodies have also

been created for other purposes, for example, to tackle crime, or to prevent environmental degradation. These have often been established by an international treaty and place obligations upon each signatory. While such international bodies directly or indirectly impact upon political processes inside nations, it is notable that there is little real advocacy on behalf of these international bodies by the politicians in nation-states. Indeed, while international sovereignty is constantly being eroded, any suggestion that this is being diminished is generally angrily denied by politicians, anxious to maintain their own influence and fully aware of the impact on their own democratic traditions. Europe has demonstrated this dichotomy most clearly in recent times with the Union and the Eurozone countries in particular, unable to escape the logic of their economic (and currency) integration – political union is the inevitable consequence of the economic interconnectedness of nation-states.

In fact, the pretence of sovereignty is maintained despite states themselves having contributed to their own loss of power – or eventual demise – by actively deregulating, privatising, dispensing with border controls and developing the technological infrastructure to support globalisation (Castells, 2006). This proactivity on behalf of states is, of course, pursued in order to become competitive, or maintain competitiveness, in a global environment. The difficulty for states is then in gaining any real democratic legitimacy for decisions taken at the supranational level. Only the power elites are involved in the decision-taking process and political systems have simply not evolved to allow democratic participation at any level beyond the nation-state. Castells (2006) points out that the 'anti-globalisation' movement is something of a misnomer, in that their slogan has been 'no globalisation without representation', again emphasising the democratic deficit inherent in the process. The powerlessness of individuals and communities in the face of globalised political economies is, then, a key issue to be addressed. In the absence of any deliberation or thought being given to formal processes of international democratisation, informal political associations and alliances such as the anti-globalisation movement, and more recently the *'indignados'* (the indignant or outraged ones),[1] have begun to gain ground.

At the same time, non-governmental organisations (NGOs) are also developing and taking on new roles, again at the expense of nation-states. Held (1989) charts the rise of these organisations in his *Decline of the Nation-state* and finds that whereas there were 176 such organisations in 1905, he calculates there were 4615 in 1984. This had risen at an even faster rate to 26,000 by 1996 (*The Economist*, 1999), although Agg (2006) suggests that the figure had reached nearly 50,000 by the end of the 1990s.

The proliferation of NGOs has had a profound impact and they have 'reshaped world politics' (McGann and Johnstone, 2006). There was a significant NGO presence at the 1992 Earth Summit in Rio, where 17,000 NGO representatives staged an alternative forum to the UN-sponsored meeting, while 1400 were involved in the official proceedings. McGann and Johnstone believe that the growth of non-state actors is the result of a number of drivers, including the perceived inability of both domestic and international institutions to respond to the social, economic and political consequences of rapid advances in science and technology, growing economic interdependence, and political fragmentation, as well as a growing number of transnational threats (pandemics, climate change, security threats). The increase in the number of NGOs, however, has not been matched by any means in which they might be made democratically accountable. Rather than this being seen as a problem, Agg (2006) suggests that the transfer of power to NGOs has been part of a deliberate strategy to move away from their previous role as small-scale welfare providers to become major players in all areas of social and political development. Further, this trend has been seen as a positive development across the political spectrum. The sustaining of an independent civil society through the growth of NGOs has been supported by the neoliberal agenda of 'rolling back the state' which has advocated diverting funds away from government control and, at the same time, by grassroots movements of the Left who also supported the growth of the NGO sector, seeing its goals of participation and empowerment as creating the potential for a change in social structures.

The state has become the mainstay and accepted unit of democratic politics but its powers are now in flux, with the speed of globalisation threatening its very existence. For many, the state, especially where it is reinforced by nationhood, has also largely defined personal and collective identity and, prior to the advent of globalised communications, was able to dominate most aspects of the information flows at a formal level and to provide the basis for cultural markers and 'flagging' of daily lives (Billig, 1995). This is under attack from both above and below. Communications are now global, with the internet in particular transforming the way in which we transmit and receive information, and rapidly developing in poorer countries, having become almost universal in the West. The control of communications is, however, heavily concentrated and Castells (2006) notes that 50 per cent of the world's audiovisual material is controlled by just seven global communication groups. NGOs have also become important communicators, increasingly exercising their influence, both at the supra-national and regional level. Yet citizenship is almost entirely conceptualised and practised at the national and state level, a mismatch which can partly explain the reduction in national electoral behaviour and sense of powerlessness.

In this new environment diasporas are also much more able to form and sustain themselves, irrespective of the freedoms, cultures and norms of the countries in which their members live. Diasporas again transcend national boundaries and inevitably foster a shared historical perspective, beliefs and values which will not necessarily match those of any one nation or state. The co-existence of diaspora identities and the many nation-states in which they are found often gives rise to the phenomenon of hybrid identities, such as 'British Muslim' or 'Black British'. Indeed, many people now claim multiple identities, generally a mixture of faith, nationality, ethnicity and place of residence. The advent of more diverse societies means that, within any given state, there are now many more cultural and social networks, which have become more influential than the traditional forms of relationships that have been dependent upon intra-national familial and parochial cultural networks.

Serious political attention is only now beginning to be given to the social impacts of globalisation. For example, a new influential group of Labour Party intellectuals in the UK have recently published (Glasman et al., 2011) a review of current political issues and commented – or lamented – that:

> Customary patterns of social life and the flourishing of persons have been threatened, as well as transformed, by unmediated forms of globalisation, industrial decline and the commodification of non-market spheres of life. The free rein given to markets has led to high levels of inequality, the exploitative use of cheap migrant labour in a desperate attempt to fuel economic growth, and a pervasive sense of insecurity. To ensure the social and economic security of the British people Labour[2] will need to recover its role as defender of society, and bring capital under national and global democratic control.

The Left-leaning Institute of Public Relations have also recently announced a major research programme on the future of globalisation headed by former UK Business Secretary Lord Mandelson, which aims to re-examine who benefits from globalisation and how a more even distribution of the benefits both between and within countries can be encouraged.

Harris (2008) sees globalisation in far more fundamental and political terms, in which the ruling class has been transformed and become transnational as a result of a global business culture and integrated activity based upon a shift from industrial to financial capitalism. This new transnational capitalist class, according to Harris, controls many of the global economic and regulatory systems, including the International Monetary Fund, the World Trade Organisation and the World Bank. Harris also suggests that this shift in power may result in a challenge to the new global order with the unification of the present disparate and emerging oppositional elements in various parts of the world. Recent events, and particularly the emergence of the *'indignados'* in Spain, drawing upon the protests in Greece and garnering support in many other European countries, in response to the public expenditure reductions brought about by the banking and Eurozone crises in 2011, may give some further credence to this. It would indeed be ironic if a new class-based global identity, which cuts across nationality, ethnicity and cultural divisions, emerges to provide some form of unified challenge to the existing order.

The impact of globalisation on the way we live our lives, how we think of ourselves and how we relate to the new 'others' in our more cosmopolitan real and virtual worlds, are perhaps the unintended consequences of the globalisation of markets, but may emerge as the most profound and challenging dimensions of the process.

Cohesion and solidarity – the 'paradox of diversity'

As a result of globalisation, societies are becoming more and more multicultural – or 'super diverse' – often despite the many attempts by nation-states to protect the integrity of their borders and to resist migration and to create higher hurdles for migrants. The anti-migration stance of Western politicians is, however, a denial of the multicultural reality. Populations are already diverse and will become much more so without any further inward migration. In England and Wales, this is recognised in the official statistics, with the 'non-White British' group growing from 6.641 million in 2001 to 9.127 million (estimated) in 2009 (ONS, 2011), a growth of over 30 per cent in eight years. As a percentage, the 'non-White British' group is now estimated at 17 per cent, and because of regional variation at over 40 per cent in London (ibid.).

However, in common with many Western states, the age distribution of the British population clearly indicates that the ethnic composition will become much more diverse. According to a study sponsored by the Equality and Human Rights Commission, almost 20 per cent (or one in five) of children under 16 are from minority groups and can therefore be expected to make up a larger proportion of the population in the future (Platt, 2009). The concentration of minorities in particular towns, or parts of towns, also means that many areas in Britain have substantial (more than 30 per cent) minority populations.

More profoundly, world populations will continue to move at an alarming rate and irrespective of economic migration. Christian Aid predicts that, on current trends, a further 1 billion people will be forced from their homes between now and 2050 and believe that forced migration is the most urgent threat facing poor people in developing countries. Their projections comprise: some 50 million people displaced by conflict and extreme human rights abuses; 50 million people displaced by natural disasters; 645 million people displaced by development projects such as dams and mines (at the current rate of 15 million a year); 250 million people permanently displaced by climate change-related phenomena such as floods, droughts, famines and hurricanes; and a further 5 million people will flee their own countries and become accepted as refugees (Christian Aid, 2007).

Political leaders cling to the hope that not only can they control their borders, against the tide of globalisation, but also that they can remain as the most significant influence over the daily lives of their citizens, with the electorate continuing to support them and be influenced by them. This is an ever more difficult challenge as the nature of international communications is now such that people can access many new channels of information and develop much broader frames of reference. The level of turnout in most elections has fallen across Western democracies, and 'identity politics' based upon spurious ideas about 'difference' has been one way in which political leaders have sought to retain their relevance and influence.

In respect of migration, many national leaders are, themselves, caught in something of a bind as they generally continue to promise and promote economic growth and know that inward migration is often the easiest and quickest way of achieving this, as migrants are generally more work-ready and work-willing – and have a lower labour cost. They will also fill gaps in the labour market and undertake tasks that are unattractive to host populations, for example, in agriculture and social care, and are more flexible on social costs, for example, in respect of housing. Nevertheless, many host communities object to increasing the population through migration, often precisely because of the advantages that they have to employers, and are constantly demanding limits, or even a complete halt, to inward migration. Extreme Far Right parties, which are enjoying rising levels of support across Europe, go still further and demand the repatriation of migrants, including those born in the countries to which their parents or grandparents migrated to and in which they are citizens. The continuing debate over diversity and multiculturalism has led to a widespread populist view that multiculturalism has 'failed' (this is discussed in more detail in later sections).

Globalisation has brought many benefits and opened up both commercial and socio-cultural opportunities on a very large scale and these can only go on increasing. However, it has created an era of super diversity in which new relationships between peoples of different background have developed and are constantly changing. Multiculturalism as we now know it is very different from its early form and the impact upon personal and collective identity and the forms of governance and mediating tensions has been profound. While it is clear that most people are now exposed to diversity in all aspects of their daily lives – either in our local communities, schools and workplaces, or indirectly through TV, social networks and other media – there appears to be something of a 'paradox of diversity' (Cantle, 2011). The more diverse societies have become and the more people have been exposed to difference and become accustomed to it, the more they seem to retreat into their own identity, embrace identity politics and support separatist ideologies. This may, in part, be due to the lack of engagement with difference, a rather wary detachment that makes us more determined to cling to our own community's certainties. The concept of 'contact theory', which has been reinvigorated through the recent programmes of community cohesion and is discussed in later sections, suggests that meaningful engagement with others does enable us to change our attitudes and behaviours towards others.

However, living alongside each other but in separate spheres, in what Sen (2006) has called 'plural monoculturalism' and where cultures may 'pass each other like ships in the night', reflected to a greater or lesser extent in all Western democracies, is not sufficient. In such circumstances, any sense of a shared society, in which common experiences can take place and an understanding of each other's needs and attributes can develop, is very unlikely. Rather, stereotypes and prejudices can flourish and irrational fears can emerge with the possibility of a demonisation of the 'other'. It is this analysis of 'parallel lives', following the riots in English northern towns in 2001, which gave birth to the programme of community cohesion (Cantle, 2001) and was reinforced in 2007 by a similar study (CIC, 2007). The idea of 'parallel societies' has been subsequently used elsewhere, for example, in the French-speaking and English-speaking societies of Canada which have been described as 'two solitudes', reading different newspapers, listening to different radio programs, watching different TV shows, reading different literature and 'generally quite uninterested in each other's culture' (Kymlicka, 2003).

There are, however, relatively few ways in which 'solidarity' can be measured. It is often based upon a number of objective indicators, such as the incidence and nature of hate crime and the level of inequalities, or the perception of people themselves about how they feel about 'others' and how well they relate to them. While this is an area that remains to be fully developed, a range of governmental and non-governmental partners did create a framework in 2004 (Home Office et al., 2004) and this later formed the basis of a national league table for local areas in parts of the UK. Robert Putnam, however, has looked at this through the lens of 'social capital' a term that has been in use for many years but made especially salient through his seminal work *Bowling Alone* (Putnam, 2000). His more recent work (Putnam, 2007) has demonstrated that social capital was inversely related to diversity – 'immigration and ethnic diversity challenge social solidarity and inhibit social capital', or, more graphically expressed, to:

> inhabitants of diverse communities tend to withdraw from collective life, to distrust their neighbours, regardless of the colour of their skin, to withdraw even from close friends, to expect the worst from their community and its leaders, to volunteer less, give less to charity and work on community projects less often, to register to vote less, to agitate for social reform *more*, but have less faith that they can actually make a difference, and to huddle unhappily in front of the television. Note that this pattern encompasses attitudes and behavior, bridging and bonding social capital, public and private connections. Diversity, at least in the short run, seems to bring out the turtle in all of us.
>
> (2007, p. 146)

Others have disputed the impact of rising ethnic diversity on cohesion, and contrasted Putnam's results in the USA with other slightly different studies in Europe (Legrain, 2011). However, the solidarity of communities is inevitably impacted by the population churn and change resulting from migration and other social factors. In the UK, for example, it is estimated that about one-third of all the 2 million foreign-born people have been in the country for less than five years and around half for less than ten years, while the proportion of migrants that had been in the UK for 20 years or more had fallen from around half in 1997 to about one-third in 2007 (Fanshawe and Sriskandarajah, 2010, p. 13).

Putnam (2007) did not suggest that the adverse impact of diversity on solidarity would remain indefinitely and that in the medium to longer term:

> successful immigrant societies create new forms of social solidarity and dampen the negative effects of diversity by constructing new, more encompassing identities. Thus, the central challenge for modern, diversifying societies is to create a new, broader sense of 'we'.
>
> (p. 139)

However, the difficulty primarily remains with those communities that are undergoing a fast 'pace of change' and it has been previously noted that this has created difficulties for cohesion (Cantle, 2004). Further, as population churn increases, the level of investment in cohesion programmes also needs to increase, but there has been little by way of vision and established policy and practice to turn this into a reality and there is, rather, a sense of retrenchment. Indeed, negative factors are easier to identify and to measure. The growth of the Far Right has been especially notable in Europe (see later sections) and as the standard bearers of anti-diversity and anti-migrant policies, they have succeeded in heightening the politics of fear and presenting the state as no longer willing, or able, to control the influx of foreigners, nor temper their alien culture.

Similarly, it is possible to chart the way in which the World has become more prone to ethnic and faith conflict with over 70 per cent of conflicts having an ethnic or faith dimension (Baldwin et al., 2007). In fact, there are indications of a rising number of divisions and more ardent separatist movements, where people no longer feel able to even share the same land or government. Around 20 nations have been created in recent years, which stem partly from the breakup of constructed federations in the Balkans and Eastern Europe, but in other continents too, for example in Sudan, which has recently divided. More divisions are possibly on the way with states like Belgium becoming virtually ungovernable as a single entity and secessionists movements in Quebec,

Scotland, Catalonia and many other places, as strong as ever. Where we might have expected more collaboration across borders and the separate identities of regions and states to give way to common or globalised identities, the opposite seems to be true. Indeed, old ideals of internationalism, often inspired by progressives, particularly following the Second World War, also seem to be on the wane amid a new 'age of fear':

> We have entered an age of fear. Insecurity is once again an active ingredient of political life in Western democracies. Insecurity born of terrorism, but also, and more insidiously, fear of the uncontrollable speed of change, fear of the loss of employment, fear of losing ground to others in an increasingly unequal distribution of resources, fear of losing control of the circumstances and routines of our daily life. And, perhaps above all, fear that it is not just we who can no longer shape our lives but that those in authority have also lost control, to forces beyond their reach.
>
> (Judt, T. quoted in Cuperus, 2011)

Younge (2010) believes that the elevation of identity is caused by the erosion of democracy which he sees as inherent in the process of globalisation. He believes that globalisation undermines the democracy and sovereignty of the nation-state and turns individuals into a 'universal tribe of consumers' who are 'economically interdependent but isolated and impotent as citizens'. Younge's argument is compelling, especially in the context of the many examples he provides, from the creation of the Euro, the globalisation of brands which reduce local corporate markers, and the recent financial crisis, enabling him to conclude that with this loss of control and access to democratic levers, we retreat more into separate identities or tribes. Younge also quotes from David Hooson's (1994) *Geography and National Identity* in support of his argument:

> The urge to express one's identity and to have it recognised tangibly by others, is increasingly contagious and has to be recognised as an elemental force even in the shrunken, apparently homogenizing high-tech world of the end of the twentieth century.

This theme is taken further by Castells (1997), who sees recent political changes, including the privatisation of public agencies and the 'attack' on the welfare state, as ones which, 'while relieving societies of some bureaucratic burden, have worsened living conditions for the majority of citizens and broken the historic social contract between capital, labour and the state' (p. 419). Castells also suggests that other social and economic changes have contributed to this trend, notably the move away from 'political ideologies based on industrial institutions and organisations', together with the 'weakening of the labour movement' and the 'practicing of a form of secularized religion' which 'diminishes capacity to enforce behaviour and provide solace'; and the decline of the patriarchal family which 'disturbs cultural codes' (p. 422).

The ongoing debate about the future of the Eurozone – a single currency for 17 nation-states within the EU, which is made up of 24 nations – illustrates the dilemma and the way in which the political arguments about national powers and loss of democratic legitimacy have been framed. The flaw the Eurozone financial crisis exposed, according to *The Times* (2011), is that 'national power cannot survive within a supranational currency union' and that it went wrong because the monetary union was established with 'none of the corresponding political structures in place'. This then creates a choice between the ceding of even more national democratic power to a supra-national body under a federal structure, or the return of national powers and national currencies. The bind of the nation-state, through its seeming hold on democratic structures, is at odds with both the process globalisation through trade and commerce and even with the attempts at limited financial union initiated by the nation-states themselves. At no point in this debate is another option – that of democratisation at an international level – or new forms of global governance, even considered.

The sense of collective identity has changed profoundly in all Western societies, but it would appear that, when the impact of increasing diversity is coupled with globalisation, it has had a more potent and negative impact upon solidarity, spurring a range of local and regional identities, separatist movements and community tensions, and that the state, which itself is under threat, is no longer able to provide an adequate basis for identity which can transcend these affinities.

Globalisation and identity

The changing nature of personal identities is not a simple matter, with many separate components shaped by increasing diversity in terms of faith, locality and ethnicity – as well as an apparently declining sense of nationality. This is reflected in a recent UK report by the Searchlight

Table 2.1 Most important element of identity: UK SET 2011

	Asian (%)	White (%)	Black (%)
Nationality	16	37	10
Country where you were born	15	25	6
Your village/town/city	8	16	11
Religion	24	6	16
Your estate/neighbourhood/community	4	5	11
Ethnicity	17	6	40
Country you live in now	15	5	5

Source: *Fear and Hope Project Report*, Searchlight Educational Trust (SET) (2011)

Educational Trust (SET, 2011), which found that, while many ethnic groups saw themselves in a similar way, 'Asian' and 'Black' groups differed significantly from 'White' groups in respect of identity (see Table 2.1).

The three components of 'country' – nationality, country of birth and domicile – were most important for White groups (67 per cent) compared to Asian (46 per cent) and Black (21 per cent), and minorities were also more likely to regard religion and ethnicity as the most important element of their identity. However, while the SET report asserted that 'national identity trumps any other notion of overall identity', this rather supposes that nationality, country of birth and country of residence are synonymous. For some people this will be the case, and may supposed to be a higher percentage among White groups, but for an increasing number of more mobile groups only one of these features might apply and might relate to national identity – and even where they are added together they may be lower than might have been expected.

Indeed, elsewhere in the report, the SET quotes Castells (1997) and his view of 'the decline of statism'. In the same publication, Castells' thesis is laid out more clearly – that the state has been bypassed by networks of wealth, power and information and lost much of its sovereignty. In later work Castells (2006) draws upon the research of Professor Norris of Harvard University who has analysed the *World Values Survey* to show that regional and local identities are also trumping national loyalties. The *Survey* compared identities at world, national and regional levels, with cosmopolitan identities in general. Professor Norris calculated that for the world as a whole, 13 per cent of respondents primarily considered themselves as 'citizens of the world', 38 per cent put their nation-state first, and the remainder (in other words, the majority) put local or regional identities first. Norris (2011) has herself commented that while national identities may be weakening, they are 'important to social cohesion and state legitimacy in multicultural communities' (p. 25). Norris contrasts cosmopolitan identities, resulting from globalisation and which might be said to be 'tolerant of diverse cultural outlooks and practices, valuing human differences rather than similarities, cultural pluralism rather than convergence and de-emphasising territorial ties and attachments', with national identities that are thought to be oppositional to this view (p. 26). However, Norris does point out that while nationalism and cosmopolitanism are theoretical opposites, 'it remains to be seen empirically whether people could hold both views, for example by having strong feelings of national pride and also favouring multilateral solutions to world problems' (p. 26). At the same time, however – and without contradiction – Norris has found that nationalist identities *are* weaker in globalised and cosmopolitan societies where 'denser and faster interconnections across territorial borders seem to gradually erode older allegiances and promote a more multicultural ethos' (p. 99).

This trend is particularly notable with regard to faith and, while the Jewish community were the only significant diaspora with a visible identity and culture that transcended the many nations in which they were to be found over hundreds of years (Cheesman and Khanum, 2009), small Black communities who were resident in a number of European cities in the early part of the twentieth century (and earlier), often settling in the major ports connected to the slave trade, failed to sustain an international conception of themselves and often only survived as a beleaguered minority. Global information and communication technologies have enabled diasporas to have much greater potency and to threaten the homogeneity and distinctiveness of national and regional identities. The salience of diaspora religious identities depends upon the social and political context and, at the current time, the focus – and often heightened concern – has been upon young Muslims, with 'new telecommunications media facilitating a global intensification of the promulgation of Islamic knowledge and in expanding public deliberation over matters of Islamic tradition and belonging' (Gale and O'Toole, 2009, p. 146). However, modern communications will help to sustain all diasporas and, no doubt, add to the wider sense of their belonging across national boundaries. The complexity of identity inherent in this is considerable, with all major faiths represented in most Western societies and with a wide range of sects and other divisions, which may also give rise to significant difference or 'otherness'.

Global communications have also helped to sustain the identities of nationals living in foreign countries, often irrespective of faith differences. These nationality-based diasporas again are not new, with Irish, Chinese and Italian communities being identifiable in many countries over the last century or so. However, while they may have been under pressure to 'fit in' during the early days of their migration, modern communications have meant that they can regularly return to their country of origin and may even do so on a semi-permanent basis without great difficulty. Further, these communications can constantly reconnect them to their homeland influences by the internet, satellite TV and social media. In some cases, the reinforcement of heritage can leave people with a historic conception of themselves which is no longer recognised and practised in their heritage country, nor connected to the one in which they now live. For example, Powell (2004) refers to the experience of Italian heritage Australians as cleaving to the real memories of their parents with a nostalgia which is both painful and clichéd which 'risks turning them into living souvenirs of an Italy that no longer exists'.

The rise of English as a global language (Crystal, 2003) spurred on by the technological developments that have used it, has also enabled interaction across national boundaries at completely new levels. This enables both minority and majority communities to connect across national boundaries in different ways, for example, in respect of British citizens who take up semi-permanent residency in Spain.

Despite these developments in the way identity is formed across national boundaries, there remains a tendency to apply reductionist principles to the notion of identity. Sen (2006) argues that conflict and violence are sustained today, no less than the past, by the illusion of a unique identity. He agrees that the world is increasingly divided between religions (or 'cultures' or 'civilizations'), which ignore the relevance of other ways in which people see themselves through class, gender, profession, language, literature, science, music, morals or politics. He challenges 'the appalling effects of the miniaturisation of people' and the denial of the real possibilities of reasoned choices. Part of the response to this is the now almost routine hyphenating of nationality, faith and ethnicity.

The inevitable consequence of people from different identity groups sharing the same society has led to the inexorable growth of 'mixed race' and the further development of hyphenated, or multiple identities.

In Britain, 'mixed race' is now the fastest growing minority. However, this group is not actually recognised as such in policy terms, there is no funding, representation, support nor champion. This is partly for practical reasons, as the boundaries of the mixed-race group are necessarily blurred and cover many different combinations of Black, Asian, White and other ethnicities, and any combination of faith and nationality. But it also suggests an overtone of racial purity, whereby 'pure breeds' in ethnic or religious terms are recognised with leaders chosen to represent their particular constituency of interest, whereas 'our mongrel selves' (Slattery, 2003), have no particular identity, nor recognition. This is also a function of the ambivalence towards intermarriage, which still faces many religious and cultural barriers in nearly all majority and minority communities and may be regarded with hostility and shame.

Hyphenated identities also arise from the mixing of the characteristics of nationality, country of origin, religion and ethnicity, for example, 'Black-British', 'British-Muslim' or 'British-Chinese', rather than as a result of intermarriage. Without the cultural bars inherent in the notion of 'mixed race', these forms of hyphenated identities may have some success in seeking and gaining state financial support and recognition, though the huge number of potential permutations makes this increasingly less likely. All types of hyphenated identity also run the risk of simply replacing the limited notion of a single identity with a multiple identity that is just as limited. As Brah (2007) points out, identity is a process and not a fixed category (though that is how many people would apparently like to regard it).

In the face of this broader diversity and changing patterns of identity, governmental responses have been ambivalent. For the most part, they have attempted to reinforce their view of national identity through such measures as the teaching of national history and promoting national citizenship and identity. On the other hand, by remaining steadfastly nationalistic and promoting the integrity of national borders and governance, eschewing any suggestion of the erosion of sovereignty and by attempting to deny the interdependence brought by globalisation, they appear to lag behind the current reality of their communities. This theme is developed in latter sections.

A national conception of 'Britishness' or 'Frenchness' or any other national approach to identity will inevitably be contested and beset by the difficulty of defining it in tangible terms, except at the blandest and therefore almost meaningless level. However, the UK's community cohesion programmes have found it possible to develop local programmes around a 'sense of belonging' and these have received widespread support and been uncontroversial (Cantle, 2008), and appear to have improved cohesion indicators (DCLG, 2011). Such programmes are, however, free of the value-laden concepts that surround nationalism and national identity and simply focus on the need for people from a given area to engage and 'get on' with each other to minimise friction and conflict and promote the common good on a local basis. They do nevertheless depend upon a positive view of diversity in which people from a wide range of backgrounds are portrayed as 'belonging' as equal members of the local community.

While it is clear that diversity does have an impact on social solidarity, in the short term and as part of a transitional process, it is less clear whether this is transitional and whether the sense of alienation and the loss of democratic power can be rebalanced in the longer term. Can the institutions of government themselves adapt, will they facilitate or hinder more fluid identities, and will the new phenomenon of social media create new transnational relationships that transcend traditional power structures?

From tribal to international affinities

While the concept of a state has been around for a long time, the modern democratic state is relatively new, perhaps originating in a meaningful sense only over the last three or four centuries. Many states are even more recent inventions, with, for example, Germany only being in its present form for around 150 years and previously consisting of a number of separate regions and nations, like Saxony and Prussia. Indeed, Europe has been subject to the constant changing of national borders and even 'vanishing kingdoms', with a shifting patchwork of territorial claims and counter-claims, especially in the East, and some areas having five new national 'owners' within just 20 years (Davies, 2011). Much the same could be said of most other continents, with many contested borders and identities. But smaller states are the current trend and in 1950 there were only some 50 nations, compared with four times that number today (McGann and Johnstone, 2006).

Britain can perhaps lay claim to being one of the older states, with the emergence of a central state-led power – the military – after the English Civil War (1642–1651). Although it remained subject to much change after that time, the Civil War started the process of the overriding of separate and divisive private armies, baronial fiefdoms and clans, and eventually enabled it to impose its will inside England's borders and subsequently on the other nations that make up the state today.

It thus passed Fukuyama's 'essence of stateness': enforcement, or coercive power (Fukuyama, 2005). This supports Weber's view (1946) that a state depends upon the legitimate use of physical force within a given territory. 'Coercive power' may be exercised in different ways, including by nation-building through the enforcement of a common culture. For example, the former Soviet Union imposed the Russian language upon the citizens of the constituent countries. Similarly, at the time of the French Revolution, less than 13 per cent of the territories now forming France spoke French (Castells, 2006), but this was gradually imposed and is still regarded as perhaps the most fundamental part of French culture.

But a state is not the same as a nation. A state is a political concept, whereas a nation is generally defined as a body of people who share a history and culture that provides them with a common identity in terms of values, mores and behaviours. A nation is a very imperfect concept and may encompass a range of differences, or be relatively uniform, even within a shared understanding. As discussed later, the whole notion of what is shared is fundamentally challenged by diversity and globalisation. A nation may coincide with a state and be a 'nation-state'. In this way, nations may be much older than the modern states, as in the 'first nation' people of Canada and Australia. Great Britain thinks of itself as a nation, but the 'nations' of England, Scotland and Wales at least, have much longer histories and deeper affinities and Britain would therefore also be difficult to describe as a 'nation-state', even though there is some degree of shared understanding, with a different level of meaning and affinity at the national levels. This is true of many states around the world, where particular groups define themselves as 'nations', seek to protect their heritage and identity and even to try to form their own states.

While it is not always the case, many of the identifiable nations within states, have often been based upon particular ethnic or religious characteristics. These differences – which are often manifest in the form of tensions with other nations or groups within those states – have often been established over centuries. Yet, these national differences now co-exist with a much wider range of multicultural and multifaith cosmopolitanism which has resulted from recent periods of mass immigration and the diversity stemming from globalisation. This has posed particular challenges for both the long-standing majority and minority nations within modern states. Do the majority and minorities abandon their rivalries and attempt to remake their nation on the basis of a much more diverse history and culture, or fit the newer groups into their existing divides?

The evidence points very much to the latter, with perhaps a reinforcement of the identities of the longer-standing groups. The basic divides between the first nation groups of Australia and the original settlers, the French- and English-speaking groups in Canada, the Protestant and Catholic communities in Northern Ireland, the Catalonian and Spanish 'nations' and many more besides, show no sign of moving away from their bicultural positions and moving to a multicultural conception. Rather, these two divides continue to exist alongside each other and are becoming even more important identifiers.

'National identity' does not therefore coincide with an affinity or emotional attachment to the state in which people happen to reside, except perhaps in the case of coherent nation-states, with clear borders and relatively homogenous populations. Such states are clearly becoming fewer in number as patterns of migration impact on all continents. For many modern democracies this 'coherence' may have been illusory for some considerable time with borders constantly contested and changed and divisions often the subject of intense debate. Belgium, for example, eventually managed to form a government in 2011, some 18 months after a general election, with language, religious and cultural differences reinforcing political divides, and reflecting the divisions since it was formed, or perhaps constructed, nearly 200 years ago. For many countries around the world still struggling to come to terms with democratic frameworks, the position is even less clear and the idea of a nation remains just that, an idea, with tribal groups, clans and regional groupings ensuring that any overall sense of state legitimacy and national affinity is still a long way off.

States have recognised the need both to develop an institutional framework to support their political and social reach and to link citizenship to nationality (Cantle, 2008). This has generally taken the form of activities to build 'citizenship' in which people are encouraged to take a more active part in the running of their communities and participation in the political sphere. This has been extended to the devising of citizenship tests for new migrants to try to ensure that they understand, and are committed to, the institutional framework and the values and mores that underpin daily life, though this has been criticised for homogenising values and behaviours and failing to recognise the diversity of cultural norms. Children have also been the focus of citizenship activities, by including the teaching of citizenship as part of the school curriculum and by attempting to provide a common historical perspective, for example, in England. States have also attempted to ban or prevent cultural markers and behaviours that they see as antipathetic to the norms of that society, for example, the wearing of the face veil in France, Belgium and the Netherlands and the embargo on minarets on mosques in Switzerland.

Outside of the Western sphere, the emphasis has been on 'nation building' to create an institutional framework that can supersede the role of tribal and other groupings. This has been particularly relevant in post-conflict situations as in Iraq and Afghanistan, but Fukuyama (2005) sees a much wider problem as 'modern states are anything but universal'. While Fukuyama recognises the contested role of the state and that they exist 'for good or ill', he believes that the 'central project of contemporary international politics' is the nation building of weak states through improving democratic legitimacy and strengthening institutions. Although Fukuyama recognises the difference between building a state and building a nation, he generally uses the terms synonymously and his focus is on the institutional framework of the state – policing, utilities, banking, education, the legal system and the political framework. Even in these terms, Fukuyama recognises that while states may seek to have a wide 'scope' of activities their 'capacity' to deliver on them may be very different.

In this varied sense, the state can take over the functions of tribes, clans and regional groupings and provide for a more rational-legal framework which depends less upon patronage and is replaced by universal state-wide administrative systems and jurisprudence. It is also true that the norms and values that underpin these systems may, over time, become internalised and accepted as part of the national value system. However, while states may create a more nationalistic system of government, which may or may not be supported by an emotional attachment to any degree, they also form a new layer of affinities – and barriers – which may also be inappropriate in increasingly globalised and diverse societies. In defining who 'we' are in national terms, we are also defining others as 'they', yet those others are a part of our society, even if only on a temporary basis.

While commentators like Fukuyama are enthusiastic about 'state building' to take over the role of tribal groups and provide administrative, legal and democratic coherence to weak and divided societies, he is very reluctant to see this as a transitional stage on the way to international forms of governance – and global affinities. Fukuyama (2005) nevertheless recognises that state sovereignty is under threat, particularly from the growth of the global economy, as a result of the increasing mobility of capital and labour. He also acknowledges that stateness has been eroded by a variety of 'multilateral and international organisations designed to take over certain governance functions from nation-states'.

However, he supports the continuation of states as the principal and continuing form of governance on two counts – they alone can enforce laws and in the absence of any clear form of international organisation there is 'no choice but to turn back to the sovereign nation-state... to make it strong and effective'.

Fukuyama seems to base his assessment on the strength of institutions rather than the identity associated with nationhood. Belgium would appear to be an exemplar in this respect, with many of their state institutions continuing throughout the 18 months without a government and following a stalemate general election result in 2010. But, both before and since the new government, there is little popular affinity to the country as a whole, with strong separatist movements and no common culture. Indeed Belgium has no national TV stations, no national newspapers and no national political parties – all are based on separate identities. However, Billig (1995) also casts doubt on the end of the nation-state despite his emphasis on the nation as 'an imagined community'. He notes that the global village is now also daily 'flagged' and 'banal globalism is supplanting the conditions of banal nationalism' (p. 132). He nevertheless suggests that the sovereignty of nation-states is actually 'collapsing under the pressure of global and local forces' and that the pre-eminence of national identity which once claimed the loyalty of individuals now has to compete within a free market of identities, including supra-national and sub-national claims. Billig, then, takes the view that rather than the development of supra-national states with commensurate forms of identity, national identity is giving way to an 'older, fiercer psychology' and an assertion of cultural identity based upon language, colour, tribe, caste, clan or region (though this can support national interests and identities in some instances). This supports the idea of a 'paradox of diversity' referred to earlier.

Nationalism has a bad name, with George Orwell famously describing it as 'the worst enemy of peace' and certainly many brutalities have been committed in the name of nationalists. Orwell used the term in the sense that it implied the superiority over another nation and contrasted it to 'patriotism' which is simply a love of one's country and represents peace rather than militancy. But as Billig (1995, p. 6) points out, there are distinctions within forms of nationalism and, for example, 'between the flag waved by Serbian ethnic cleansers and that hanging unobtrusively outside the US post office'. He describes the latter as 'banal nationalism' which is an endemic condition, as daily 'the nation is flagged in the lives of its citizenry'. Nationalism is not, in any event, the same as national identity and the creation of strong nations does not in itself create problematic forms of identity. Yet, as Billig also points out, political rhetoric has often been used to turn national identity into nationalistic fervour and to justify hostility towards other nations. It remains to be seen as to whether this task would be as easy with the present climate of diversity in which so many other nationals are found within states and in which intermarriage between nationals has become commonplace.

Despite the strength of national identity and nationalism to date, identity is no longer so clearly and directly related to place. This is hardly surprising, given that people are able to live and work away from their country of birth on a temporary or permanent basis and may also see themselves on a number of other levels, for example, as gay or straight, Black or White, Hindu or Christian and in any combination, hyphenated together or with a national, sub-national or supra-national interest. A more general trend appears to have been identified by Stone and Muir (2007), at least in the UK, in that as people have become wealthier and gained access to higher levels of formal education, their collective identities have weakened, particularly in relation to social class, political party and national identity.

Identity politics can develop across borders, without reference to place or with it as only a limited or secondary consideration. While there is scepticism about the challenge to national identity, these new forms of identity may develop much more quickly and the pace of change would appear to be accelerating with the advent of global communications – especially the growth of social media – which offer new forms and levels of contact, across all established boundaries. The successful markers of statehood have taken some considerable time to impose themselves, probably unknowingly, upon citizens and to create an emotional attachment. It may therefore be the case that it will take time for such attachments to break down and for allegiances to become more international or global, but the opportunities are now much more evident and accessible and while retrenchment may have been the experience of globalisation to date, a positive encouragement of an intercultural perspective could provide for a much faster transition. Indeed, the process may be far more developed than supposed – the effectiveness of the state may well be better judged by the affinity that people feel towards it and how far they see their identity influenced by it, as compared to other influences. Table 2.1 indicates that even in Britain, one of the more established states and separate nations, relatively few people are prepared to say that 'nationality' is the most important form of identity to them. Norris (2011) found that only 38 per cent of the sample for the *World Values Survey* identified the nation-state first and a surprising 13 per cent primarily considered themselves 'citizens of the world'.

The impacts of future change are likely to be even more profound – responding to a new scale of global problems requires the development of new systems of global governance, which recognise the interdependence of nations and the commonality of humankind – as Martin Wolf, Associate Editor and Chief Economics Commentator at the *Financial Times*, explains:

> The affluent economy enjoyed until recently by just a small proportion of the world's human population is now becoming global. Billions of hitherto poor people not only aspire to the standards of living of the advanced countries, but expect to achieve them within their lifetimes. But such a leap will, on anything like current trends, impose vastly greater demands on the planet's resources and threaten profound changes in the global environment. Is this tension between human aspirations and natural limits manageable technologically, economically, socially and politically? A way must be found to combine economic dynamism with respect for natural limits. This, in turn, will demand profound changes not just in the economy, but in governance at all levels. Of all these challenges, climate change is the most intractable. This is the most difficult collective action problem in all of human history – inherently global, extremely long term, technologically demanding and replete with deep distributional questions.
>
> (Wolf, 2011)

Identity has, in the past, been strongly associated with tribal and regional affinities. This has been transformed by the development of modern nations and states that have provided a unifying force, based upon a common political and legal framework, which conveys associated values and the banal flagging of everyday life. But with national identity and nationalism has come conflict based upon national divisions. As the role and influence of the state wanes, the central challenge for humankind will be (and with due acknowledgement to Tariq Ramadan[3]) how to ensure that the new 'we' of the nation, which replaced (to some extent at least) the old 'we' of the tribe, can become the future 'we' of the international and global community.

3
Reforming the Notion of Identity

Most of the academic debate revolves around the way in which different identities are conflicted or accommodated *within* nations and in particular the relationship between minority and majority communities. In the light of globalisation and super diversity, however, this now seems to be somewhat outdated and potentially irrelevant. The debate had emerged in the context of post-war migration and was therefore also focused almost entirely upon 'race'. Notwithstanding the constantly changing landscape of national borders within continents, there has been an overwhelming coincidence of nations and 'race' which only began to break down, relatively slowly at first, from the early years of multiculturalism. The whole idea of 'race' became untenable in the light of scientific evidence that dispensed with the remnants of the Eugenicist movement, but has seamlessly become transposed to ethnicity and faith, with these social and political constructs still being conceptualised in the form of primordial distinctions, while failing to recognise many other aspects of individual and collective identity. Nevertheless, even in this form, 'race' continues to dominate the conceptualisation of multiculturalism and remains rooted in the past.

Identities have also generally been discussed as though they are fixed and given, rather than transitory and chosen – they are fundamentally about past heritage, rather than future personal and collective development. This had been understandable in the previous context of strong national identities with minimal internal visible differences, and especially in an era that had emerged from a state of war between nations and the sensitising of national identities. It also has to be said that, when the frame of reference of national populations is confined to national borders, or even more limited to regional, tribal and local communities within them, people have had little real choice other than to simply absorb and affirm their process of socialisation.

In terms of identity choice, then, there is a huge difference between those that live in a small community, where everyone looks and speaks like themselves, believes in the same god, has only one version of history given by their community or taught in their education system, has a limited diet of food, culture and ideas, and those that live in a globalised city, with many ethnic cultural and religious influences, who are able to travel to many countries and can connect via the internet to a worldwide information system. The latter are far more able to exercise real choice than the former and far more likely to reform and change their ideas about identity.

The changing national context of identity

The era of super diversity means that it is no longer possible to think about identity in terms of bounded identity 'blocks' that attempt to find accommodation with each other, either between minority and majority, or between the distinct minorities. Whereas 50 years or so ago most European countries were able to think about 'race' in terms of the handful of distinct groups of migrants from their former colonies, this is simply no longer possible. In terms of the recent impact of migration, there are now 20 cities with more than 1 million foreign-born residents, which combined means these metropolitan areas have 37 million foreign-born residents accounting for 19 per cent of the world's foreign-born stock. These few points on the globe are the destinations for one in five of the world's immigrants. There are another 59 cities worldwide with a presence of 100,000 or more foreign-born residents, including 11 cities with an immigrant presence of between 500,000 and 1 million people: Atlanta, USA; Boston, USA; Buenos Aires, Argentina; Montreal, Canada; Phoenix, USA; Riverside, USA; San Diego, USA; San Jose, USA; St. Petersburg, Russia; Tel Aviv, Israel; Vancouver, Canada (Clark, 2008, p. 27). Many other countries have similarly high rates of internal migration and cross-border movement.

In Britain's case the ethnic classification in official terms has nevertheless remained more or less the same, with the census and other formal record systems persisting with a few 'tick boxes' for Black-Caribbean, Black-African, Pakistani, Bangladeshi, Chinese and Irish, though a small number of mixed categories have been added, which combine some of the above groups together, or with the White category. This suggests that the perception of ethnicity is still based around a relatively small number of groups with 'mixed' elements added. In this way, 'accommodations' can be negotiated on a bilateral or multilateral basis, with the mixed groups largely omitted from the identity politics. However, in the present reality, the number of ethnic, national, religious and cultural groups and combinations thereof, runs into many hundreds and has created resistance to simplistic categorisation and given rise to 'You Can't Put Me in a Box' (Fanshawe and Sriskandarajah, 2010).

Super diversity means that nation-states, as well as communities and individuals, have to begin to think about their identity in much more nuanced and complex ways. Multicultural policies have hindered this development, tending to reinforce fixed concepts of cultural difference built around past patterns of diversity, and the negotiation of accommodations has hardened and homogenised those identities by promoting 'plural monoculturalism' (Sen, 2006), as a small advance from a singular monocultural identity. Interculturalism can potentially offer a more dynamic model, capable of coping with ever changing patterns of diversity and hybrid identities.

Nation-states have of course attempted to reinforce their own sense of nationhood and allegiance by seeking to prop up their ailing cultural and political identities, built around nationhood. As described earlier, this has often taken the form of citizenship programmes, tests and oaths of allegiances, alongside specially devised or reformed education programmes, using the notion of unification through history, literature and language. This has become increasingly difficult as globalisation and diversity have already undermined any real consensus about what actually constitutes 'national identity'. Further, it has tended to alienate minority cultures and hardened their separate identities, and is often perceived as homogenising and exclusive. In addition, the state actually provides or supports a number of institutions that themselves instrumentalise particular identities and cultures, through support for a particular religion, faith-based schooling, funding for ethnic specific groups and even identity-based policies, like those developed for anti-terrorist programmes (and that David Cameron, the UK prime minister (Cameron 2011), may have unwittingly redefined as 'state multiculturalism') (see Chapter 4).

The concept of 'culture' has, in any event, always been difficult to define and the extent to which a 'common culture' actually existed in any state can be challenged. Today, 'culture' is often associated with 'race', ethnicity and religion, simply because they have become the modern fault lines in multicultural societies. But this follows an era in which 'culture' was much more closely aligned with social class and was value-laden in the sense that 'high culture' represented good taste and refinement with the unsaid assumption that other culture was by definition 'low' and associated with poorer people. Since the Second World War, the cultural divide has become much more closely aligned with 'race' and more latterly with ethnicity and faith. Many of the previous markers of social divides, such as those based on language, accents and dress codes, have all but disappeared in modern Britain at least. For example, the 'proper' language of the BBC has been supplemented and supplanted by regional accents, and in terms of dress, the establishment of a huge range of high street fashions – often based upon global brands and the 'casualisation' of clothing – has removed many of the visual cultural codes. More markedly, the end of deference to our class 'betters' has long since removed visible class-based social hierarchies and repositioned them, for example, in respect of celebrity status. The age of 'deferential worker', identified by Lockwood (1966), is over, partly due to social change and especially the impact of mass communications, which have democratised information and enabled all bastions of power to be challenged. Inglehart (2008) has confirmed that, at an international level, the rise of 'self-expression values' represents a shift away from deference to all forms of external authority.

Further, the working class has been dramatically reduced at the expense of a massive increase in the middle class. As in any definition of 'class' there are a number of ways of defining 'middle class', Diana Farrell suggests that the middle classes begin at roughly the point where people have a third of their income left for discretionary spending after providing for basic food and shelter. This allows them to begin to take vacations, buy consumer items like mobile phones, fridges and even cars. They may also be able to improve their health care, or plan for their children's education. On this basis, and for the first time in history, more than half the world is middle-class, largely because of the exceptionally rapid growth in emerging countries (Farrell, 2009). However, this average figure masks much higher levels in the West with middle-class proportions around 80 per cent in the USA, Germany, the UK and Canada and thereby easily forming the majority. The developing middle-class growth rates now mean that, in numerical terms, China has the biggest number of *bourgeois* households in the world (Adler, 2008). The numbers of middle-class people in all countries is expected to continue to grow at a rapid pace, especially in the emerging economies of India and China, with an estimated 3 billion more middle-class consumers over the next 20 years (Kharas, 2010).

The growth of the middle class, of course, stands in contrast to the continuing high number of people who subsist on less than one US dollar per day. And, many middle-class families will have over extended themselves, or may fall prey to unemployment and other crises in their finances and are by no means financially secure. But the growth of the middle class across the world will profoundly alter the way people see themselves and others, both within and between nations. Middle-class people are able to use their discretionary spend to travel, to invest in communications, especially the internet, read more widely and develop their education – and in so doing to learn about others. As suggested previously, a more wealthy and better educated population seems to imply a weakening of collective identities (Stone and Muir, 2007).

The rapid *embourgeoisement* of the world's population is surely something to be celebrated, especially the growth in developing countries where hundreds of millions of people have been lifted out of poverty for the first time. And, for example, the fact that 3 million Chinese can now enjoy skiing, a sport that was completely unavailable to them 15 years ago, simply affirms the right of those in the developing world to grasp the opportunities that have long been available in the West. But alongside the opportunities for greater personal fulfilment and the relief from grinding poverty, the more profound change is that people are now beginning to connect with one another in new ways and to transcend national and cultural barriers at unprecedented levels. It would appear that middle-class people from different countries are beginning to share affinities in ways that have been almost impossible in the past. This could of course be no more than being able to buy the same Nike, Sony or Burberry item, or follow the same Barcelona or Manchester United football team, or simply to meet in Paris or Bangkok, but improved intercultural understandings and relationships are the almost inevitable result of this new interconnectivity.

There is also some evidence that identities are becoming less 'vertical', as characterised by national forms built around social class and defended by political and community leaders, and that they are shifting towards more 'horizontal' forms, with greater emphasis on cross-community and international linkages. Mansouri (2009), drawing on research in Australia and some other countries, indicates that contemporary migrant youth in Australia share much with migrant youth globally, and also more generally with all youth growing up conversant with new media and in multicultural surroundings. Mansouri also suggests that young people from a range of ethnicities, including Turkish and indigenous Australian and Pacific Islanders, can now focus on the connections between young people, rather than their particular ethnicity. Young people in the UK also seem inclined in this direction with a UK survey indicating that some 93 per cent of young people think it is important to learn about issues affecting people's lives in different parts of the world (Ipsos-MORI/Geographical Association Survey, 2009). Though the potential of social media, particularly among the 'Facebook generation', is yet to be assessed, the dramatic events in the Middle East, or 'Arab Spring' in 2011, appear to suggest that people are increasingly willing and able to connect across borders. And while the number of users of Facebook is open to some conjecture among commercial sources, it is reportedly heading towards 1 billion people and other social networking sites are also growing. The potential for new affinities, less hidebound by familial and parochial patterns, therefore appears to be very significant.

McGhee (2005), however, is determined to challenge any notion of the emergence of cosmopolitan identities, and associates it with the politics of New Labour. Under this doctrine, of which he evidently disapproves, he suggests that 'identity, culture and tradition are seen as conducive to prejudice, antagonism, polarization, mistrust, hatred and overt (fanatical) loyalty associated with preservationist or past-orientated orientations'. He believes that emotionally 'hot' patterns of identity are, unfortunately, being replaced by 'a calmer cosmopolitan mentality which is characterised by flexibility, "cool" loyalties and thin patterns of solidarity' (p. 172). Even though McGhee acknowledges that this form of cosmopolitan citizenship is not aimed simply at minorities and requires everyone to change (p. 167) (thus negating one of his, and others', principal concerns about community cohesion – see later), he still attempts to find fault with an approach that he is deeply suspicious of, on political grounds.

McGhee (2005) is so concerned by what he then sees as the illiberal agenda of the New Labour government, that he pays little or no attention to the impact of international and global trends and focuses on the relationships between minorities and majorities within nations. McGhee is not alone in this approach and it emerges in many different contexts, for example, in respect of the French-speaking Quebec province and its relationship to wider Canada, where Bouchard (2011) is concerns with the 'legitimate' interests of the majority culture, and the desire to perpetuate and maintain itself in the face of pressure from minorities and immigrants. Burnett (2004) sees the debate in the same political terms as McGhee and similarly detects assimilationist tendencies in any reform of the notion of identity and does not look beyond the rather historic boundaries of the majority/minority binary position within nation-states. Of course, these boundaries are still important, but are no longer the only driver of identity, especially for younger people growing up in an era of super diversity (Ali, 2003).

McGhee (2005), again like a number of others, also seems to ignore the possibility that identity is layered, dynamic and contextualised rather than monolithic. It is, then, either integrated to the point of assimilation, or diverse with protected separate domains, and faced with this simplistic choice that he has created for himself, chooses the latter. But identities are not simply 'hot' or 'cold' in the way that McGhee suggests – nor related wholly to 'race'. Identities consist of many components, and some of these components feature more strongly in the overall conception and vary in strength at different times and in different contexts. These 'layers' have been set out in detail previously (Cantle, 2008) and include the way people define themselves in relation to employment, language, culture, faith, ethnicity, nationality and locale. It is also clear that entirely new components are emerging as a result of national and international media, diaspora influences, intermarriage and travel. This is not surprising as societies are dynamic and constantly in flux with the salience of particular differences changing over time – for example, in Great Britain 'Irish' is still used as an ethnic group, but no longer has any real justification as such, at least no more than the many other national groups such as 'Polish' or 'Romanian'.

This is precisely the problem for the conceptualisation of identity in many Western nations. Previous conceptions of identity still linger on, even though the historic position may have altered or moved on completely. This is ironic as most academics are only too keen to support Hall's (1992) view that identities do not exist in isolation and accept that, like 'race', ethnicity and culture, are socially and politically constructed. However, they then appear to defend a static view of identity and seem to regard it as primordial, with any attempt to question or challenge any aspect of it as a government or illiberal plot to undermine real programmes of social and economic change. And actually, the very idea of 'Black', 'White', 'Muslim' or another generic term to describe a 'culture' is homogenising. In the same way that countries had in the past defined themselves by their overwhelming 'sameness' and had seen themselves as a 'race', any generic descriptor will mask as much difference within that culture as between them and other groups. Even when they are broken down to reflect more varied conceptions they can, again, become rigid and homogenising. For example, Modood's (1988) apparently reasonable attempt to conceptualise 'Asian' identity as separate and distinct from 'Black' political culture, simply results in him creating a new reified category 'which suppressed the cultural diversity within this category' (Solomos and Back, 1996, p. 135).

'Mixed race': the legacy of racial constructs

It is though, the classification of people as 'mixed race' which perhaps best illustrates the inadequacy of the way in which race (and ethnicity, faith, culture and nationality) are conceptualised and discussed. It is an unfortunate legacy of our racialised past, rather than a basis for reflecting our present diversity. Until recently, it had been difficult to even discuss the concept of mixed race with interethnic sexual relations still heavily bounded by taboos and in which intermarriage was either legally or socially barred. Miscegenation was actually against the law in a number of countries, including the USA, until the 1960s. Indeed, it has always been a 'left over' form of identity for those that did not conform to the standard categories and is rooted in our past racial history with unfortunate connotations of racial purity:

> the historical and contemporary neuroses about intercultural union, which circulate especially (though not exclusively) where the peoples involved display visible signs of difference such as skin colour, are inevitably grounded in the impossible assumption of original unity and racial purity.
>
> (Coombes and Brah, 2000, p. 4)

But governments around the world, often supported by civil society bodies, religious leaders and community organisations generally support the notion of 'preference of purity' by awarding funding to single-identity groups, creating special forms of social status, or by recognising and privileging such groups for consultation and negotiations. No such recognition or support is provided for mixed-race groups. Despite this, the fastest growing ethnic minority, in Britain at least, is that of mixed race. There is not, nor can be, any pretence of homogeneity within a group that is so encompassing of all manner of nationalities, ethnicities, faiths and cultures, but we apparently still believe that this is possible within almost equally homogenising generic terms such as 'Black', 'Asian' or 'Muslim'. The main function of the mixed-race category is, then, only to record the number of people who are not considered to be of some particular 'pure' origin.

The term 'mixed race' is, unsurprisingly, also contested. For some, it carries derogatory overtones and suggestions of racial impurity, and for others that the identity of mixed-race people is presented as confused and mixed up. 'Mixed race', however, has at least been more of a neutral term than those like 'half-breed', mulatto, or 'half-caste', which were clearly offensive. Alternatives, such as 'dual', or 'multiple heritage', are now preferred in some quarters, but they still imply a lack of recognition in the identity stakes, being somehow 'in between' pure and unfettered origins.

Moreover, in most Western countries, people who are of mixed race are routinely classified as 'Black', based on the racialised assumption that they are not of 'pure' White descent and must therefore be Black. This applies to President Obama, who is habitually described as 'Black' in the press and media, even though he has a White mother and Black father.

Despite the social taboos, the legal restrictions that inhibited inter-racial sexual relations for so long and the institutional preference for 'pure' origins, the number of mixed-race people is growing at a fast rate and rejecting the societal concerns: they are at least apparently willing and able to see beyond skin colour and other socially constructed differences. This is not, unfortunately, a celebrated trend but intercultural union is fast becoming the peoples' choice and is impossible to ignore.

In the UK, mixed-race people were not even identified and counted prior to the 1991 census and the full extent of the changing circumstances have only recently begun to emerge. England and Wales had nearly 700,000 mixed-race people in 2001 and this had risen to nearly 1 million only eight years later in 2009 (ONS, 2011). This is a huge rate of growth and it would appear that this category is the fastest growing of all minority groups, with around 9 per cent of children now living in families that contain mixed or multiple heritages (Platt, 2009). It is likely, however, that the categorisation of mixed race is still underestimated. In the first place, people are not encouraged to self-identify and the UK census's category suggests only four groups for 'Mixed': 'White and Black Caribbean', 'White and Black African', 'White and Asian' and 'Other Mixed'. While people can write in any combination, including multiple heritage, they are only guided to the above particular groups and there is little to suggest an idea of 'mixed-ness' in respect of faith and nationality, let alone the many other ethnicities.

Interestingly, there are few, if any, attempts to promote the growth of mixed race as a means of developing intercultural understanding and reducing the tensions between groups. Despite Coombes and Brah

(2000) seeing the idea of preserving racial purity underpinning much of the debate about cultural and social intermixing, they tend to dismiss past attempts to encourage racial intermixing as 'assimilationist', though these attempts were largely to secure advantage in a colonial context. And indeed, there are fears about the creation of some sort of undifferentiated mass of White, Black and other ethnicities, a 'coffee coloured people by the score', to quote the pop song *Melting Pot*.[1] One may wonder if this is such a bad ambition given the present failure to see the common humanity across divisions. However, it also points to a false choice between assimilation, often presented in culinary terms such as a 'soup', in which every ingredient is mixed up and infused together and loses its distinctiveness, and a diversity model in which ingredients are part of the same dish but keep their distinction as in a 'salad bowl' or 'stir fry'. This again suggests a simplistic all-or-nothing choice in which there are no 'layers of separation' (Cantle, 2008) and in which culture is viewed as static, rather than dynamic and contextualised.

In 'the real world', Ali's research with young people (2003) has found that children cope very well with connotations of 'mixed race' and are reluctant to be put into specific boxes. They recognise that identities are contextualised and 'for the most part, were free of adult "visual politics... using creative approaches to belonging"' (p. 168). For many young children, 'race' is not always the most salient feature of their lives (p. 170) and that 'what the children understand from their teachers is limited to static and confining notions of monocultural and ethnic positions' and 'with a very simplistic ideal of "tolerance" of "other" cultures, which inadvertently reinforced very static and hierarchical notions of what culture meant' (p. 168).

Unfortunately, even well intentioned anti-racist teaching can reinforce static concepts of race and identity and Ali (2003) suggests that there is an 'urgent need for anti-racist teaching to involve recognition of multiplicity', which she reluctantly calls 'hybridity' (p. 178):

> such complexities in cultural forms coupled with the children's cultural expertise in readings and performances in these areas, will require skilled navigation on the part of teachers. The need to consider more reflexive models of new ethnicities is essential for this process.
>
> (p. 179)

Fanshawe and Sriskandarajah (2010) are equally concerned about singular identities and the title of their publication 'You Can't Put Me in a Box' for the Institute for Public Policy Research makes their position clear from the outset. They point out:

> In an age of super diversity where people do not identify around single identities and feel conflicted allegiance (if any allegiance at all) to predefined groups, activism around particular 'strands' seems irrelevant to many people and may not even be that effective in addressing the true causes of inequality. Even the very categorisations that we rely on (for example, 'black', 'gay', 'Asian' or 'disabled') no longer seem to be able to tell us much about who people are, what lives they lead, who they identify with, or what services they need from government and society. And the tick box approach seems to be missing out on growing numbers of people who fall outside or across standard classifications. Yet society seems to treat ethnic identities as if they are clearly bounded, static and meaningful, and public bodies insist on a tick box classification.
>
> (Fanshawe and Sriskandarajah, 2010, p. 5)

The policy response to super diversity, however, has simply been to create even more categories, often based upon combinations of faith, ethnicity and nationality. Ali (2003) chides previous commentators for their failure 'to deconstruct and evolve' their post-race framework and creates these 'comma-ed or hyphenated identities that plague multiplicitous positions and hold to some sort of composite, constructed version of mixing some sort of singular "racial" identities' (p. 18). In the UK, we have seen the ethnic classification categories grow to encompass a limited number of mixed-race groups but these do not begin to reflect the complexity of super diversity and, although religion has also been given greater prominence in the census, 'mixed race' is still almost entirely focused on ethnicity rather than interfaith unions. But the more categories are created, the more it becomes clear that they too are inadequate descriptors, in which many people are still 'left over', and this only increases the pressure for more categories to recognise the 'difference' of ever more discrete groups. Most Western countries could easily develop several hundred identity categories and even then would fail to provide a suitable 'box' for everyone.

The implications for policy are profound. First, many public and private sector organisations now routinely monitor the ethnic origin, faith, gender, sexual orientation, disability, age and caring responsibility of their staff and customers. This intelligence has informed a range of measures to promote equality and prevent discrimination (see Cantle, 2008, pp. 174–178). These measures have undoubtedly had some success, both in terms of outcomes and in terms of developing greater transparency and thereby improving the confidence in the fairness of institutional arrangements, particularly on behalf of the minority communities. It has, however, also led to accusations of 'political correctness' and the focus has often been more on process than on outcomes. But there is also no doubt that there has been a failure to adjust and adapt equalities programmes to the current realities of super diversity and mixed-race hybridity. Nowhere is this more evident than in the policy and practice of adoption, where the search for the perfect ethnic match of prospective parents and the child to be adopted has denied many children the opportunity of a loving home. Transracial adoption has been bound up with concerns about national and ethnic identifications and has assumed, in particular, that Black people have a different and bounded culture, derived from distinct 'roots' that are different from those of White Britons (Ali, 2003, p. 8). However, it is based on an even deeper sense of division too, in which it is assumed that people of one 'race' cannot provide love and support to a person of another 'race' and that their identity will be in some way compromised or confused, leading to psychological problems. While it is true that some mixed-race adoptions have been unsuccessful in the past racialised context, the present policy simply fails to recognise the current reality in that many 'natural' families are in fact 'mixed race' in some way and when wider domains of heritage are taken into account, 'mixed' is very much part of the new 'normal'. Adoption policies have simply failed to recognise that the divisions upon which such assumptions have been based, are now part of a post-race set of social constructs and therefore only exist if adoption policies choose to instrumentalise them.

In many respects, social arrangements have moved ahead of policy and practice and support Ali's (2003) findings in respect of younger people. Brynin et al. (2008) believe that the decline in co-ethnic partnerships will continue with new generations reflecting a general view that similar education, friendships, attitudes and beliefs provide a more meaningful basis for the selection of a partner, rather than ethnicity. There is also evidence of a general trend for younger cohorts being more likely to form relationships with, or marry, those of a different religion compared to older cohorts (Platt, 2009, p. 9). And the dramatic growth in mixed-race unions and children bear out these projections.

Muslim communities and retrenchment

Another – and perhaps even more pressing – reason to dramatically reform our accepted notion of identity relates to the way in which the West has come to view the Muslim communities through the lens of a hardened and homogenous identity.

In ten years since the tragic events of 9/11, a number of strategies have been developed at a national level to try to reduce the threat of Al Qa'ida terrorism, though it is doubtful whether they have made the world a safer place. The UK's Prevent programme (HM Government, 2008),[2] which has been emulated in many other countries, has been exceptional in the way that it has focused on a single identity group and created a Muslim-centric industry that has homogenised and hardened Muslim identities. The homogenising of communities is not only the province of governments, and Demirbag-Sten (2011) points out that Swedish public TV station 'Halal TV' is a striking example of how the media, like our politicians, entertain the belief that it is only possible to communicate with Muslims through Islam, an approach that 'intensely stigmatises Muslims'. This is, however, consistent with the idea that there is a 'Muslim problem', which pre-dates the so-called 'war on terror' and has enveloped whole nations and communities. Indeed, the international context is critical and has determined much of the way the 'West' sees the Muslim communities around the World and the way in which Muslim communities, including those in the West, see their Western identities. At the same time, Al Qa'ida and other extremist organisations claiming to be acting on behalf of Muslims everywhere, also promoted the notion of 'war'. The 'war on terror' thus gained political currency after 9/11 and was widely used by politicians' and in the press and media. In entering common parlance it came to mean that, in popular terms, Muslims were the enemy and that Huntingdon's thesis (Huntingdon, 2002), the 'clash of civilisations', had become real.

More generally, Muslims have been associated with the supposed 'failure of multiculturalism' at the highest level (see Chapter 4) and Muslims are constantly projected as one homogenous community and portrayed in a bad light, with many stories in the popular press about the wearing of the veil, hard-line preachers and attacks on gay rights. And of course the portrayal of Muslim communities from around the world has generally been even more negative: 'we' are at war with 'them' and 'they' are at war with 'us'. The extent of this 'stigmatising' was revealed and evidenced in a recent study by Cardiff University (Moore et al., 2008) of 1000 newspaper articles, which has shown that references to radical Muslims outnumbered references to moderates by 17 to one. The most common nouns used in relation to British Muslims were 'terrorist', 'extremist', 'militant' and 'Islamist'. Indeed, a coincidental development has been the rise of Far Right groups in England, such as the English Defence League, which are specifically constructed as 'anti-Muslim' organisations and have found common cause with other Far Right groups and garnered popular support across Europe.

The Prevent Strategy did not include any plans or programmes to develop a portrayal of Muslim communities which represent their wider diversity and views but, rather, had the effect of reinforcing the mythology – a programme of constant alertness and surveillance still roams across the entire Muslim community. There have been many allegations of spying on the Muslim community (Kundnani, 2009) and though some may have been exaggerated or mistaken, the perceptions were, and remain, very real.

The previous government had itself also acknowledged that Prevent was in trouble. The then Communities Secretary, John Denham, said:

> We have recognised that the label originally attached to the funding – preventing violent extremism was seen by some as stigmatising for Muslim communities as a whole and in particular for those who participated in the Prevent work.
>
> (Denham, 2010)

The new government took a similar view and were initially very keen to rectify what they also saw as this counter-productive approach. Baroness Neville-Jones, the new secretary of state for security, in her first interview (which was interestingly with the Islam TV Channel) immediately indicated a review of Prevent and other security measures that had been seen to disproportionately impact upon the Muslim community (Neville-Jones, 2010). However, under the banner of Prevent, there are still many programmes that are not intelligence-led nor based upon evidence and, rather, take the form of generalised surveillance in which hundreds of thousands of public officials are being asked to keep an eye on Muslims in their employment, in their schools, colleges or universities, or in their communities, and identify those that may present a potential threat. There is little that could be objected to in the original aims of Prevent:

To be successful we need to ensure that:

- The voices of violent extremists do not go unchallenged.
- People are able to access a wider range of alternative, authoritative views about Islam and participate in debate.
- Communities have an increased range of tools and support to help them in rejecting violent extremism.
- Mainstream voices overseas are amplified to resonate with counterparts in the UK.

(HM Government, 2008)

Similarly the upgraded version in 2009 (HM Government, 2009) added the objectives of 'disrupting those who promote violent extremism', increasing 'resilience of communities' and to 'address the grievances that ideologues are exploiting'.

However, the way in which this was applied through Prevent meant that it appeared to target the whole Muslim community. Khan (2009), on behalf of the An-Nisa Society, summed up the views of many Muslim and other organisations:

the government's approach to dealing with terrorism by targeting the whole Muslim community as 'potential terrorists' in its Prevent Strategy is flawed and fraught with perils. We believe that rather than creating community cohesion and eliminating terrorism it has the potential to create discord and inflame community tensions.

The most glaring concerns of the Prevent strategy are the targeting of the whole Muslim community as potential terrorists, the fusion of counter terrorism with community cohesion and community development initiatives, and the mainstreaming of Prevent in the core services of local councils.

Prevent's sole focus on Muslims through their faith identity has limited, rather than broadened, their perspectives. Amartya Sen (2006) confirms that the present approach has been paradoxical in its effect and has actually helped to bolster religious identities and power structures:

The confusion between the plural identities of Muslims and their Islamic identity is not only a descriptive mistake, it has serious implications for policies for peace in the precarious world in which we live [...] The effect of this religion-centred political approach, and of the institutional policies it has generated...has been to bolster and strengthen the voice of religious authorities while downgrading the importance of non-religious institutions and movements.

(Sen, 2006, pp. 75, 77)

Gary Younge (2009) expressed this very clearly and in more practical terms:

...the government continues to approach Muslims as though their religion defines them. It rarely speaks to them as tenants, parents, students or workers; it does not dwell on problems that they share with everyone else; it does not convene high profile task forces to look at how to improve their daily lives. It summons them as Muslims, talks to them as Muslims and refers to them as Muslims – as though they could not possibly be understood as anything else.

The House of Commons Communities and Local Government Select Committee (2010) also very much endorsed this view and pointed out the interconnectedness of identity:

The single focus on Muslims in *Prevent* has been unhelpful. We conclude that any programme which focuses solely on one section of a community is stigmatising, potentially alienating, and fails to address the fact that that no section of a population exists in isolation from others.

Bartlett et al. (2010, p. 23) confirm that there has been a 'growing identification among Muslims in Western democracies along religious lines, both within the media and by Muslims themselves'.

Thus, the political agenda, coupled with the anti-terrorist programme under the banner of Prevent, has served to deny the diversity within the Muslim community and stand in contrast to the studies that have revealed the extent and nature of this diversity – indeed the Muslim communities in the UK are among the most diverse in the world (iCoCo, 2008). Despite the huge variation in nationality, ethnicity, sect, tribal, clan, political and community affiliations, it has created a situation that has defined a whole series of distinct and separate communities by their 'Muslimness'.

The focus on Muslim communities has not only served to harden and homogenise Muslimness but has also obscured the threats of violence in other communities and meant that governments have failed to take sufficient account of those from the Far Right and lone wolf killers and to anticipate more general social unrest – the UK was certainly caught napping by the August 2011 riots. While the new Prevent Strategy (HM Government, 2011) does belatedly suggest a wider role and will begin to encompass sectarian and Far Right violence, in practice little has been done to give any effect to monitoring these threats and there are no programmes that would reach into the growing number of Far Right organisations and their increasing numbers of supporters, nor a widespread programme of surveillance, to prevent the transition from extremism to terrorism. The tendency to essentialise minority identities has also helped to create wider barriers between minorities and the majority population, because it camouflages similarities between minorities and majorities and makes it difficult for alternative and, ironically, often more moderate, dissenting voices to be heard from within the minority groups (Jurado, 2011).

Despite the overbearing focus of Western governments on their Muslim communities, the main thrust of change in the way Muslim identities are formed and portrayed has come from Muslim communities themselves in the form of the 'Arab Spring', which has had the effect of presenting them as freedom fighters and 'democrats' in opposition to the oppressive regimes led by despots, who also happened to be Muslims. This has confounded the usual portrayal and aligns the rebels with at least some 'Western' values. Further, the rebels became allies with the NATO-led forces in Libya and received other less tangible forms of support from a number of other countries. Suddenly, Muslims in the Middle East had become friends of the West, brave freedom fighters and supporters of democracy, and the fact that they were Muslims was hardly mentioned, except to voice the fear that after the conflict they may turn into Muslims again, by adopting a new Muslim fundamentalist identity!

Western governments, themselves, have done little to try to change perceptions of the Muslim communities, and indeed have often reinforced the negative identity, justifying the international conflict and counter-terrorism activities at home. It is remarkable that in the UK and other countries with significant Muslim populations nothing has been done to try to counter the negative images of so many of their own citizens – around 2 million in the UK alone. Rather, they continue to be portrayed in some sections of the popular press and media as a 'fifth column' who hold values incompatible with those of mainstream society – and this popular view is constantly reinforced by government initiatives to counter (their) terrorist threat.

Multiple, dynamic and choice-based identities

The relationship between multicultural policies and ideas about identity has been problematic on a number of levels. Both 'defensive' and 'progressive' forms of multiculturalism (see Chapter 4) have tended to resist notions of universalism in relation to identity and values. Proponents of multiculturalist policies have viewed these calls for universal values as a coded attack on minorities and an attempt to portray their values as inferior or invalid. Thus, the promotion of universal values has been limited because it could be portrayed as a vehicle for assimilation. This approach has meant that progressive ideas and values that are generally held as universal, most notably the rights of women and girls, have not been advanced at the same rate across all communities. In this protected arrangement, minority communities too have been encouraged to cling to past conceptions of their heritage, eschewing opportunities to change and adapt to both changing circumstances within Western societies and the wider context of globalisation and super diversity. Indeed, some minority communities have clung so rigidly to past idealised views of their heritage, that they have failed to keep pace with the social and cultural changes within their countries of origin, or as suggested earlier, become living souvenirs of a past that no longer exists (Powell, 2004).

'Values' are not, of course, the same as 'identity', but how we see ourselves and others does depend to some extent on whether we hold ideas in common. Again, the choice between 'all or nothing' integration in which people are able to 'integrate' at some levels and remain separate and distinct at others, is the key issue. Because multiculturalism has been dominated by a racialised debate since its post-war inception, identities have also tended to be bounded by visible differences, in which all distinctive features are treated as the single most important or sole determinant of identity. Globalisation and super diversity are changing the terms of this debate.

'Race' continues to provide fault lines that impact upon conceptions of identity, though racism has already significantly shifted from a biological basis to more nuanced and subtle forms utilising cultural rather than racial determinants. The binary Black/White axis has therefore also been weakened, with many more complex patterns of assumed superiority/inferiority emerging within and between minorities as well as on the more traditional majority/minority basis. But the idea of 'race' not only dominates the thinking of the Far Right, but also that of anti-racists who give credence to the binary divide by defending essentialist racial identities.

The 'race' context does not, however, simply revolve around minority communities, and majorities within Western societies have also generally clung to a monocultural conception of themselves – White, Christian, and based upon a single (or possibly several) historic language groups – in the face of post-war multiculturalism, which was viewed as a threat to this collective identity. Ironically, the policies of multiculturalism that evolved at the time to provide a defensive shield around minorities to protect them against racism and discrimination and allow them to hold on to their former heritage, have also hardened the host community's monocultural conception at the same time. For example, many Western nations see themselves as being peculiarly Christian and have failed to notice that the Christian world is now quickly changing, to the extent that the majority of the Christian population now live outside the Western world. The growth of membership in Africa and Asia is especially notable and more than two-thirds of Christian church communities are outside Western Europe and North America (Seko, 2004).

There have been few attempts to engage with the 'layers of difference' (Cantle, 2008) across communities, nor to end the assumption of 'singular affiliation' in which any person belongs to only one 'collectivity' (Sen, 2006, p. 20) and, rather, to conceptualise identity as a straight line with assimilation at one end and complete separation and absence of a collective sense of belonging at the other. Despite the antipathy to more mixed and hybrid forms of identity and those that can change over time, an increasing number of people are no longer bound by fixed ideas of themselves. This is most apparent in the case of mixed-race relationships, in which 'race' is no longer important, or at least far less important than other ideas about what people have in common. It is clear that, as ideas about the biological superiority of one 'race' over another continues to decline, the position of people of mixed race will change and ideas about being a 'left over' second class category should be erased. However, while it is only to be expected that community and faith leaders are still trying to steer people into their flocks and to hang on to their influence, change will only occur if the institutions of the state are prepared to stop privileging pure or single forms of identity (see later chapters). This may lead to a change in the practice of ethnic classification and monitoring – should we have a new tick box for 'not defined by any identity' or even, 'member of the human race'? Alternatively, as some commentators have begun to argue, perhaps calls for the cessation of ethnic classification and monitoring altogether on the basis that the more sensitised to race we become, the less we are able to see each other as 'human beings with similar hopes, aspirations and problems' (Mirza, 2010), will be heeded. Yet, the task of seeking to ensure 'fairness' through policy instruments is still relevant and is far from finished business, with virtually every assessment of equality indicating that ethnic minorities remain significantly disadvantaged. The implications for practice of a new model of interculturalism are discussed in Chapter 8.

While multicultural policies are still rooted in the, largely, colonial migration history and the past focus on 'race', they are unable to cope with the implications of globalisation and super diversity in several respects. First, the sheer number of recognisable groups – whether based on language, ethnicity, faith, nationality or a combination of some or all of these differences – means that it is simply not practicable to separately seek representation and negotiate accommodations with, let alone fund, the hundreds of distinct and combinational forms. Nevertheless a cadre of single-identity community leaders, based largely on the colonial migration patterns, has been created over the years and they continue to promote their 'difference', with the formal or tacit support of the state, rather than create a broader sense of commonality. Newer migrant groups who are facing different issues – and often more pressing concerns – threaten these relationships and underline the need for multicultural political processes based upon dynamic and new patterns of interaction. For example, the Irish community in Britain is no longer regarded as 'other', experiences little discrimination (though it is still classified as an ethnic group) and now receives little by way of recognition in identity terms. The Italian community has similarly slipped below the political radar in the USA. Meanwhile, the Roma community has moved to the forefront of multicultural concerns in the UK, along with many European countries, and since 2001 those communities that had been identified as 'Asian' or 'African', or perhaps denoted by their national origin, are now interacted with under their newly discovered 'Muslim' identity.

Indeed, as the salience of 'race' has diminished, it has partly shifted to ever more divided ethnic and hybrid identities that combine ethnic, faith and nationality which are often presented in the same primordial context and as discrete categories in Sen's 'plural monoculturalism' terms (Sen, 2006). The transposition to faith has, to some extent, been no more than a continuation of the racial vilification, by using faith as a proxy for race in which the Muslim communities bear the brunt of the attacks by the Far Right and where Muslims are readily identified as a visible and largely non-White minority and as 'others'. However, all faiths have also emerged much more clearly and prominently into the 'public realm' even though this has been strongly contested (Dinham and Lowndes, 2009), and become a more important component of collective and personal identities in Western states, despite lower levels of formalised worship in many of those same countries. The Western rhetoric of the 'war on terror' and the equation of this in peoples' minds with the Muslim communities has, no doubt, also served to harden and homogenise faith identities on both sides of this divide. As noted earlier, diaspora influences, which are generally faith-based, are also now able to sustain themselves across national and continental boundaries by using technology and by taking advantage of the more generally affordable cost of travel. Faith thus provides a frame of reference, which is no longer particularly constrained by national influences, in most Western states, despite some attempts to restrict visible symbols such as the face veil, as in France, the Netherlands and other countries.

There have also been equally profound social changes that have enabled people to identify themselves in other ways, most notably with regard to sexual orientation and moving beyond the homosexual/heterosexual divide to lesbian, gay, bisexual, transgender and intersex (LGBTI) distinctions. The Women's Movement, which has successfully established the recognition and categorisation of gender on a routine basis in the UK and other countries, has, of course, been longer standing and politically vociferous for more than a hundred years and has continued to make gains and to be able to assert a distinct set of identities, with rising economic and political power. This is reflected in rising levels of tolerance among 'Western publics', particularly among the young, confirmed by Inglehart's (2008) findings that values had changed between 1970 and 2006 with a much greater emphasis on gender equality as part of a broader syndrome of tolerance of outgroups, including foreigners, gays and lesbians. Groups representing people with disabilities have also become more assertive and identifiable, especially as disability has increasingly been accepted and based upon a social rather than medical model. The same could also be said of those groups who will gain some recognition in the identity stakes as a result of the UK's single Equality Act 2010 which described nine 'protected characteristics'. The previous anti-discrimination laws were replaced with this single Act to make the law simpler and to remove inconsistencies. The protected characteristics, which cannot now be used as a reason to treat people unfairly, are age, disability, gender reassignment, marriage and civil partnership, pregnancy and maternity, race, religion or belief, sex and sexual orientation. On this basis, everyone will fall under one or more of the protected characteristics, so it could be said to regard all people as diverse, or 'different'.

'Race', of course, remains an important aspect of identity – and is still used in legal definitions to cover ethnic, faith and national groups – but it has been diffused by a much wider range of social, national and language groups and developed in many hybrid forms. To some extent, these additional characteristics now compete for attention and their very recognition in the public sphere means that it is easier to discuss those differences on a more positive and rational basis, in which 'race' has far less salience. Interculturalism has the potential to consolidate the change from the race-based forms of identity under multiculturalism, to much more multifaceted forms, but must avoid merely creating yet more forms of 'plural monoculturalism' in which there is no connection or empathy between them.

States must also realise that, while collective and national identity is threatened from below and people are much more able to choose to live their lives in different ways and to form new associations, they are also threatened from above. International influences are now stronger than ever in political and social terms, and compete with both formal and informal national and local influences. Indeed, states are losing their sense of legitimacy as it is becoming clear that they have limited power to control global forces and the exercise of democratic processes at a national level has a limited impact on global outcomes. This 'democratic deficit' is fast becoming a political problem as much as a social one and may well lead to further unrest. There are now calls to 'repatriate powers' to nation-states and a number of political parties and movements are specifically devoted to this, particularly in Europe with an added impetus following the financial crisis. The hope is a simple one – that nation-states and their political parties will regain control of their economies and realign democratic political processes, enabling citizens to engage with this power (largely by reversing the downward trend of voter turnout) and thereby also develop a closer association with nationhood. Retrenchment is, however, an unlikely outcome as globalisation cannot be easily thrown into reverse. These backward-looking aspirations also confound any attempt to give serious consideration to a more progressive option of developing democratic systems at an international level and the building of more global collaboration and transnational forms of identity.

People are able, to a greater extent than ever before, to choose their identity, or at least some aspect of that identity. They are also more likely than ever before to come into contact with people from different national, religious and ethnic backgrounds and to develop personal relationships that challenge communal structures and essentialist or pure forms of race or faith identity and recognise that these have been socially and culturally constructed in the first instance. The notions of identity are no longer bounded by the differences within nation-states, nor by the post-war preoccupation with the accommodation of 'racial' differences between majority and minorities.

The impact of globalisation and super diversity upon personal and collective identities is, then, profound, with individuals and communities able to draw upon heritage, faith, language and local, regional, national and international ideas about identity and to create hybrid or multiple identities that are dynamic and change over time and in different contexts. The political processes inherent in multicultural policies clearly need to develop more flexible responses to the dynamic – and increasingly complex – salient features of identity. The 'intercultural' model as a new conceptual framework for policy and practice is discussed in later chapters.

4
The 'Failure' of Multiculturalism

The notion of the 'failure of multiculturalism' has confused rather than assisted a debate about how we learn to live together in an increasingly interdependent and interconnected world. 'Multiculturalism' can simply describe the modern reality of most countries in that, alongside the majority population and indigenous peoples, there are now a large number of migrant groups from different ethnic and faith backgrounds at various stages of permanent settlement. This is a descriptive reality for most countries around the world. In this sense – and save for the most exceptional and extreme views – the argument that multiculturalism has failed simply because of the multicultural nature of modern societies, has seldom been advanced. The reference to 'failure' is based upon the perception that the *policies* of multiculturalism have been an inadequate response to the changing composition of societies. The debate about 'failure' has nevertheless contributed to a popular view that it is indeed the very presence of people from many different backgrounds that somehow poses a threat to social stability and solidarity. It is also the case that multicultural policies have, as yet, failed to deliver fair, stable and harmonious societies, at least as judged by both the objective reality (significant levels of inequality, racism and community tensions) and the subjective reality (continued emotional resistance to diversity and a desire to halt or reverse the trend). In particular, these views have been based upon a view that multicultural policies have promoted separate communities within nation-states.

The more recent suggestions of 'failure', however, relate to the current political and international context and specifically refer to the relationship of Muslim communities within Western democracies. The UK prime minister (Cameron, 2011) focused his suggested failure of 'state multiculturalism' almost entirely on the Muslim community and this

53

formed the major part of his speech. Chancellor of Germany Angela Merkel, in referring to the 'utter failure' of multiculturalism in Germany (Merkel, 2010), also set her remarks in the context of various reports and comments by political colleagues that 'people from different cultures, like Turkey and Arab countries, find it harder to integrate'. Nicholas Sarkozy (2011), the French president, also remarked upon the failure of multiculturalism. This has brought a new dimension to the debate, rather than changing its basic nature.

A recent report by the Council of Europe (2011) illustrates the current difficult debate about multiculturalism in its report *Living Together* and only felt able to provide a range of principles and policy guidelines rather than a conceptual framework:

> We are of course well aware of this debate, but find that the term 'multiculturalism' is used in so many different ways, meaning different things to different people and in different countries – is it an ideology? a set of policies? a social reality? – that in the end it confuses more than it clarifies. We have therefore decided to avoid using this term and instead to concentrate on identifying policies and approaches that will enable European societies to combine diversity and freedom.

This rather prosaic approach, which is explored later, has already begun to shape a new approach to the way diverse groups share a common society.

Early and 'defensive' forms of multiculturalism

Early forms of multiculturalism were inevitably 'defensive'. The focus was both on protecting minorities from racism and discrimination and on developing positive action programmes to begin to provide minority communities with some semblance of equal opportunities. However, this approach depended upon a significant degree of separation as a means of avoiding contact and conflict. Also, while the positive action programmes did narrow inequalities, they ironically also had the effect of reinforcing differences and promoting separate development. On a more positive note, in countries like Britain this process did give effect to a commitment to protecting the heritage of minorities and reflected the rejection of assimilation and promoted an appreciation of diversity and a commitment to tolerance and fair play.

While migration has only recently developed on a mass scale, it is not new and has taken place over the centuries (see, for example, Winder, 2004) and consequently resulted in many controversies based on 'race'. But the focus of the host community's hostility changes over time. For example, in Britain it was focused upon the Jewish community prior to the First World War, while concerns about the Irish minorities stretch back still further, but have almost disappeared in the last 20 years. The state's relationship with the Black-Caribbean community has also been difficult – they experienced a high level of racism at least up to the 1970s, were the centre of riots in the 1980s, but appear to have become almost universally accepted in recent times. By contrast, the Muslim community has become demonised since 2001, but this has taken place within a period of super diversity in which relationships are formed not only by reference to migrant communities but also within diaspora and transnational frames of reference.

The idea of multiculturalism developed as post-war migration grew. This migration was both on a different scale to previous migratory episodes, but also much more 'visible' and clearly determined by 'race'. Britain's journey to multiculturalism over this period has not been an easy one. In common with many other European countries, the influx of minorities provoked resentment and hostility. Like migrants before them, the new wave of predominantly Caribbean and South Asian people in the 1950s and 1960s found themselves pushed into manual occupations, linked to poor housing, often clustered around those employers which provided low-skilled and low-paid employment.

The new migrants were received with great suspicion and ambivalence. The fact that migrants were needed to fuel the post-war reconstruction effort and provide essential public services did little to assuage the resentment of the majority, who had been nurtured on the idea that Britons were a superior 'race' and that 'coloureds' – a term used in official reports at that time, as well as in popular discourse – were, by definition, inferior. Demands to limit migration were often repeated and many administrative restrictions were agreed in response. Even though anti-discrimination legislation was eventually introduced in 1965, the atmosphere remained highly charged, perhaps culminating in Enoch Powell's 'rivers of blood' racist rallying call which gained considerable popular support in 1968. Not surprisingly, minorities built defensive support systems around themselves and anti-racist supporters, often associated with the Left, were quickly rallied when any criticism of minorities began to emerge.

A defensive and protective policy based upon multicultural separateness gained support from both sides of the political divide. The Right opposed integration and racial mixing in principle and the left feared that it would precipitate further hostility and that the cultural heritage of minorities would be undermined in a wave of assimilation. There were, nevertheless, attempts to 'promote good race relations' – which were actually enshrined in legislation in 1968, and remaining on the statute book until the present day – but these were never implemented with any real sense of purpose (for discussion of the limited measures, see Cantle, 2008) and any discussion of the emerging multicultural model appeared to provide an opportunity to excite even more racist sentiment and to give greater oxygen to the Far Right. Demands for social justice were, however, impossible to ignore and during the late sixties an assertive 'Black' political consciousness, with support from developments in the USA, began to gather steam. This gave rise to a number of remedial programmes, often targeted at geographical areas and neighbourhoods where minority ethnic groups were concentrated. This was also supported by a range of equal opportunity policies, mainly aimed at tackling discrimination in the workplace and key services like social housing. Positive action programmes, though more controversial, also gathered ground – for example, the introduction of Black-led housing associations from the late 1980s became one of the most well-regarded investments in Black and minority leadership in Europe. These initiatives had some success and some of the values and ideals behind them were internalised and became more widely adopted as part of the 'fair play' associated with British liberal multiculturalism. However, they also inadvertently reinforced the notion of special and preferential treatment, which caused resentment from sections of the poorer majority community.

Given that in the immediate post-war period racism and discrimination were rife, the policies of that time almost inevitably had to attempt to impose tolerance and equal opportunities through legal and regulatory frameworks, and to minimise conflict and tensions by reducing or avoiding contact between different communities. It could be argued that the policies were right for the time, and the 'failure' may therefore simply have been the subsequent lack of action to modify the approach and to take account of changing social, economic and political circumstances.

The failure to adjust policies in the UK, at least, may have been due to the belief that while there had been a continual level of racism and xenophobia over the years, this was far less overt and directly discriminatory in nature, supporting the view that cultural diversity had become more generally accepted. This appeared to be confirmed by the growing success of many people from minority backgrounds in just about every professional sphere, increasing levels of intermarriage and little by way of Far Right political organisation within the majority community.

This view turned out to be somewhat complacent and was challenged by the community cohesion reviews in 2001 (see Chapter 5), which followed the riots in a number of English northern towns. The reviews focused on the 'parallel lives' led by different communities, the reluctance to promote interaction between them and the consequent fear misunderstanding of the 'other'. The reviews pointed out that, while there appeared to have been a lack of real opposition to the then policies of multiculturalism, it was apparent that there had been little by way of positive support for them either, and that the deep-seated resentment of minorities by the majority community had never really been dealt with and what was seen as an overbearing culture of 'political correctness' had kept the hostility below the surface.[1] The reviews also suggested that the policies of multiculturalism up to that point had had the impact of institutionalising separation and had limited the opportunities for people from different backgrounds to learn about each other and to disconfirm stereotypes and myths.

Previous policies had not in any way set out to promote or encourage separateness. Indeed, most of the policy interventions were focused upon preventing discrimination and were essentially 'defensive' in nature to provide protection to minorities who were faced with racism and discrimination and the hostility from the host White community who had not, or could not, come to terms with the change. Separation was, however, the consequence of these policies as Ranjit Sondhi (2009) has explained:

> Concerned less with the complexities of integration, the practice of multiculturalism came to be centred largely on managing public order and relations between majority and minority populations by allowing ethnic cultures and practices to mediate the process. Minority languages, religions and cultural practices were encouraged, and gradually the right to be equal was overshadowed by the right to be different.
>
> Such multicultural policies led, albeit unwittingly, to the creation of culturally and spatially distinct communities fronted by self-styled

community leaders who traded in cultural, as opposed to social capital. The scale and depth of difference became the very currency by which importance was judged and progress made. In other words, in the distribution of goods and services, there was everything to be gained from difference and non-mixing. This resulted in the tendency at the neighbourhood level to live in entirely separate ethnic worlds, a kind of self-imposed apartheid, a cocooned existence in which whole generations could exist without ever having to get engaged in wider social issues, or to read about and experience other people's cultures, or even to have dinner with families other than those from one's own ethnic, religious, cultural or linguistic background.

As a result, far from being a system that spoke to the whole of society, multiculturalism spoke only to each specific minority in isolation. This served to maintain the exoticism and essentialism of minority cultures hindering a two way conversation with the majority culture. It was also silent on the question of what to do with the deprived and disadvantaged sections of the indigenous community, driving its members further away from the goal of tolerance and into the arms of extremists.

Sondhi makes a number of very important points here, which go to the heart of this debate. First, the 'right to be equal' was overshadowed by the 'right to be different'. This does not imply any sympathy for assimilation and the loss of heritage and distinctiveness of minorities, merely that all communities should be able to develop commonalities with others, without losing their distinctiveness. Such a view is widely shared among commentators and apart from some extreme positions, is also shared across the political spectrum. The problem, however, remains as to how this, almost universally agreed, principle is put into practice. Parekh's (2000, p. 56) vision of Britain as 'one Nation – but understood as a community of many communities...based on a commitment to core values both between communities and within them', seemed to offer such an approach.

However, Hasan (2010) illustrates the depth of disagreement, chastising Parekh for advancing 'tendentiousness and specious arguments' in this same *The Future of Multi-Ethnic Britain* report (Parekh, 2000) and makes a similar criticism of Parekh's book *Rethinking Multiculturalism* (Parekh, 2000a). Hasan is particularly critical of what he sees as Parekh's desire to put up a 'do not disturb' sign around minority cultures, paying lip service to any real sense of critical engagement with other cultures that would enable them to adapt and change. He sees Parekh as wanting to create a special and separate place for minorities, in which 'Western states must veer away from their public commitment to liberal universalism so as to accommodate these minority cultures and faiths'.

In much the same way, Hasan also criticises Modood in his *Multicultural Politics* (Modood, 2005) for trying to redefine secularism in a way that accommodate Muslim demands for differential treatment. Indeed it is the case that Modood goes somewhat further in a later contribution to the debate (Modood, 2011), arguing in support of a concept of political secularism and a secular state that 'is more empirically based and sociologically apt in that it recognises where the power lies' (ibid., p. 102). This, he explains, should 'destigmatise public religion' and 'pluralise the institutional recognition of religion' (ibid., p. 104) – a concept of secularism that has little by way of underlying principle and is liable to change and contextualisation.

The 'right to be different' has political as well as cultural drivers. In this sense it can perhaps be characterised by the notion of identity politics (which is further discussed in later sections) and is played by both political and community leaders who seek to heighten differences in order to create a political advantage for one group or another, or by communities themselves, who have been quick to learn that the recognition of difference carries with it rewards in terms of representation and resources. Identity politics therefore militates against community collaboration and encourages competition and has even contributed to communal conflict (Cantle, 2001). This phenomenon was difficult, though manageable, when the number of minorities was small in number and could to some extent be negotiated on a bilateral basis, but is extremely problematic in an era of super diversity.

Second, there has been considerable debate about whether 'self-segregation' really exists, with much of the denial based upon the view that the very idea is tantamount to 'blaming minorities' for the problems of multiculturalism. This approach is perhaps best exemplified by Finney and Simpson (2009) who are intent on dismissing any notion of segregation as a problem and seem to see almost any discussion of segregation as part of 'the myths and the litany' about race and immigration (p. 162). However, in the very next page of their tirade they do concede that 'segregation is increasing when it is measured by the size of minority populations' (p. 163) (and even though it is only they who have attempted to measure it by anything else). Simpson, with others (2007), has, in fact, also produced research that, while emphasising that many young Asian people wanted to live in mixed areas in two northern towns in England, 'clearly shows that White and Asian young adults identify

and favour areas partly in terms of factors they associate with racial composition'. This is one of the few studies that have actually sought the
views and preferences of the local community themselves – and apparently this study did not add to the 'litany and myths'. In the context of
a racialised society, or where historic divisions are based around faith,
social class and other affinities, it is not surprising that people seek to
congregate with others who share the same idea of themselves and have
a common bond of personal and collective identity. What matters is
whether this common bond is regarded as primordial and 'natural', to be
preserved at all costs, or whether connections and bonds with others can
be established and built on the basis of a more universal conception of
identity. This reflects the fundamental difference of perspective between
multiculturalists and interculturalists, which is developed below and is
further discussed in Chapter 7.

Trying to understand why particular groups congregate together in
housing and other terms, is not the same as 'blaming them' for the
problems of multiculturalism. In fact, it could be rather the reverse.
Herman Ouseley, a former chair of the Commission for Racial Equality
and himself from an ethnic minority, found in his study of Bradford
(Ouseley, 2001):

> different ethnic groups are increasingly segregating themselves from
> each other and retreating into 'comfort zones' made up of people like
> themselves. They only connect with each other on those occasions
> when they cannot avoid each other, such as in shops, on the streets,
> at work, when travelling and, perversely, in Asian-owned restaurants
> by choice. Education in schools that are racially self-segregated is the
> most vivid reflection of this state of affairs.

and

> self-segregation is driven by the fear of others, the need for safety
> from harassment and violent crime and the belief that it is the only
> way to promote, retain and protect faith and cultural identity and
> affiliation.

'Self-segregation' does not apply only to minorities and the majority
population could be said to self-segregate when 'White flight' takes place
(see Cantle, 2008, pp. 80–81). But when applied to any group, 'self-
segregation' is not an adequate term as the reality of self-segregation,

particularly when exercised by minority populations, is neither unconstrained nor an entirely free choice. The implied voluntary nature does not reflect the institutional constraints, socio-economic factors and the social and emotional bonds that result from the process of socialisation. Sondhi's approach to the issue of self-segregation is, then, mature and realistic. He recognises that it is a real phenomenon – but that blame is not appropriate as choices are constrained and contextualised – and is therefore to be discussed dispassionately and openly. As with all discussions of 'race' there remains a chance that the debate can be hijacked and exploited by the Far Right, but suppressing discussion also means that the Far Right's arguments remain unchallenged.

A criticism of Sondhi's approach (and that more generally of community cohesion) is that it downplays economic disparities. This argument, supported in particular by a body of academic opinion (see Chapter 5), is based on the view that tensions and conflicts between communities are almost entirely attributable to poverty and deprivation, and were these to be somehow magically wiped away people would apparently live in harmony. For some, this is based upon a classic Marxist position, but there are a number of arguments that are often conflated and presented on a very simplistic basis without regard to supporting evidence. In particular, this critique has failed in the following respects:

- Assertions that poverty is responsible for poor community relations and, specifically, for racism, do not distinguish between the concepts of relative deprivation and absolute poverty. Most commentators equate 'poverty' in the most general way with the competition between majority and minority communities over jobs and resources, although it is often presented as a function of people being deprived or 'poor'. In some cases, the element of competition is a key factor in differences, but the level of hostility between groups can vary from place to place and in different contexts, even though relative deprivation of the different communities is the same. It would also not explain why the response to the relative deprivation of one group is to attack another relatively deprived group rather than seek common cause with them or take some other form of action. Goodwin's studies of the Far Right across Europe have firmly concluded that 'feelings of cultural threat ultimately trumped feelings of economic threat in driving public reactions to immigration' (Goodwin, 2011c).
- The suggestion that racism and other divisions are attributable to absolute poverty is equally spurious, with the implicit suggestion that

poorer people are likely to be more racist, and is often based upon no more than stereotypes about poorer people, rather than on evidence.

- To recognise that ethnicity (and all difference) is an independent variable from that of class and socio-economic position and that the suggestion that governments prefer to ignore the real problems of racism and focus instead on the relations between groups in order to gloss over fundamental inequalities, again turns on the notion that all prejudice and discrimination has an economic root (and that all governments are simply duplicitous). The causation of prejudice and predictors of community cohesion are still relatively under-researched, but there are an increasing number of evidence-based studies that clearly indicate that prejudices can be autonomous and transcend socio-economic position. As Laurence and Heath (2008) have shown, there are a range of factors, including having friends from different ethnic groups, a broad mix of ethnicities within an area as well as disadvantage and deprivation – and even then 'not all deprived areas have low cohesion'.

- There are fundamental differences of ideology and values that are independent of levels of the socio-economic scale. These can be international, or diasporic, as much as local or national and completely outside the context of the socio-economic structure. Most discussion of multiculturalism has revolved around accommodation between majority and minority populations rather than reflecting the current reality of super diversity and global communications.

- 'Differences' are not confined to ethnicity and also encompass sexual orientation, special needs and disabilities, faith and sects and other characteristics and therefore have deep socio-psychological roots that are not part of the economic structure. For example, it is seldom asserted that homophobic violence, intergenerational conflict or hate crimes against disabled people are simply due to poverty. Rather, it is accepted that prejudice and ignorance play a strong part.

- Positive attitudes to difference and 'otherness' appear to be related to exposure to people from different backgrounds and the opportunity to engage and interact with them is crucial. It should be noted that poorer people will, in general, have fewer such opportunities, but there are many others who live and work in very insular environments, where difference is more likely to be seen in negative stereotypical ways, based upon myths rather than realities. But this is a function of lack of opportunity and broader life chances, rather than poverty itself.

These arguments are explored in greater detail in Chapter 5, but it is appropriate to point out at this stage that the programmes designed to improve community relations have produced positive results and 'contact theory' in particular (Hewstone et al., 2006, 2006a, 2007, 2008, 2008a) is enjoying a period of renewed interest, based on this success. Similarly, programmes that have been developed to produce a positive image of diversity in schools, workplaces and communities, based upon a common sense of belonging, appear to be having some impact. Again, these are under-researched, but the results from participants are promising and some communities appeared to have responded well to more positive images of a diverse and united society (Cantle, 2008, pp. 178–188).

None of this is to deny the impact of inequalities and deprivation in some instances. It would also appear, however, that the *perception* of unfairness in the allocation of resources, or access to jobs and services, can trigger hostility towards others when one group appears to be gaining some preferential treatment or advantage – and it is of course more likely that poorer people will be more dependent upon resources allocated by the state and less self-reliant. Further, the political arguments, especially Far Right and anti-migrant sentiment, produce a more general hostility towards minorities, which is irrespective of socio-economic position and has become pervasive (see later section in this chapter). Indeed, anti-migrant hostility is now shared by longer-standing minority residents.

Progressive multiculturalism

Progressive forms of multiculturalism have been developed with a view to both avoiding the assimilationist tendencies of some European countries, perhaps most notably France, and at the same time avoiding the reliance on the separationist British model. The Canadian approach perhaps most exemplifies this model (though this conception has been challenged by the French-speaking provinces of Canada: see later sections). The Canadian government,[2] who believe that in 1971 they were the first in the world to adopt multiculturalism as an official policy, set out their vision in these terms:

> all citizens are equal. Multiculturalism ensures that all citizens can keep their identities, can take pride in their ancestry and have a sense of belonging. Acceptance gives Canadians a feeling of

security and self-confidence, making them more open to, and accepting of, diverse cultures. The Canadian experience has shown that
multiculturalism encourages racial and ethnic harmony and cross-
cultural understanding.

Mutual respect helps develop common attitudes. New Canadians, no
less than other Canadians, respect the political and legal process, and
want to address issues by legal and constitutional means.

Through multiculturalism, Canada recognizes the potential of all
Canadians, encouraging them to integrate into their society and take
an active part in its social, cultural, economic and political affairs.

All Canadians are guaranteed equality before the law and equality
of opportunity regardless of their origins. Canada's laws and policies recognize Canada's diversity by race, cultural heritage, ethnicity,
religion, ancestry and place of origin and guarantee to all men and
women complete freedom of conscience, of thought, belief, opinion,
expression, association and peaceful assembly. All of these rights, our
freedom and our dignity, are guaranteed through our Canadian citizenship, our Canadian Constitution, and our Charter of Rights and
Freedoms.

... As Canadians, they share the basic values of democracy with all
other Canadians who came before them. At the same time, Canadians
are free to choose for themselves, without penalty, whether they want
to identify with their specific group or not. Their individual rights are
fully protected and they need not fear group pressures.

The Canadian multicultural vision is indeed progressive and emphasises
'cross-cultural understanding', 'common attitudes', a 'sense of belonging' and being 'open to, and accepting of, diverse cultures'. While it also
offers the right to 'keep their identities' and 'pride in their ancestry',
the emphasis is clearly upon collaboration and identification with others, rather than the construction of a defensive barrier around diverse
groups. Further, and more progressively still, it suggests that Canadians
are individuals who 'are free to choose for themselves, without penalty,
whether they want to identify with their specific group or not... they
need not fear group pressures'. This contrasts with the British model
which has supported community group leaders, enabling them to speak
on behalf of their communities as though they are a homogeneous
group defined by a single faith or ethnic identity (and may be part of
'state multiculturalism' – see below).

The British approach to multiculturalism has not been codified in the same way – it has developed by a series of legalistic and political interventions, subject to many twists and turns, largely in response to events, rather than as a positive vision. The nearest it has been to a vision statement has been that offered in 1966 by the then home secretary Roy Jenkins and again at a time when racism and intolerance was leading to real community tensions:

> Integration is perhaps rather a loose word. I do not regard it as meaning the loss, by immigrants, of their own national characteristics and culture. I do not think that we need in this country a 'melting-pot', which will turn everybody out into a common mould, as one of a series of carbon copies of someone's misplaced vision of the stereotyped Englishman.

> I define integration, therefore, not as a flattening process, but as equal opportunity accompanied by cultural diversity in an atmosphere of mutual tolerance. This is the goal. We may fall a little short of its full attainment, as have other communities both in the past and in the present. But if we are to maintain any sort of world reputation for civilized living and social cohesion, we must get far nearer to its achievement than is the case today.
>
> (Jenkins, 1966)

This statement may also be seen in a 'defensive' sense in that it dwelt more on 'what not to do', with a clear commitment to try to avoid assimilation, though the commitment to recognising that diversity is to be valued and maintained and that there are many different ways of being an 'Englishman' is more suggestive of a 'progressive' policy. Unfortunately, these generalised statements and commitments were not translated into a more nuanced and layered approach to consider what was actually meant by 'national characteristics and culture' nor any other meaningful appreciation of the components of difference. The term 'culture' has been used very loosely to encompass differences in faith, lifestyle choices, political views, familial and social structures, community traditions, linguistic, artistic and musical preferences, occupational and business patterns, historic precedents and more general ideas about 'values'. Multiculturalism has, then, become associated with the 'creation of culturally and spatially distinct communities' (Hussain et al., 2007), very much in accord with 'the future for multi-ethnic Britain' still envisaged by Parekh's 'community of communities' in his report of 2000 (Parekh, 2000).

Some recent attempts have been made to distinguish 'the layers of separation' (Cantle, 2008) though generally within the context of the debate on segregation and integration (discussed in greater detail in Chapter 6), though any attempts to consider the relative importance of these spheres have again been met with hostility by ardent multicultural theorists, like Lentin and Titley (2011, p. 45). However, attempts to end distinctiveness in some spheres, especially in terms of employment, have long been seen as a desirable aim of multiculturalism and laid out in successive government plans (see, for example, Home Office, 2005) but it is the language of 'inclusion' rather than any ideas about 'integration' that appear to have been more acceptable and compatible with the then multicultural theory. Ratcliffe (2004) presents his vision for 'race', ethnicity and difference as 'imagining an inclusive society', though he concedes from the outset that this is 'not easy to conceptualize' (p. 7). Indeed, Ratcliffe struggles to do more than suggest a number of 'key features' for his inclusive society and these amount to 'culture of respect for difference' supported by a 'condemnation of racism and discrimination'; a 'greater degree of material equality', the removal of the 'rigid separatism... [which] leads to suspicion and hostility of the "other"', but with 'the right of individuals to opt out' (p. 166).

Ratcliffe draws back from the more obvious conclusion that 'inclusion' also requires a level of integration and that this need not imply an 'all or nothing' basis from separatism to assimilation. In order to be 'included', a practical level of integration is required: individuals will find it necessary to communicate on a common basis, work alongside 'others' and attend the same training or educational facilities. Further, individuals will have to share some aspirations and values, for example, the aspiration to grow socially, economically, educationally and politically in order to achieve some semblance of equality. 'Inclusion' therefore is a way of presenting integration activities as putting the onus on the majority or 'host' community to reach out and 'allow in' minorities (and other disadvantaged groups), whereas 'integration' is regarded with suspicion because it appears to demand that the minorities adapt and change – or even assimilate – in order to become part of society. Similarly, 'exclusion' has been used in a way that implies that minorities are being denied equal opportunities by exclusionary behaviour on the part of the majority (see, for example, the Social Exclusion Unit, 2004) whereas 'segregation' is thought by some commentators to imply the blaming or 'scapegoating' of minorities for wanting to be separate (for an extreme view, but one that is shared in part by a number of others, see Finney and Simpson, 2009).

The language of multiculturalism is therefore heavily coded and any attempt to develop more progressive forms of multiculturalism, which have sought to the promote cultural distinctiveness alongside commonalities and a sense of belonging to a shared society, have found it hard to gain consensus, partly because the terms are understood in so many different ways. The Communitarian Network (2002) attempted to create a more progressive conception of multiculturalism, set out as 'diversity within unity', in which 'over-arching' values would bind the community together, but would allow cultural distinctiveness to flourish. This approach was taken further with more specific proposals developed under the banner of community cohesion. This emphasised the commonalities of language, shared values developed through inter-action and debate and the creation of institutions that were mixed and facilitated mutual trust and understanding, while also proposing the retention of cultural distinctiveness and the tackling of inequal-ities (Cantle, 2001). Community cohesion became almost universally adopted by practitioners on a local basis across the UK but it was, ini-tially at least, objected to by some academics (see Chapter 5) because of what they see as the underlying political agenda to undermine minori-ties (Lentin and Titley, 2011, p. 45). However, an intercultural critique of multiculturalism, which suggests that the latter has been based upon a 'notion of culture linked to personal autonomy or to claims of differ-ent contexts of universalism' (Hammer, 2004) has begun to create a shift in the thinking of avowed multiculturalists like Meer and Modood who feel compelled to re-examine the 'provenance of multiculturalism as an intellectual tradition' (Meer and Modood, 2011) and are now calling for a 'rebalancing of multiculturalism' (Meer and Modood, 2008), rather than an acceptance of a new intercultural model.

However, this is not an academic or theoretical debate and many countries around the world are struggling with the balance between the rights and essentialist distinctiveness of minorities on the one hand and the core values, commonalities and responsibilities to which they feel all citizens should subscribe on the other. The Netherlands have already broken with their more liberal form of multiculturalism, in favour of new policies that 'ignore ethnic differences' (Meer and Modood, 2008) and debates such as whether to ban the wearing of the face veil in France, prohibit the building of minarets in Switzerland, allow the pub-lication of cartoons depicting Mohammed in Denmark, to intervene in alleged child abuse cases among indigenous peoples in Australia, or impose the French language on English speakers (especially new migrants) in the province of Quebec, have caused real controversy in those countries and reverberated around the world. The Far Right, in particular, have capitalised on these controversies and begun adjusting their appeal to reflect cultural, rather than supposed biological, difference (Cantle, 2011).

Unfortunately the paradigm of multiculturalism has been, then, even as a progressive conception, largely confined to a limited debate about the accommodation between majority and minority communities within states, reinforcing the binary Black/White perspective of 'race' and failing to recognise the multifaceted process of accommodations within minority and majority groups and between diasporas, national and international boundaries. It is not difficult to see why the Commission for Integration and Cohesion (CIC) declined to use the term 'multiculturalism' and felt that it had a confusing quality and that their focus should be on the practical policies to make a complex society work, where race, faith and culture are important, but not the only elements of that complexity. This was enshrined in the title of the CIC report *Our Shared Future* (CIC, 2007a, 13). The Council of Europe (2011) similarly declined to even use the word 'multiculturalism', preferring the concept of 'Living Together', and again preferred to focus on more practical application. It is possible that, against this background, a new and more forward-looking concept of interculturalism can prosper, free of the baggage of multiculturalism and provide a new vision for diversity in an era of globalisation.

'State multiculturalism'

Prime Minister David Cameron (2011) introduced a new term into this discourse with the concept of 'state multiculturalism', which he defined in the following terms:

> Under the doctrine of state multiculturalism, we have encouraged different cultures to live separate lives, apart from each other and the mainstream. We have failed to provide a vision of society to which they feel they want to belong.

and

> We have even tolerated these segregated communities behaving in ways that run counter to our values.

Cameron's concept of 'state multiculturalism' was simply that the state itself had encouraged minority communities to remain separate. He did little to indicate what mechanisms the state had actually used to promote separatism and, rather, most of his comments appeared to be focused on what he saw as the problems of the Muslim communities in the UK that indulged in the 'horrors of forced marriages', the 'preachers of hate in mosques' and extremist views shared in internet chatrooms.

It is true that the state, in the UK at least, has promoted separatism at least in so far as it has sought to control conflict and tensions by keeping communities apart, as in the approach of 'defensive multiculturalism'. It is also true that, apart from the policies of community cohesion, little has been done to provide a vision of a society in which minority communities feel included – again as discussed earlier.

However, the prime minister did not appear to acknowledge the way in which a number of government policies support separation and therefore continue to promote 'state multiculturalism'. Further, the speech did not suggest that there should be any attempt to close the separation of lives, nor to encourage people to live together (and no specific measures were subsequently introduced in the government's 'integration strategy' (DCLG, 2012)). Rather, the focus was on 'values' and this was presented in very simplistic terms in respect of a small number of extreme – and largely Muslim community – practices and as the failure of 'them' to integrate with 'us'. In this sense, he saw integration as a one-way street in which little or no accommodation was made by more established communities, and by 'integration' he clearly intended that Muslim communities should be willing to change their values and adopt those of Western cultures. This approach does tend to reinforce the idea of a 'clash of civilisations' (see earlier), even though in the same speech Cameron claimed that he wanted to avoid any generalisation about the Muslim communities.

The concept of 'state multiculturalism' does have, however, some potential use in establishing whether the state sponsors, deliberately or unwittingly, the separate lives of different communities inherent in the earlier and defensive forms of multiculturalism. For the most part, the state has intervened on behalf of minorities to either protect them from discrimination or to support them with initiatives that enable them to access employment, education, health and other services, on a more equal basis. This has generally been provided on a culturally separate basis, which has either created a distinct framework or simply reinforced that based in other spheres. This 'single identity' provision or funding of services has been challenged since 2001 (Cantle, 2001), and the development of community cohesion and this challenge was reinforced in 2007 by a further review of cohesion (CIC, 2007). The former Labour government effectively ducked the issue and largely left decisions to the local level (DCLG, 2008) and the new Coalition government has yet to offer a view, despite the prime minister's comments and their recent integration strategy (DCLG, 2012).

However, the state also sponsors a number of institutional arrangements that directly or indirectly promote the separation of cultures and faiths, in a number of spheres. The most notable of these is the provision of education that has been specifically developed along faith (and ethnic) lines. This is especially true in Northern Ireland where around 95 per cent of schools are either Protestant or Catholic based, but in England too many schools are both formally and informally divided, with support from the state. Thirty-six per cent of primary schools and 18 per cent of secondary schools in England had a religious character in 2007 (Department for Children, Schools and Families, 2008). Most of these are under the auspices of the Church of England (205 secondary and 4441 primary) with a larger number of secondary schools run by the Catholic Church (343), who also control 1696 primary schools. There are also over 100 primary schools and around 55 secondary schools run by other Christian faiths and by Jewish, Muslim and other faiths (ibid., p. 15). Concern has been expressed about the impact of school segregation on community cohesion (Cantle, 2001) and research continues to demonstrate how existing levels of ethnic segregation between schools continue to be exacerbated by selection on the basis of faith (Osler, 2007) and to divide society (Kymlicka, 2003; Runnymede, 2008).

Faiths in Britain are 'race coded' in the sense that there is a strong coincidence between ethnicity and faith. Further, school selection practices more generally, including those for non-faith schools, have allowed processes to develop that advantage or disadvantage particular communities. For example, those more popular schools that are oversubscribed, simply default to local neighbourhood preferences, and where these are segregated the school will also be segregated. This coincidence of school and residential segregation is apparent in other countries too, such as the USA (The Eisenhower Foundation, 2008). In addition, the advent of parents' choice in the UK, in which parents are able to choose schools outside of their neighbourhood, has meant a higher degree of choice is exercised along ethnic and faith lines. This has become more problematic in recent years, so much so that a national study of school pupil segregation in 2006 found that school segregation is now greater than that found in the residential areas in which they are situated (Johnston et al., 2006).

The role of the state is not limited to supporting a faith basis of divisions in schools, it also privileges and sponsors faith groups as influencers and providers of welfare services. This 'privileging' of faith groups is extended in many other ways, both in general terms and with regard to particular faith groups, which gives credence to faith identities. By treating with faith groups, meeting with them to discuss their particular point of view and by granting them special roles in the decision-taking process, they institutionalise the role and place of faith and ethnic groups and solidify and homogenise identities, most recently and notably in respect of the Muslim communities (Jurado, 2011). Indeed, faith-based groups also receive funding to enable them to participate in such processes and to develop and support engagement and to provide services to their communities. These arrangements have rarely been questioned, except by secular groups who often seek a similar position of influence – which would only serve to further perpetuate the identity basis of political arrangements, even if on what might be seen as a fairer basis. With regard to schools, but with clear wider application, Gallagher (2004) points out that the 'mere fact of separation sent implicit messages to young people that they were fundamentally different'.

Separate faith-and cultural-based provision has developed over many years, with little recognition of the way in which multicultural societies have changed and the new challenges that they now face. In terms of education, for example, the churches in the UK provided education long before the Forster Education Act of 1870 which marked the moment at which the state accepted its responsibility to run schools, but then only on the basis that it filled up the gaps in provision, rather than introducing a new system (Howard, 1987, p. 111). The dual basis of school provision has continued to this day, overcoming a number of challenges (see, for example, Runnymede Trust, 2008), and, rather, the institutional arrangements have enabled them to develop strong lobbies and to present the case for the 'value added' they believe they provide, whenever the status quo is questioned (see, for example, Catholic Education Service for England and Wales, 2010).

The present privileging of faith provision based on the past faith composition of the population means that these arrangements are increasingly untenable and counter-productive. Governments have recognised that the faiths that are relatively new and growing in the UK would be treated unfairly if they were unable to enjoy the same privileged position in relation to state support for faith-based schooling. The number of faiths that are now therefore able to draw upon this support and institute their own schools is growing, thereby increasing the divisions within and between communities and taking advantage of 'state multiculturalism'.

The French principle of *laicité*, which has been enshrined in French law for about a hundred years and has underpinned the separation of the state and church, and was seen as part of the French support for a regressive assimilationist model of multiculturalism, has enabled France to cope better with the shift from a largely homogenous and monocultural society to a multiethnic and multifaith community. The institutional separation in France has meant that it has at least partially avoided controversies about the role of faith in schools and government institutions generally, though the French model has involved the almost complete negation of faith in the public sphere and this position is quite distinct from state support for faith service provision. It has also led to more difficult debates about the denial of the expression of faith preferences, principally in relation to the banning of the face veil and head coverings.

Faith has become a major component of multiculturalism, rising in the public sphere in many Western states and as an inevitable result of inward migration, which has meant that all modern states now consist of a substantial number of people from minority faiths. Despite a relatively strong separation of faith and state in the UK and the suggestion that the government does not 'do God',[3] Britain does have an established church and does privilege the Church of England in particular in terms of representation – for example, there are 26 of its Bishops in the House of Lords. Christian faiths more generally are also privileged, again through representation, prominence and participation in major ceremonies and arrangements for public holidays. More recently, efforts have been made to develop the representative capacity of other faiths, most notably those of Muslims, in order to try to combat extremism in accordance with the Prevent agenda. Despite this, the level of influence wielded by faith organisations is relatively light, preserving the claim of secularity in the UK, and stands in contrast to that of the USA where, such is the presence of the Christian faith in the public sphere, no mainstream politician could hope to get elected if he/she suggested that they did not 'do God'. This is despite the fact that the USA does not have an established church.

Faith groups are, then, not only in the public sphere in the sense of visibility, and are now seen as part of the fabric of multicultural societies in which religious identities are recognised alongside those of 'race' and ethnicity. Indeed, our present system of multiculturalism encourages these increasingly divergent identities to emerge by rewarding them with specific funding and representation, although faith groups are generally not funded for work that might be seen as proselytising (though their very presence and supported work gives their faith a public credence). Previous concerns have been expressed about this 'single group funding' or 'single identity funding' (Cantle, 2001; CIC, 2007 and NICVA, 2004, p. 200), but neither the present nor previous government have felt able to do more than question the practice.

Once again, single identity funding was developed under a progressive conception of multiculturalism. It was justified largely on the basis of providing resources to disadvantaged groups, to ensure that they had sufficient resources to develop leadership and advocacy on their own behalf; that they had access to public services on a more equal basis, and that they were better able to identify and fill in any gaps in mainstream provision; and that they could protect their own heritage (Cantle, 2008). In an era of super diversity, however, the policy and practice of single-identity funding has become almost impossible to manage with so many groups competing for attention and funding and with separate advocacy and provision resulting in a substantial increase in resources. It has also been challenged on the basis that it is counterproductive as it enables mainstream provision to 'continue to fail' minority communities and to remain inflexible and insensitive to minority needs, rather than to change and recognize the reality of diversity (Miah, 2004, p. 90). Others have argued that single-identity funding has reinforced a model of multiculturalism that promoted separation and militated against bridge building and collaboration between communities (Hussain et al., 2007).

There are strong arguments in support of some targeted funding to new migrant communities, to enable them to build their capacity and to fully engage in the process of governance and in civil society. However, the continued funding on the basis of their identity, rather than an identified need (and one that would almost certainly be shared with other communities to some degree), means that the state is instrumentalising particular identities. The funding of groups on the basis of ethnicity and faith had become endemic in a bid to stimulate a fairer level of representation and provision, bearing in mind that mainstream providers had been perennially criticised for failing to provide equal opportunities and entitlement. These deficiencies remain today and a recent comprehensive review that asked the question 'How Fair is Britain?' (EHRC, 2010) found evidence of numerous inequalities associated with different communities and interests; perhaps most worryingly they found 'particularly large differences' for those not in education, employment or training, for some ethnic and religious groups, and that people from most ethnic minority backgrounds earn less than might be expected, given their qualifications, age and occupation, with the most significant variation in pay rates for Muslim men and women (ibid., p. 671).

The Equality and Human Rights Commission (EHRC) are also clear that identity also determines disadvantage to a greater or lesser extent:

> Yet all too many of us remain trapped by the accident of our births, our destinies far too likely to be determined by our sex or race; our opportunities far too often conditioned by the fact that our age, or disability, our sexual preferences, or deeply held religion or belief make us lesser beings in the eyes of others. And far too many of us are still born into families without the material or social capital to give us the right start in life.
>
> (EHRC, 2010, p. 7)

Not surprisingly, therefore, funding has continued to be made available to particular identity groups for projects in the fields of employment and training, arts, sports, history and heritage, health, housing, education and many other areas, although the challenges to this method of funding referred to earlier, and especially the newly imposed public expenditure reductions, have tended to curtail this approach to some extent. However, partly in response to the growth of the Far Right and partly because of the concern about the privileging of minority faith and ethnic groups, the majority White community is now also beginning to be seen as a singular identity, with calls for targeted support, competing with minority focused initiatives and broadening the salience of particular identities (Runnymede, 2009).

The response then, to the relative deprivation and discrimination associated with particular ethnic and faith groups has been to treat with them through that lens and as though they are homogeneous and with the impact of hardening this particular conception of their identity, in the same way that Younge (2009) and Sen (2006) suggested in respect of the Muslim community in Western countries. This form of positive action has generally stopped short of action that might be described as 'positive discrimination', as it is presented as enabling groups to compete on a more equal basis, rather than creating a more direct form of advantage. It remains to be seen whether newly identified disadvantage associated with particular groups, for example, the Roma community, will be responded to in a way that is based upon their identity as Roma people, or whether different approaches will be developed.

Positive action has, however, been very clearly exercised in relation to the Muslim community. As indicated in Chapter 3, there has been a widespread recognition that the 'Prevent' programme of intervention that until very recently was focused exclusively upon the Muslim community in Britain (and replicated in many other Western countries) has been counter-productive, given credence to religious rather than other leaders in the community and hardened and homogenised Muslim identities (Jurado, 2011). In the same way, other programmes can create 'suspect communities' (Hillyard, 1993), in which their internal and external identities are heightened, as during the height of the Northern Ireland conflicts with regard to Irish communities, especially those living in other parts of the UK.

Identity is also supported and 'flagged' in less tangible ways. In particular, ethnic and faith monitoring has now become routinised and people are invited to indicate how they see themselves on a limited number of themes, particularly 'race' or ethnicity, faith, gender, sexual orientation, age and disability. This information is gathered by most public agencies and by an increasing number of private businesses anxious to hone their marketing opportunities and to demonstrate fair recruitment practices. Ethnic and faith coding are particularly prevalent in education, housing, health, employment and other public services. This monitoring has again been developed as a means of addressing disadvantage and identifying gaps in services and problems of discrimination, but also has the effect or creating a social and economic salience for these particular identities. Identities are also flagged negatively, by attempts to restrict expressions of identity in the public sphere, as in the banning of certain items of clothing, but again by indicating that these markers are important enough to be of concern.

'Identity politics' has been conceived as a means by which specific communities or groups can marshal forces on behalf of their own interests and influence the provision of services and facilities in their favour and often with the support of politicians who see it as 'natural' to garner support in this way (Demirbag-Sten, 2011). However, Muir (2007, p. 6) identifies a new wave of identity politics in which the government attempts to rein back 'the older politics of multiculturalism – which, it is argued, encouraged an emphasis on difference at the expense of solidarity' – and to now emphasise the importance of shared national and local identities. In this way, the state attempts to create a renewed sense of identity to counteract the many distinct identities with their own competing loyalties. This has been behind much of the previous government's support for citizenship (see Cantle, 2008, pp. 162–170) and has been an attempt to undo some of the state's own sponsorship of separate identities.

The role of the state has been to respond to and regulate divisions and tensions within and between communities and, in respect of modern multicultural societies in particular, to negotiate accommodations between the 'host' majority community and newer migrant communities as part of the 'concentrated reflexive monitoring they both permit and entail' (Giddens, 1991, p. 16). The necessary regulatory role the state provides is complex and continuous, involving both legislative programmes and more subtle influencing strategies (for further discussion see Cantle, 2008, pp. 95–100), though the key issue has often revolved around whether the state should be able to maintain a cultural advantage for the majority community as advocated by Wolfe (2002) and Bouchard (2011). The state is not a neutral actor and not only takes on the role of referee, but also writes the rule book and 'state multiculturalism' is an inherent part of the modern landscape. However, the state's power and influence has become limited as a result of the changes discussed in earlier chapters, and even states that are outside the sphere of Western democracies struggle to offer any real and effective control over international communications, as China's constraint of Google has demonstrated.

The role of the state under an intercultural model would need to become that of a proactive change agent in which populations are encouraged to adapt and adjust to the new multicultural modernity. Instead of looking backwards and focusing almost entirely on the negotiation of ideas about fairness, largely within its' borders, it will need to consider a more forward looking agenda that takes account of globalisation. However, even at a national level we are some way from what Muir (2007, p. 17) describes as 'a new discourse around shared identity' which he sees as being very much in its 'early stages' and being 'difficult territory, especially for the left' because of their antipathy to exclusionary jingoistic flag waving. However, it is a more significant challenge at the international level and cannot in fact be situated within a narrow-minded flag-waving culture, as it inevitably entails a more fluid and overlapping idea of national identities and politics, in which interdependency has to be embraced. And, as David Cameron (2011) perhaps unwittingly indicated, 'state multiculturalism' has lacked any sort of vision of the future society in which everyone wants to belong. This, then, is the task of a new intercultural model.

Multiculturalism and 'race'

Multiculturalism has been essentially about 'race', in most Western countries at least. The context of the 1950s and 1960s made this inevitable, and the panoply of measures introduced to mediate the early problems associated with an influx of largely non-White migrants were almost entirely designed to help cope with racial tensions and con-flicts. The principal legislation in the UK, for example, was through a series of 'race relations' acts, and the various commissions and regulators were built upon improving race relations and tackling discrimination on racial grounds.

Over the years and especially since the atrocities of 9/11, the focus has shifted to faith differences and, of course, especially in response to the supposed Muslim/Christian divide. The 'culture' part of multicultural has also begun to be understood in many different ways and now revolves around ethnic, faith, nationality, language or any other dimen-sion that has a social or political salience. It may also be a combination of some or all of these differences.

The concept of 'race' – and therefore of racial difference – has, then, failed the test of time. Indeed, since the Second World War we have wit-nessed the complete demolition of the pseudo-scientific proposition of the geneticists who had attempted to establish fixed racial distinctions and a hierarchy of superiority. The advances of understanding on the human genome have largely put paid to any idea of significant racial distinctiveness, in a primordial sense. In populist terms, it is also clear that the notion of 'race' is no longer sufficient in itself to constitute 'difference' in the eyes of most people and this has been recognised by Far Right parties across Europe who are modifying their appeal and focusing on cultural, rather than 'racial', difference (Goodwin, 2011a).

However, 'race' has been reinvented as ethnic difference, at least in so far as it is presented as primordial, bounded and fixed. This is also true of other differences that are based upon visible characteristics, par-ticularly those associated with the distinctiveness of faith and largely based upon associated forms of clothing. Indeed, in the UK some faith groups, notably Jews, are formally designated as a 'race' because of the extent of the visual distinctiveness of the dress of the small number of orthodox Jewish groups, rather than their visibility in terms of phys-iognomy. The policies of multiculturalism have then been built upon, and are a response to, racial and other visible differences. They have remained rooted in this notion of difference and have not adapted to the wider diversity agenda of sexual orientation, gender, age, disability and other characteristics. They have also failed to recognise that what society understands as 'difference' is part of a dynamic process, and while each era tends to see the present boundaries of difference as permanent and fixed conceptions, they are all liable to change. It is suggested that 'interculturalism' (see later sections) is able to recognise all aspects of diversity as a dynamic process and respond to the changing components of 'difference' and the wider impacts of globalisation.

Within most discourses on multiculturalism, 'race' is presented as binary Black/White opposites, mutually exclusive and occupying no common ground (Chek Wai Lau, 2004, p. 122). The emphasis has also been placed firmly on the history of racism in a colonial context and the continuing discrimination against Black and ethnic minorities by White people or by institutions still infected with racist and discriminatory attitudes and procedures, as expressed by the title of Paul Gilroy's book *There Ain't No Black in the Union Jack* (Gilroy, 2002). Of course, these views still have considerable validity and Black/White racism remains a significant factor in the so-called 'post-race society'. Indeed, the 2002 version of Gilroy's book has an introduction that Gilroy has added to the original 1987 version. This recognises that race politics have been greatly changed, with

> an historic turn away from the simple efficacy of blackness – a bridging term that had promoted vernacular cosmopolitan conversation and synchronised action among the victimised – cannot be separated form the pursuit of more complex and highly-differentiated ways of fixing and instrumentalising culture and difference
>
> (Gilroy, 2002, p. xiv)

Gilroy also recognises that Black communities 'are being actively recomposed' by the internal and external pressures upon them and 'by the new arrivals whose experience of racism leads them to seek or refuse political allies' (ibid., p. xii). The solidarity of 'Black' communities – the term was used politically for many years to encompass all non-White minorities – has indeed long since broken down. The idea of a universal Black identity was described by Modood (1988, p. 399) as a 'meaningless chimera' and he viewed the Asian culture as separate and distinct, perhaps underpinned by religion as powerful a factor in identity as class or race. In the last decade, and especially since the events of 9/11, the Muslim identity has, in particular, been identified as a separate component of the term 'Asian', but other distinctions are now commonly used and it is now rarely used as a form of collective identity.

The Lozells riots in Birmingham in 2005 also brought a new dimension to race relations in the UK. This was the first significant example of interethnic conflict or 'Black-on-Black' violence. The violence between the Asian and African Caribbean communities within the north-west area of the city resulted in two deaths and 347 crimes, including five attempted murders (Latchford, 2007). These riots are hardly mentioned by multicultural theorists and regarded as something of an aberration in which the solidarity of Black and minority communities unfortunately broke down. In fact, even the term 'Black on Black' violence is disapproved of and again regarded as undermining the solidarity of Black communities who need to stick together and find common cause against racism. In reality, of course, racism is practised at many levels and is certainly found within and between ethnic minorities and within and between different faith communities – as well as within and between different White communities. Although not as serious as the Lozells incident, there are many other examples of tensions and violence between different communities. This is hardly surprising given the long-standing enmity between different groups and in a super-diverse society many such communities now find themselves living alongside people with whom they have been in dispute for many years, possibly even centuries.

The idea of a 'Black' identity was homogenising, but served a political purpose for ethnic minorities and was not disputed by the White community who seemed happy to regard all minorities as 'non-White' – that is, as distinct and, for the most part, inferior to themselves. However, the White community has also been homogenised and this too, is breaking down. Indeed, the definition of 'White' is, in any case, problematic with clear divisions having emerged along cultural lines, or based on faith or national differences. Immigration from Eastern to Western Europe has created many distinct groups, some of whom have had long-standing feuds with other groups, perhaps especially from the Balkan countries and, again, find themselves in close proximity after emigration. In Britain, the White Irish are still designated as a separate ethnic group within the 'White' category, though the tensions of the past have all but disappeared. However, new tensions have emerged both between the newer White migrant groups and with the White 'host' community (and with the BME early migrants). Evidence from the UK government's *Place Survey* (DCLG, 2009) shows that many of the most tense communities, where people do not believe that 'they get on well with those from different backgrounds', are in areas with large White majority and Eastern European communities. These are often rural county areas that are unused to any form of diversity. They have a relatively high number of Eastern European migrant workers, who are often in very separate employment, typically in the food picking, processing and packing and horticultural industries, where their accommodation is also often provided on a separate basis in all manner of temporary units close to their workplaces. The UK has also witnessed some of the worst violence between White groups, in the form of sectarian conflict between Protestant and Catholic communities in Northern Ireland. This is also evident to a lesser degree in Scotland. None of the disputes and conflicts within the White community have been termed 'White on White' violence, nor seen as 'racist'. However, they are clearly part of the 'complex and highly differentiated ways of fixing and instrumentalising culture and difference', which Gilroy (2002) described above.

The spurious notion of a White or Black identity and the ways in which they have both been differentiated and socially and politically constructed (see Cantle, 2008, pp. 101–122) means that they are constantly in a state of flux and heavily contextualised. Further, whereas multicultural policy has also tended to assume that what constitutes 'multi' and what constitutes 'cultural' is conceived and understood in much the same way around the world, the nature of multicultural societies is very varied and covers a wide range of situations from those largely monocultural societies with a very small number of people from just one or two vaguely distinguishable minorities, to a high number of highly distinct and separate groups who comprise the majority of the population.

Bouchard (2011) identifies four types of society that all have a very different history and population composition and have therefore developed different understandings of the 'management of ethno-cultural diversity'. Bouchard's typology is:

- where the nation is composed of ethno-cultural groups placed on equal footing and with no recognition of a majority culture. Bouchard believes that the 'nations' of Australia and Anglophone Canada are included in this category, though it is possible to argue that, even in largely all-migrant countries, the dominant Anglo/Celtic population has to some extent taken on the role of the majority or 'host' community;
- a paradigm of homogeneity (commonly seen as the assimilationist model) which fundamentally asserts an ethno-cultural similarity in public life for all groups, irrespective of minority or majority size and

history (nations such as France, Italy and Japan are included in his examples);

- a bi- or multi-polarity set of societies composed of two or more national groups or subgroups, sometimes officially recognised as such and granted a kind of permanence (nation-states such as Malaysia, Bolivia, Belgium and Switzerland are included here);
- a paradigm of duality, where diversity is conceived and managed as a relationship between minorities from a recent or distant period of immigration, and a cultural majority that could be described as *foundational*. Bouchard suggests that the French-speaking province of Quebec is in a similar position to Aboriginal or First Nation communities;
- a paradigm of *mixité*, founded on the idea that, through miscegenation, the ethno-cultural diversity of a nation will be progressively reduced, eventually creating a new culture separate from its constituent elements (examples are primarily in Latin America, notably in Brazil and Mexico).

Bouchard's particular preoccupation is with the distinction between French- and English-speaking Canada – and where language is almost the only differential marker of 'culture' (and might be said to represent an audible rather than visible difference). In other countries, however, where language differences create or underscore other historical and cultural differences, the countries would not necessarily regard this as part of the multicultural paradigms of polarity or duality. Such countries would include those from the former Soviet Union, like Estonia, which have now very significant divides between Russian and Estonian language speakers, and countries like Belgium, where the language divides are equally marked and longer standing, but both tend to understand multicultural distinctions as those associated with new and visible ethnic minorities. In other words, for most countries the idea of multiculturalism still revolves around 'race', rather than culture.

Although Bouchard's typology does still tend to rely upon some form of ethnic or national basis of culture, he does attempt to develop an 'intercultural' conception of societies and begins to draw in other forms of diversity.

Community cohesion programmes in the UK have taken this somewhat further, however, and while they were initially devised as a response to 'race' riots in northern England, they went on to recognise all forms of difference, including those based on social class, age, disability and sexual orientation and have devised interventions to address these divides[4]. While some of these characteristics might be stretching the definition of 'culture', they do recognise the more recent ideas about personal and collective identity and about how societies may now attempt to promote solidarity across all divides. Multiculturalism has understandably and necessarily been preoccupied with 'race'. It has failed to recognise that other differences have divided societies in the past and continue to do so and, moreover, that newer ideas about difference (also discussed in earlier chapters) have become part of the public sphere and now form a significant component of personal and collective identity. Interculturalism is more able to respond to that challenge and to recognise that 'difference' is not confined to minorities, nor defined by 'race'. In the meantime, and as Gilroy (2002) suggests:

> there are other stories about 'race' and racism to be told. They are defined by a liberating sense of the banality of the inter-mixture and the subversive ordinariness of this country's convivial cultures in which 'race' is stripped of meaning and racism just an after-effect of long gone imperial history
>
> (p. xxxviii)

Far Right and populist appeal

Opposition to both the policies of multiculturalism and the very principle of multicultural societies has been most fervently expressed by Far Right groups who share a common bond in this respect. However, while they have also been preoccupied with race and immigration and have traded on the supposed threat of 'others', they have perhaps been a little more adept than proponents of multicultural policies in adjusting their approach in recent years. As suggested above, the Far Right have found that their appeal, based on the supposed biological superiority of the White 'race', no longer resonates as well as it has done in the past and they have now begun to focus on the cultural dimensions of difference.

Goodwin (2011a) illustrates this with regard to the growing support for the Far Right across Europe and suggests that, while some of these groups, which he refers to as populist extremist parties (PEPs), still subscribe to a more strident form of biological racism, this is arguably more prevalent in Central and Eastern Europe.

> Increasingly ... this biological racism is becoming socially unacceptable among European populations. As a consequence, the most successful

> PEPs have steered clear of this discourse in favour of framing minority groups as a cultural as opposed to racial threat
>
> (Goodwin, 2011, p. 13)

Goodwin explains that, while the Far Right still see minority groups as biologically inferior to the majority group and 'still exhibit biological racism among an inner circle of followers (the "back-stage"), in the quest for votes (the "front-stage")' (ibid., p. 13), these arguments are downplayed in favour of claims that minority groups are culturally threatening and incompatible with Western values and societies.

The Far Right understand the change in attitudes that result from the impact of globalisation – and have, perhaps, better adjusted to the new circumstances than centrist politicians. Marine Le Pen, the leader of the French *Front National*, sums this up as 'now the real divide is between nationalism and globalisation', and complains that 'France's sovereignty has been "sucked dry by the EU" ', with 'cultural identity under attack through massive immigration' (Le Pen, 2011).

This does not mean that the Far Right no longer opposes migration on any other basis than that of 'wanting to protect the racial purity of the majority group, a crude form of racism that is often combined with anti-Semitic claims, such as that secretive Jewish-led groups control international relations or that the events of the Holocaust have been exaggerated' (Goodwin, 2011a, p. 13).

Rather, the Far Right have adjusted the way in which they present arguments and seek to ensure that:

> minority groups are seen as threatening in several ways, namely as:
>
> - a threat to national identity;
> - a threat to social order;
> - a threat to economic stability;
> - a burden on public services and the welfare state.
>
> Particular emphasis, however, is placed on the threat that immigrants and minority groups present to national culture, the national community and ways of life.
>
> (Goodwin, 2011, p. 13)

Goodwin (2011) illustrates this change of direction with the example of Norway, where PEPs in the 1980s typically framed opposition to immigration along economic lines, while in more recent years they have developed a discourse that has increasingly embraced a cultural dimension. This approach is also evident in the UK where the British National Party (BNP) has developed campaigns that focus particularly on Muslim minorities and do not specifically draw attention to their ethnicity. The Muslim focus enables them to tap into the present Islamophobic discourse in which Muslims are presented as a threat, seen as 'others' and generally thought to have values that are inimical to Britishness. This approach also recognises that the old concepts of racial superiority now resonate with fewer people, especially younger groups who have grown up in a diverse society.

Far Right parties are growing, however, at least partly on the basis that mainstream politicians no longer appear to represent the less affluent sections of the White 'host' community and they have consequently become a significant electoral force in many European countries. In the UK, they have also grown significantly, though they have generally failed to achieve any significant electoral success. Nevertheless, they gained more than ten per cent of the vote in no fewer than 52 local authority areas in 2010, and overall they won around 560,000 votes. Only a year earlier they had received 1 million votes as two BNP candidates were propelled into the European Parliament (iCoCo, 2011). As a result, Goodwin (2011) suggests that the BNP has now become the most successful extreme right party in British history and points out that since 2001 its support in general elections has grown 12-fold; support in local elections increased by a factor of 100 and membership by seven fold. It is very clear that, despite some year-on-year ups and downs, their overall trajectory has been rapidly upward for the last ten years or so and, as the Institute of Community Cohesion (iCoCo), which monitors Far Right activities in the UK as part of an ongoing concern for tackling community tensions, found in its most recent report (iCoCo, 2011), that they have succeeded in broadening their appeal, even within rural and suburban areas.

Across Europe the Far Right have grown and in the same 2009 European parliamentary elections that saw the BNP in the UK win two seats, Austria, Belgium, Bulgaria, Denmark, Finland, France, Greece, Hungary, Italy, Romania and Slovakia all sent representatives of PEPs to the European Parliament (Goodwin, 2011a, p. 2). The size of the support for these Far Right parties has enabled them to enter government in support of other parties, in a number of European countries including Austria, Belgium, the Netherlands and Italy. This has even been the case in the traditionally more liberal countries of Scandinavia, which has seen an unprecedented growth in Far Right support in Norway,

Finland, Denmark and Sweden, and forming part of the government in Denmark (where it is the third largest party) and Norway. At elections in Vienna in 2010, the Austrian Freedom Party (FPÖ) increased its share of the vote to more than 25 per cent, and in the Netherlands support for the Party for Freedom (PVV) increased almost three-fold to 1.5 million votes or 15.5 per cent of the vote (Goodwin, 2011c). There has been a similar growth pattern in Eastern Europe where the Far Right are perhaps even more anti-democratic and aggressive in their approach (Minkenburg, 2011) and where substantial popular support is now evident in Poland, Hungary, the Czech Republic, Romania, Bulgaria, Slovakia and Slovenia (Goodwin, 2011a). Far Right parties are now part of the political infrastructure across Western and Eastern Europe.

Messina (2011) seeks to distinguish the types of Far Right party with a comparative European perspective. He offers a distinction between 'generic groups' that are exclusively obsessed by animus towards settled and new migrants; 'neo-Fascist groups' who are inspired by an overarching ideology, embracing the core tenets of pre-Second World War Fascism; the 'opportunistic Right' who are driven by a calculated desire to win votes rather than an obsessive race-centred ideology; the 'new radical Right' who aspire to govern and have more formal membership and regular electoral activity; and the 'ethno-national Right' who are primarily single-issue parties, placing ethno-nationalism centre stage, with anti-migrant appeals in second place. The BNP are placed in the neo-Fascist camp.

What they all share, however, is hostility towards settled and new migrants, or as Griffin (2011) suggests, 'Fascism's adaptation to the transformed historical conditions' and the growth of 'neopopulism', possibly inspired by France's *Front National*. This exploited populist concerns about the threat to 'Frenchness' and the French way of life, and endorsed the rallying call of Le Pen for 'immigration to be stopped and cultural identities to be preserved' (Le Pen, 2011), as though it is possible to halt any single aspect of the process of globalisation that has been gathering pace for many decades. But her kind of political leadership also depends upon appealing to one section of the population over another and building a power base to represent their 'difference'. Gary Younge (2010), a staunch opponent of the Far Right, clearly understands the relevance of 'identity' in this political discourse. In his book *Who Are We?* he points out that when it comes to identity, the global and the parochial have a symbiotic relationship – the smaller the world becomes and the less control we have over it, the more likely we are to retreat into the local spheres where we might have influence.

As a result of the growth of the Far Right, mainstream politicians frequently feel obliged to try to head off support for the Far Right by at least appearing to listen to the concerns of their electorate on these issues. New and tougher controls on migration are periodically announced, particularly in the run-up to elections, and mainstream politicians have used emotive terms like 'swamping'[5] to suggest that they are in line with popular opinion, notwithstanding attacks from the Left who claim that this only enhances Far Right support. The hope that this sort of language would assuage public opinion because the concerns about multiculturalism were being understood and addressed (Kymlicka, 2003a, p. 206; Ouseley, 2004) has not been well founded. Indeed, mainstream politicians have generally been very mistaken in their belief that the hostility towards 'others' is in some way confined to extremists and they have failed to recognise that the resentment towards multicultural policies in general and migration in particular goes a lot deeper. In the sense that cultural diversity and migration do not enjoy popular support multiculturalism can also be said to have 'failed'. This lack of support cuts much deeper than the overt support for the Far right, as evidenced by the recent *Hope and Fear* report (SET, 2011).

This report, commissioned by the Searchlight Educational Trust set out to explore the issues of English identity, faith and race. With 5054 respondents and 91 questions, it is one of the largest and most comprehensive surveys into attitude, identity and extremism in the UK to date. It concludes that:

> there is not a progressive majority in society and it (the survey) reveals that there is a deep resentment to immigration, as well as scepticism towards multiculturalism. There is a widespread fear of the 'Other', particularly Muslims, and there is an appetite for a new right-wing political party that has none of the fascist trappings of the BNP or the violence of the English Defence League. With a clear correlation between economic pessimism and negative views to immigration, the situation is likely to get worse over the next few years.
>
> (SET, 2011, p 30)

Copsey and Macklin (2011) have produced a timely review of the UK's BNP. As Neil Copsey's introductory section points out, despite the obvious rise in electoral support for the BNP, academic research is only now beginning to catch up. But the BNP are only one part of the UK's growing Right, which has been further boosted by the activities of the UK Independence Party (UKIP) who also appeal to anti-migrant and xenophobic populism (Goodwin et al., 2011). They have grown as the 'polite alternative' to the BNP and are fast becoming 'a powerful outlet for controversial Far-Right views'. UKIP garnered over 900,000 votes in the 2010 general election. In addition, when the small but very vociferous English Defence League support is added to this, the popular and street-level impact of the Far Right as a whole becomes even more significant.

Further, the SET report (2011), referred to earlier, demonstrated how limited the support for multiculturalism is at present. They identified what they call six 'identity tribes' in modern British society. These are: 'confident multiculturalists' (found to be 8 per cent of the population); 'mainstream liberals' (16 per cent); 'identity ambivalents' (28 per cent); 'cultural integrationists' (24 per cent); 'latent hostiles' (10 per cent); and 'active enmity' (13 per cent). Those identified as 'identity ambivalents' could apparently easily be pushed further towards the Right, unless mainstream political parties tackle the social and economic insecurity that dominates their attitudes. This report therefore, somewhat alarmingly, suggests that only one-quarter of the population are comfortable with our present model of multiculturalism.

Goodwin (2011) appears to confirm this rather depressing attitudinal picture, providing a really useful analysis of the opinion polling on migration and race-related issues over the last ten years or so. Over this period, the public have generally viewed the government's performance on immigration in a negative light. The views have not been ambivalent, with around 80 per cent supporting suggestions that 'immigration is not under control'; that the government is 'not being open and honest' about the scale of migration; and that immigration policies are not sensible or credible. Even more worryingly, when opinion polls have asked which political party have the best policies on immigration, the majority of those polled generally feel that none of them do, or they don't know. These results suggest that the ground is wide open for the Right to cultivate.

As discussed in Chapter 2, there appears to be something of a 'diversity paradox' in that the more diverse societies are and the more people become engaged with difference, whether in personal terms, or virtually, through the media and communications, the more they seemed to embrace identity politics and support separatist ideologies. Moving from a multicultural model to one based on interculturalism therefore requires a change to the way in which societies conceive of, and instrumentalise, identity through policy and practice. This is developed in later sections.

The transition of multiculturalism to interculturalism

The early forms of multiculturalism were necessarily defensive, both to protect minorities from the hostility and racism they faced and to stake a claim for fairness and social justice. Clearly, both elements remain pertinent and need to be part of any new model. However, this approach depended upon a preoccupation with 'race' and mostly concerned the extent and nature of accommodation of minorities within each country, based on a static conception of culture that is positioned on a linear 'segregation to assimilation' pathway. As both majority and minority communities came to terms with living side by side, the early policies failed to adjust and to develop the notion of 'a shared society' – language that has only recently begun to emerge and largely as part of a critique of multiculturalism. The advent of community cohesion in the UK in 2001 led this process with a series of progressive measures to create dialogue and interaction, while still retaining the principles of fairness and rights. Interculturalism can provide a new paradigm to take this process still further and respond to the challenges of globalisation and super diversity.

Table 4.1 therefore indicates the way in which ideas about multiculturalism have changed but can be built upon to reflect the increasing complexity of our multicultural societies and develop into interculturalism. Both multiculturalism, in its more progressive form, and interculturalism, can underpin the necessary characteristics of a cohesive society, as indicated in Table 4.1. However, it should be noted that community cohesion programmes in the UK at least, have largely been conceptualised and implemented on a localised and contextualised basis. A new paradigm, or metanarrative, of interculturalism would develop a new national and international perspective to both support and facilitate cohesion.

Some components of multiculturalism are common to community cohesion and interculturalism. However, while the 'defensive' form was perhaps an appropriate response to the intolerant and racist attitudes and behaviours of the early stages of multicultural societies, it inevitably led to separation, ignorance and mistrust of the 'other'. Anti-discrimination legislation and equal opportunities programmes were certainly required to deal with the many injustices experienced by minorities (and by women, older people and those with disabilities),

Table 4.1 Components of multiculturalism and interculturalism and characteristics of a cohesive society

Components of multiculturalism	Characteristics of a community cohesion	Components of interculturalism
Protection of distinctive cultural heritage	*Values diversity*	Support for distinctive cultural heritage, on iterative and dynamic basis
Anti-discrimination legislation	*Prevents and undermines discrimination*	Anti-discrimination legislation, supported by experiential learning to address causes of discrimination and incitement of hatred
Promotion of equal opportunities and silo-based positive action	*Promotes equality of opportunity*	Promotion of equal opportunities and positive action across all differences
Focused on 'race' and ethnicity	*Positive relations across all forms of difference*	Builds positive relations for race, ethnicity, age, disability, sexual orientation, nationality and all forms of difference
Focused on majority/minorities within countries		Majority/minority focus and within and between minorities; together with diaspora, national and international dimensions
Institutional support for distinct identities and communities		Promotion of interaction, cross-cultural contact and understanding; contestation of stereotypes
	A strong sense of national, regional or local belonging	Promotion of 'belonging' and values of diversity
	High levels of knowledge and understanding about diversity, rights and responsibilities	Formal and informal citizenship and cohesion learning programmes

Table 4.1   (Continued)

With constant debate and dialogue to recognise the dynamic nature of globalisation and super diversity	Promotion of fluid and dynamic identities
	Support for international and intercultural learning and competences
In which the state is secular, neutral and outward looking and collaborative	Withdrawal of state support for promotion of particular cultural and religious identities
	Support for International collaborative agencies and leadership, based upon democratic processes
Democratic processes recognise the fluid nature of communities	
	Horizontal, cross-boundary community leadership and broader engagement

but may have also reinforced ideas of political correctness, rather than succeeding in changing underlying attitudes. In an intercultural model, therefore, the way in which these policies are operationalised would be very different and are discussed in later chapters.

Community cohesion emerged as a response to weaknesses in the multicultural model but nevertheless built upon the framework of rights and equality programmes and developed a more ambitious approach to try to change attitudes and behaviours by promoting interaction and developing a sense of belonging, especially on a local basis, and by creating a more positive picture of the nature and value of diversity. An intercultural model, however, would recognise that the era of super diversity and globalisation can no longer be considered on a simple national or local basis and that the state must adjust the way it mediates between many different groups and recognise the impact of transnational and diasporic influences. Interculturalism therefore values – and actively develops – dynamic identities through the encouragement of broader networks, the learning about others and collaborative styles of open leadership, which transcend insular patterns of understanding and behaviour.

5
The Contribution of 'Community Cohesion'

The concept of 'community cohesion' was established following a number of riots and disturbances in England in 2001 and with the subsequent *Report of the Independent Review Team* (Cantle, 2001). It represented a fundamental challenge to the then multicultural model. It was, unsurprisingly, initially resisted by a number of commentators and academics (see below) who were so used to responding to what they saw as attacks on diverse and minority communities that they reacted with knee-jerk opposition to any change in approach. Nevertheless, policy-makers and practitioners were much more favourably disposed and cohesion programmes were introduced from 2002 onwards. Though these were initially on a limited and piecemeal basis, they gradually developed across the UK and have now also become part of many 'mainstream' activities – for example, as part of a statutory duty in all schools in England.[1] Community cohesion programmes have attempted to build understanding between different groups and to build mutual trust and respect by breaking down stereotypes and misconceptions about the 'other'. In many cases, there are clear and measurable impacts of such programmes and these assessments are generally based upon attitudinal and behavioural change in the programme participants, or in the wider local community. Recent research indicates considerable success in this regard (Thomas, 2011; DCLG, 2011).

In addition to the small-scale programmes focused on divided communities, community cohesion was also developed at a city-wide or area level to encourage a broader consensus in support of diversity. The latter often included high-profile campaigns featuring people from a range of backgrounds who 'all belong' and contribute to the economic and cultural life of the area. These campaigns were important in that they tried to present a new positive picture of diversity, and, while recognising the value of cultural heritage and distinctiveness, placed a new emphasis on the commonalities between groups, thereby contributing to a less defensive and more progressive form of multiculturalism.[2]

Indeed, from the outset, community cohesion attempted to develop a positive vision for diverse societies (which was turned into a formal definition – see below), in which people from all backgrounds would feel that they belonged and were valued, enjoyed similar life opportunities and interacted with people from different backgrounds to break down myths and stereotypes and to build trust. This contrasted with the development of multiculturalism, which was still conceptualised as being largely defensive and negative – to try to stop the worst effects of a racist and colonial past. It was difficult to find any positive vision for multiculturalism before 2001, other than the 1966 statement of the then home secretary, Roy Jenkins (referred to in Chapter 4), in which he suggested that 'integration' should not be 'a flattening process, but as equal opportunity accompanied by cultural diversity in an atmosphere of mutual tolerance' (Jenkins, 1966).

Community cohesion has then, developed as positive vision of a diverse society and has been supported by a wide range of programmes to improve community relations. However, like multiculturalism, it is still largely based upon national and local institutions and programmes, and often implemented in many contextualised ways at city or local area level. Interculturalism provides the opportunity to develop a much wider vision.

Conceptual and practical development

There have been at least three formal national definitions of the concept, each building upon the other over the six-year period from 2002 to 2008. These are shown below. All refer, however, to the need for strong and positive relationships between people from different backgrounds, tackling inequalities and developing a positive climate of opinion to support diversity. There are also a large number of local definitions, which draw upon the formal national definitions but tend to add a local context.

The first formal definition built directly on the Cantle (2001) and Denham (2001) reports, and was constructed by representatives of the co-authors of the Guidance on Community Cohesion: the Local Government Association (LGA), the Office of the Deputy Prime Minister, the Commission for Racial Equality and the Inter Faith Network:

A cohesive community is one where:

- there is common vision and a sense of belonging for all communities;
- the diversity of people's different backgrounds and circumstances is appreciated and positively valued;
- those from different backgrounds have similar life opportunities;
- strong and positive relationships are being developed between people from different backgrounds in the workplace, in schools and within neighbourhoods.

(Local Government Association (LGA) et al. (2002))

Some five years later the Commission for Integration and Cohesion (CIC, 2007) proposed a number of amended and additional points, which offered a more complex and somewhat convoluted definition and sought to add concepts of 'trust', 'rights' and 'responsibilities' – perhaps owing more to ideas about citizenship which was a government preoccupation at the time:

The commission's new definition of an integrated and cohesive community is that it has:

- a defined and widely shared sense of the contribution of different individuals and groups to a future local or national vision;
- a strong sense of an individual's local rights and responsibilities;
- a strong sense that people with different backgrounds should experience similar life opportunities and access to services and treatment;
- a strong sense of trust in institutions locally, and trust that they will act fairly when arbitrating between different interests and be subject to public scrutiny;
- a strong recognition of the contribution of the newly arrived, and of those who have deep attachments to a particular place – focusing on what people have in common;
- positive relationships between people from different backgrounds in the workplace, schools and other institutions.

(Commission for Integration and Cohesion (CIC, 2007))

A further layer of complexity was added by the Department of Communities and Local Government (DCLG, 2008) in response to the CIC report:

Community cohesion is what must happen in all communities to enable different groups of people to get on well together. A key contributor to community cohesion is integration which is what must happen to enable new residents and existing residents to adjust to one another.

Our vision of an integrated and cohesive community is based on three foundations:

- people from different backgrounds having similar life opportunities;
- people knowing their rights and responsibilities;
- people trusting one another and trusting local institutions to act fairly.

And three ways of living together:

- a shared future and sense of belonging;
- a focus on what new and existing communities have in common, alongside a recognition of the value of diversity;
- strong and positive relationships between people from different backgrounds.

(DCLG, 2008a)

It is doubtful that either of these later definitions have added much to the original and have tended to blur the focus of cohesion rather than simply being based on belonging, equal opportunities and positive inter-action. However, the policy domain has been particularly productive in producing supportive guidance and documentation. This in itself can be organised into three phases. First, following the disturbances in Burnley, Oldham and Bradford in 2001 a range of interventions at a national and local level were generated. These included Ouseley (2001), Ritchie (2001) and Clarke (2001) as well as the Cantle Report (Cantle, 2001). The initial reports stemmed from inquiries into the various disturbances (though the Ouseley Report was commissioned prior to the disturbances in Bradford) and, together with the government's response (Denham, 2001), established a set of common themes that have framed much of the debate on community cohesion over the last decade or so. These reports are, hereinafter, collectively referred to as the '2001 reports'.

The second was a formalisation of community cohesion from 2002 onwards, with a focus on defining community cohesion, generating guidance to support local government and related agencies to imple-ment strategies and assess their impact. Guidance issued on commu-nity cohesion emphasised the importance of 'common values' and cross-community and cross-disciplinary working, as well as the need to continue to tackle inequalities and disadvantage. Moreover, the UK government established a Community Cohesion Unit (CCU) in 2002 to co-ordinate national work and implement programmes directly or to provide funding to statutory and voluntary agencies where they felt it necessary to do so. The CCU was supported by an independent panel of practitioners who helped to develop guidance and best practice on cohesion. Its work concluded with a final report, 'The End of Parallel Lives?' (Cantle, 2004), which stressed the importance of mainstreaming cohesion into local government services. Much of this thinking was brought together by the Home Office (2005) publication 'Improving Opportunity, Strengthening Society' and similar subsequent reports on an annual basis over several years, which promoted the building of community cohesion as one of the four key themes alongside addressing inequality, promoting inclusiveness and tackling racism and extremism.

The third phase concentrated on the importance of integration and identity as advocated by the then home secretary (Blunkett, 2004). The CIC was established in 2006 to further review the policy area, which was still new and had yet to be evaluated. It published its findings in the following year (CIC, 2007). This gave further weight to the community cohesion programme and was also forward looking, emphasising a stronger sense of 'shared futures'. The CIC report was more explicit than the previous reports in 2001 in its call for a positive vision, and advocated a 'national shared futures campaign,' in which the 'government openly make a case for the sort of society we want to be in' (CIC, 2007, p. 48). CIC also urged a debate on the definition of community cohesion in order to broaden the approach and to encompass a wider range of local contexts. In response, DCLG announced a raft of new initiatives including an amended definition of community cohesion (see above). In short, the policy literature on community cohesion is rich in its breadth and demonstrates how themes have developed since 2001.

In contrast to the policy literature, the number and scope of academic publications were much more limited and, on the whole, they tended to be critical of the concept of community cohesion from its inception following the publication and government acceptance (Denham, 2001) of the Review Team's 'Cantle Report' (Cantle 2001). However, this now appears to be changing fundamentally (discussed below). The initial concerns in this literature were about the political positioning of the concept. Lentin and Titley (2011) believe that the development of community cohesion was a means of reining back race relations policies on the part of government (p. 45), while Burnett (2004) suggests that the then New Labour government used community cohesion and the idea of communitarianism as a 'bridge between the concept of citizenship (and its obligations) and ever widening notions of criminality'. Burnett's argument is hard to follow and even he concedes that 'it is difficult to trace' just how the term 'community' has become used as an 'art of the rhetoric of political ideology'. In the absence of any real evidence, Burnett relies upon the conjuring up of a fear of a 'new moral order', which he says the government was trying to impose and in which 'individuals' rights are to be matched with social responsibilities'. He is not specific about what the possible impacts are likely to be, nor why such a shift would be problematic for those directly involved, or for society in general; but, he also attacks communitarians like Etzioni (2002) for advocating what he sees as a similar shift in direction.

However, Burnett's main thrust is to suggest that the impact of a communitarian/cohesion approach, which he lumps together, was the result of the government trying to change 'the dominant stereotype of the Asian' from 'communal, protective, secretive, private' and in some way to associate it with criminality. In Burnett's rather tendentious account of the 2001 reports into the riots and the events that surrounded them, he adduces no evidence from the reports in support of this proposition and simply relies on the way the tabloid press reported the disturbances as 'race riots' and the statements and activities of the Far Right, both of which he believes 'pointed the finger' at the Asian community. Burnett's criticism is somewhat baffling as a great deal of care was taken by the authors of the 2001 reports, most of whom had spent many years working to improve race equality, including the former head of the Commission for Race Equality, to avoid identifying minority communities as the problem. And, as Burnett himself later acknowledges, community cohesion policies did actually put a particular emphasis on the need for White majority communities to change (Burnett, 2006), and the principal report (Cantle 2001) was clearly critical of the host White majority communities and particularly of civic leadership and government agencies.

The 2001 reports also drew attention to structural inequalities and disadvantage faced by all communities. However, Burnett, supported by others (McGhee, 2008, Kundnani, 2002a), seems to overlook these aspects of the reports and, in the belief that the conflicts were almost entirely reducible to economic factors, they are concerned that the focus on community cohesion moves the agenda away from these key issues. However, Thomas (2011, p. 91) dismisses this charge in the first academic study based upon real evidence from the operation of cohesion in local communities. The assertions are also contradicted by the government policy statements at the time and particularly the annual series of Building Opportunity, Strengthening Society reports from 2005 (Home Office, 2005). The commitment to tackling inequalities and 'making social justice visible' was also reaffirmed by the review of community cohesion in 2007 (CIC, 2007).

From a similar perspective, there is a view that tensions and conflicts between communities are almost entirely attributable to poverty and deprivation (also see Chapter 4), and were these to be somehow magically wiped away, people would apparently live in harmony and all forms of racism would fade away. For some, this is based upon a classic Marxist position, but there are a number of arguments which are often conflated and presented on very simplistic terms without regard to supporting evidence. While poverty and deprivation clearly play a part in community divisions, this critique has failed in a number of respects. First, assertions that poverty is responsible for poor community relations and, more generally, for racism, do not distinguish between the concepts of relative deprivation and absolute poverty. Most commentators equate 'poverty' in the most general way with the competition between majority and minority communities over jobs and resources, although it is often presented as a function of people being deprived or 'poor'.[3] In some cases, the element of competition is a key factor in differences, but the level of hostility between groups can vary from place to place and in different contexts, even though relative deprivation of the different communities is the same. It would also not explain why the response to the relative deprivation of one group is to attack another relatively deprived group rather than seek common cause with them or take some other form of action. Competition between different communities was recognised in the 2001 reports, as one of the 'most consistent and vocal concerns' (Cantle, 2001, p. 25) as a contributory factor and this view was reinforced in the later cohesion review (CIC, 2007) and has been found in other studies (Semyonov et al., 2007). However, the perception of the unfair distribution of resources, public services and life chances can be present at different levels in society and is not limited to the poorest of sections.

The suggestion that racism and other divisions are attributable to absolute poverty is equally spurious, with the implicit suggestion that poorer people are likely to be more racist, often based upon no more than stereotypes about poorer people, rather than on evidence. The support for the Far Right in the UK is certainly not limited to the poor in an absolute or relative sense and many 'dissatisfied democrats' have been rallied by the Far Right over 'rising diversity and more culturally distinct Muslim communities' (Goodwin, 2011, p. 61) and widespread opposition to migration is evident (ibid., pp. 62–66). The Far Right parties like the BNP and newer EDL have very wealthy backers who, despite their wealth, are also willing to espouse racist views as well as support racist causes. However, the discussion of poverty and deprivation in this context also confuses the position of individual actors and those of particular communities. Laurence and Heath (2008) point to a connection between disadvantaged areas and lower cohesion scores, although they are careful to also point out that some of the most deprived areas have high cohesion scores and that living in an area with a broad range of diversity was positively associated with cohesion. Their findings reinforce the idea that poorer monocultural areas fare worse in this respect. The most recent attitudinal research in England (DCLG, 2011, p. 9) also confirms that the 'ethnic composition of the households in the area was the most significant demographic predictor of respect for ethnic differences' and that 'in areas where 5 per cent or more of the households were ethnic minority households, the greater the likelihood that people felt ethnic differences would be respected'. Further, contrary to the simple link with poverty proposed by some, the research also indicated that lower socio-economic groups had 'a greater chance of feeling that their local area was an area where people from different backgrounds got on well together' (ibid., p. 9).

The association between poverty and racism and community tensions illustrates a more general problem for social science: the linking together of two variables, where a strong statistical correlation is apparent, but the relationship rests upon the explanatory 'intervening' variable. In this case, there appears to be more support behind the idea that it is not 'poverty' *per se* that provides the explanation but, rather, that poorer people will, in general, have lower formal educational achievement and informal experiential opportunities to learn about others. Positive attitudes to difference and 'otherness' appear to be related to exposure to people from different backgrounds and the opportunity to engage and interact and to disconfirm negative stereotypical views based upon myths rather than realities. This, then, becomes a function of lack of opportunity and broader life chances, rather than poverty itself.

In a similar way, the debate over whether 'race' or ethnicity (and perhaps all difference) is an independent variable from that of class and socio-economic position is a long-standing discussion in sociology. Gilroy's review of the 'three basic tendencies' of relationship between race and class (Gilroy, 2002, pp. 2–40) is comprehensive and while he explains the interaction between the two, he concludes that 'race' must be viewed 'as a distinct order of social phenomena *sui generis*' (ibid., p. 19). As discussed above, much of the previous critiques of community cohesion rested upon the suggestion that governments prefer to ignore the real problems of racism and focus instead on the relations between groups in order to gloss over fundamental inequalities, which again turns on the notion that all prejudice and discrimination has an economic root (and that governments are simply duplicitous). The causation of prejudice and predictors of community cohesion are still relatively under-researched, but there are an increasing number of evidence-based studies which clearly indicate that prejudices can be autonomous and able to transcend socio-economic position. Further, it has now been clearly established that prejudice towards others can be reduced through contact (Hewstone et al., 2006, 2006a, 2007, 2008, 2008a).

In particular, the recent debate about Muslim communities within Western states has highlighted the limitations of viewing race relations and difference through national lenses. Islamophobia is now rife across Europe and yet Muslim communities embrace 'many different cultures and ethnicities, and spans myriad beliefs and traditions' (Bartlett et al., 2010, p. 23). As discussed in earlier chapters, the globalisation of communications has enabled ideologies and values to transcend national boundaries, independently of levels of the socio-economic or class position. These can develop at the international or diasporic level, and geo-political considerations can have a far greater salience, and contrast with the limited national concept of multiculturalism which has revolved around the accommodation between majority and minority populations rather than reflecting the current reality of super diversity and global communications.

Further, 'differences' are not confined to ethnicity or faith, and also encompass sexual orientation, age, special needs and disabilities, and other characteristics and therefore have deep socio-psychological roots which are also independent, though sometimes related, to the economic structure. It is seldom asserted that homophobic violence, intergenerational conflict, or hate crimes against disabled people are simply due to poverty. Rather, it is accepted that prejudice and ignorance play a strong part in discriminatory behaviours, including harassment and violent hate crime and intimidation. Mike Smith, the lead commissioner for the Equality and Human Rights Commission (EHRC) Inquiry into disability-related hate crime was shocked by:

> the horrendous things some disabled people have experienced. In the worst cases, people were tortured. And apparently just for fun. It's as though the perpetrators didn't think of their victims as human beings.
>
> (Smith, 2011, p. 5)

And Smith himself, in his flat in a 'smart tree-lined avenue' also

> regularly had 'NF', 'cripple' and swastikas painted on my front door. I had wooden stakes pushed under my front door at night, and the ramp for my wheelchair moved. I had offensive graffiti painted on my bedroom window while I slept.
>
> (ibid., p. 5)

The EHRC Inquiry, although focused on disability, attempted to understand the causation of hate crime, which could perhaps explain the antipathy towards, and hatred of, people with other types of difference to ourselves:

> Disability-related harassment incidents and crimes are not motiveless – they often stem from deep seated animosity and prejudice which feeds off the wider cultural devaluation and social exclusion of disabled people. [...] Many of the witnesses who gave evidence thought harassment was linked to prejudice against disabled people. Some suggested that the historical representation of disabled people as in need of charity ('handicapped') is still embedded in the stereotype of disabled people as objects of pity rather than as equal members of society. This was seen by some as being exacerbated by the differences in power – disability-related harassment as a manifestation of a much wider power dynamic that socially excludes, marginalises and discriminates against disabled people.
>
> (EHRC, 2011, p. 163)

The lack of contact with, and segregation of, disabled people was seen as a key determinant of the fear of difference (p. 164). It is tempting to substitute 'people of a different race' (or ethnicity or faith), for 'disabled' in the above quote. This would recognise the interplay of prejudice with historical perceptions of inferiority and power positions (Cantle, 2008,

p. 101). It would also recognise that it is not possible to simply 'eradicate poverty' as a means of combating discrimination and prejudice, however helpful it would be to do so. The 'difference' of people has to be addressed as much as, or in addition to, their socio-economic position.

The suggestion that the responses to the disturbances in Oldham, Bradford and Burnley in 2001, together with any negative debates on asylum and immigration which ensued, could be seen as counter-productive to the goals of shared identity and citizenship, do of course have to be taken seriously and more especially if this had amounted in some way to 'the blaming of minorities'. If this were the case then it is likely that minorities would feel under a lesser obligation to contribute to community cohesion (and thus engagement) when they are being identified as being part of the problem. The identification of disability hate crime in the EHRC Inquiry (2011) was, of course, no more tantamount to blaming disabled people for their disability than the 2001 reports were blaming minorities for the riots.

Some of the critical response to the early stages of the development of community cohesion simply reflected the 'defensive' nature of multicultural policy discussed earlier, in that almost any discussion involving minority communities was always likely to be seen as a hostile attack. Further, they were part of a general, partly understandable, belief that any discussion of 'race' presented the Far Right with the opportunity to stir up trouble. Again, as discussed earlier, this is a rather outdated view and most people, in Britain at least, no longer support the naked racist views of the Far Right. When they are given the 'oxygen of publicity' their ridiculous views are now derided – as was the case when the leader of the BNP, Nick Griffin, appeared on BBC's *Question Time* on 22 October 2009 – even though his appearance was opposed at the time on the same defensive basis. The 'anguished outrage from the political establishment and media' extended to the refusal to participate by some established and mainstream politicians who clung to the 'no platform' position of the Far Right in the media (Copsey and Macklin, 2011a, p. 86).

A new an important book by Paul Thomas has also validated the community cohesion concept and given credence to cohesion practice. In *Youth, Multiculturalism and Community Cohesion* (2011), Thomas describes a number of areas as having 'profound ethnic segregation, and the separate, oppositional and potentially dangerous ethnic and religious identities' and sets out 'grounded evidence around the implementation of community cohesion...and the reality of ethnic tension'

(p. 5). This is the first academic appraisal of community cohesion based upon empirical evidence. Thomas points out that community cohesion has been out of step with most academic analysis, but that analysis has been 'completely free of empirical evidence, resting instead on national governmental reports and discourse' (p. 4).

Thomas chides the critics of cohesion for developing 'evidence free' views and for failing to collect and utilise empirical data. He aims to correct the 'academic deficit' which has resulted from this and the failure to draw upon the 'lives, opinions and identities of young people, or the reality of policy impacts on those young people and their communities' (ibid., p. 6). And even where empirical evidence has been produced, Thomas says that 'it is often ignored by critics' (ibid., p. 93). Further, Thomas dismisses the charges that cohesion was in some way a return to assimilationism, or a shift away from tackling inequalities. He found that 'community cohesion practice accepts and works with distinct ethnic and social identities, while augmenting them with overarching identities based on common connections, needs and experiences' and was simply 'a critique of particular forms of multiculturalism policy formation and operation that have focused exclusively on the needs, identities and concerns of each separate ethnic group without consideration of relations, links and experiences shared between those groups' (ibid., p. 91).

Thomas concludes that, while the term multiculturalism has 'become tainted and unhelpful, no longer offering a constructive way forward', the approach offered by community cohesion 'recognises a renewed focus on commonality and on community relations and is recognised and supported on the ground' (p. 195).

Cohesion and interaction

Cohesion programmes represented the first real attempt in the UK to promote meaningful interaction between communities from different backgrounds and to promote trust and understanding and to break down myths and stereotypes.[4] These were introduced on a localised basis across the UK from about 2003, but with an initial concentration in England and a gradual development in Wales, Northern Ireland, and to a lesser extent in Scotland, a few years later. While most were developed by local authorities and voluntary agencies, there were some nationally recognised programmes, notably the school twinning programmes which brought together children of different backgrounds from monocultural schools. General guidance was issued nationally by the Department for Communities and Local government (DCLG, 2009a) on the basis that:

> The human need to connect with others is as important to our wellbeing as it ever was. Yet we all lead busy lives, concentrated around our immediate families and friends. We don't always have time to get to know the people next door – let alone people living further afield. And where people are living individual, isolated lives, problems can arise. In the worst cases, people can become suspicious and hostile, especially towards individuals or groups they see as 'different' or 'not belonging'.
>
> Encouraging interaction is one of the simplest, most straightforward ways in which we can overcome these barriers. When people have the chance to get to know each other, they focus on what they have in common, rather than their differences. This helps to break down prejudice and stereotypes, fostering instead mutual respect and understanding.

Initially, these programmes were regarded as 'cross-cultural' interaction, though this began to give way to, or be used interchangeably with, 'intercultural' and the notion of intercultural dialogue gathered pace from about 2008 (see Chapter 7).

While interaction programmes were clearly part of a broader agenda to improve community cohesion, a number of critics seized upon them to again try to suggest that they were implicitly driving an assimilationist and political agenda. McGhee (2005), for example, was scornful of the process of dialogue, describing it as a means of 'cooling down' cultures, traditions, identities and values, and as a means of shifting from a rights-based concept of citizenship to one based upon participation and where 'identity, culture and tradition might obstruct the emergence of actively engaged citizens' (p. 173). McGhee goes on to highlight a number of community-based projects aimed at reducing hate crime by broadening people's experiences of 'others' and, in the light of their evident success, in desperation asks 'how do you dismiss (these) initiatives?' and can only go on to suggest that they might not be for everyone and might have some moral imperative behind them for those 'outside the normal run of things' (p. 179).

Part of reason for the divergence of views between academics stems from the divisions within social sciences. Social psychologists are more likely to focus on personal interactions and the consequent change in attitudes and behaviours. 'Contact theory', championed by Allport and others from the 1950s, has demonstrated how prejudices can be reduced and behaviours changed (Allport, 1954), and more recently Hewstone and others have applied this approach directly to race and other identities in support of community cohesion programmes (Hewstone et al., 2006, 2006a, 2007, 2008, 2008a). Sociologists, on the other hand, rarely seem to draw upon the work of social psychologists and continue to see interaction programmes as a new model of forced assimilation and heralding a new and nationalistic policy agenda. McGhee even takes the view that 'active citizenship' is an integrative concept replacing assimilationist and multiculturalist strategies (2008, p. 52) and takes the same view about attempts to develop English on a more pervasive basis. Rather than it being a means by which diverse communities can communicate and interact, the promotion of the use of English is, to him, merely an extension of the government's 'linguistic nationalism' which focuses on the 'easiest signifier of sameness and difference' (McGhee, 2008, p. 53).

The same approach has been taken by activists and commentators that support the race-based conceptions of a divided society. Kundnani (2002), for example, claims that the changing nature of debates on 'race' has helped to shift the imperative to integration and by building shared norms, common identity and stable communities, diverse groups would be expected to 'buy into' British institutions, organisations and processes. Harrison (2005, p. 91) takes a similar view, fearing assimilation 'in which the entrenched barriers and values of white communities pass relatively unchallenged'. These concerns, however, owe more to political positioning than to the evidence, including that from social psychologists referred to above. They also fail to recognise the academic and practical work on peace and reconciliation that has demonstrated that intergroup relations can be rebuilt by going through painful processes of discussing and resolving differences (see, for example, Lederach, 1993, 1997); the application of 'co-existence work' as a means of addressing contemporary ethnic conflict (Weiner, 1998); the work of social capital theorists like Robert Putnam which has emphasised the importance of 'bridging' social capital (Putnam, 2000, 2007); and the more recent evaluation of community cohesion by Paul Thomas which directly contradicts these concerns (2011). The critics of community cohesion also ignore the specific research study of *What Works in Community Cohesion* (DCLG, 2007), which reviews the practical application of cohesion programmes.

The critics of community cohesion have, then, constructed their own idea of the concept, which largely equates to reducing it to interaction programmes and wilfully ignoring the broader aspects of the programme in order to try to align it to political processes of which they disapprove. Since its inception, community cohesion has been founded on the idea of promoting interaction *alongside and contemporaneously* with the tackling of inequalities and the promotion of the value of diversity and a common sense of belonging (LGA et al., 2002). While community cohesion has been used to improve interpersonal relations by promoting cross-cultural interaction, it has been used much more widely to address community-level divisions and tensions. The impact of cohesion programmes has been, therefore, to directly challenge racist and xenophobic narratives and to demand a more positive portrayal of diversity, largely in the British context, through promoting a new local narrative of place.

Developing a commitment to cohesion and a new narrative of place

From the outset, then, community cohesion programmes have been developed on a wider basis than one-to-one contact or cross-cultural interaction. The first formal definition (LGA et al., 2002) also recognised the need to 'positively value' the 'diversity of people's different backgrounds' and to 'promote a common vision and sense of belonging for all communities'. In other words, individual contact and interactions needed to be supported by wider social and political commitments – and actions.

The evidence in support of this contention is overwhelming. All of guidance issued to public agencies reflected this wider approach, often supported by case studies and examples which displayed a surprising amount of innovation and determination. Despite the challenges in the UK over the last decade, especially the rising hostility to the latest wave of inward migration, the demonisation of the British Muslim communities and the rise of the Far Right, the latest attitudinal surveys show that the proportion of people agreeing that their local area was a place where people from different ethnic backgrounds were respected had increased from 79 per cent in 2003 to 85 per cent in 2009–2010 and the findings over this period also revealed an increase in strength of feeling (DCLG, 2011, p. 9).

From the outset of the community cohesion programme in the UK, the formal guidance reflected the need for wide ranging measures that promoted an inclusive sense of belonging at the community and individual levels (LGA et al., 2002). This was soon reinforced by a government announcement that it would monitor progress on community cohesion at a local level and that this would be based upon a range of indicators including the perceptions of local people about the respect for difference, as well as objective inequality indicators (Home Office et al., 2003). This gave an imperative to local authority and partner agencies, who were also exhorted, for the first time, to provide a visible commitment to diversity and clear leadership.

The leadership message was reinforced by other guidance (LGA et al., 2004; Home Office, 2005a) and with a specific guide for local leaders, supported by practical examples, on a cross-party basis in 2006 (LGA et al., 2006). The emphasis on vision and leadership was particularly welcome and necessary given that the 2001 reports were very clear in their criticism of the failure of local political leadership in this respect and the continuing absence of any real attempt to promote the value of diversity. However, the role of all local partners was stressed, with leadership and commitment demanded of all members of 'local strategic partnerships', which were emerging at the time as the driving force behind regeneration of local areas and included representatives of local businesses, faith and voluntary agencies, police and other public bodies, as well as political and civic leaders.

The commitments were reinforced by pressure from central government, who also made the connection with the specific statutory duties and moral concerns to promote equality and social justice. These came in particular through the annual statements and reports for 'improving opportunity and strengthening society' (Home Office, 2005, 2006; DCLG, 2007).

The production of practical guidance, support programmes and exhortations during this period was frenetic. Hardly a week went by without a conference or workshop, or a new publication on community cohesion, or some specific aspect of local and national programmes. Guidance was issued for many professional areas, for example, in respect of cohesion in relation to regeneration (Home Office and the Office of the Deputy Prime Minister, 2004), housing (Blackaby, 2004) and schools (Home Office, 2004a). Some additional finance was also provided by central government to resource particular schemes and programmes, but more importantly they began to emphasise the importance of 'mainstreaming' cohesion work, so that it became part of everyday practice, integrated into existing programmes and professional activity. This responded in particular to the criticism of the final report of the

Independent Panel on Community Cohesion 'The End of Parallel Lives?' (Cantle, 2004), and to a number of House of Commons Inquiries into local and professional practice (House of Commons, 2003, 2004, 2004a). The government also made the very significant step of trying to embed cohesion practice into all 23,000 state-maintained schools in England through the introduction of the 'duty to promote community cohesion', supported by formal guidance (DCSF, 2007). This meant that every school-age child, from entry to primary school at around four years of age to around 17 years when they left, would be introduced to 'others' virtually or actually, and provided with more positive experiences of difference.

The support and guidance of national government and agencies was augmented to a considerable extent by the work of other professional and independent agencies. This included the scrutinising of performance (LGIU, 2005) and the countering of myths and misinformation about minorities (LGIU, 2006). It also included a range of practical measures, supported by case studies, to 'understand the stranger' (ICAR, 2004): to use 'the power of sport' to bring communities together (iCoCo, 2006); to develop new communications strategies to promote inclusion and a sense of belonging (iCoCo, 2006a); to more effectively map and engage with diversity in local areas (iCoCo, 2006b); to anticipate tensions and conflicts within and between communities (iCoCo, 2007); to develop professional skills to understand and respond to cohesion issues (iCoCo, 2007a); and to improve the relations with, and integration of, new European migrants (iCoCo, 2007b).

The development of the commitment to community cohesion at a local level in particular, soon began to bear fruit and the new capacity and competence of local authorities and other agencies was reflected in comprehensive local reviews and studies. The first of these was in the multicultural city of Leicester (IDeA, 2002) which had had a good track record on cohesion and diversity issues and is one of Britain's most multicultural cities. The Institute of Community Cohesion has now conducted around 50 local reviews and all have demonstrated progress on cohesion, often at a substantial level, and this includes the riot town of Oldham, which was reviewed some five years after the 2001 riots (iCoCo, 2006c). The research study into ' "What Works" in Community Cohesion' (DCLG, 2007) also found clear evidence of improving community cohesion in six example areas of England and developed a range of learning points for other areas to build upon. However, a further and more fundamental review of community cohesion was undertaken by a specially appointed commission headed by Darra Singh, to examine the issues that raise tensions between different groups, consider the role of political leadership and build the capacity of local people and professional agencies to respond (CIC, 2007). This review reinforced the concept of community cohesion and helped to further develop the understanding of the approach and promulgate good practice. The new academic work of Thomas (2011) has also supported the principles and practices of community cohesion and any doubt as to the effi-cacy of cohesion as a new framework for race and diversity has been expunged. Indeed, as indicated earlier, recent research (DCLG, 2011) indicates growing support, acceptance and respect for difference, despite considerable challenges in the current climate, and a similar study indi-cates that people felt that both racial and religious prejudice had reduced (DCLG, 2011a).

However, one of the key messages from the CIC report (2007) was that community cohesion had to recognise that local context was very significant and that highly localised initiatives were necessary to reflect the particular circumstance associated with each place. Further, the CIC emphasised that cohesion was also about differences of disability, sex-ual orientation, social class, health and disability, as well as faith and ethnicity. Their list of ingredients for an integrated and cohesive com-munity and the emphasis on particular places, neighbourhoods and communities was part of the CIC's strategy of introducing new models of integration and community cohesion (McGhee, 2008, p. 51). How-ever, it represented a more profound change in that it underlined the shift from the promotion of civic values at a national level, to the devel-opment of 'building a sense of commonality around real life issues, such as life ambitions and local problems' (DCLG, 2007, p. 6). This meant that the focus of the 'belonging' debate shifted from the nationalistic and contested ideas about 'Britishness' to developing more benign forms of local identities.

The debate about Britishness has, of course, always been challenging for the British Left, who have generally opposed nationalism and tended to fight shy of patriotism of any form, whereas in other parts of the world the Left have often led struggles for national liberation or viewed the building of a national culture as a progressive project (for instance, as part of anti-colonial struggles across Africa, Asia, Latin America and the Caribbean). The British Left have tended to be wary of waving a flag which has been historically viewed as symbolising empire and monar-chy (Muir, 2007, p. 5). However, while the Far Right have no hesitation in jingoistic flag waving, based on past monocultural and exclusionary ideas about identity, centrist Right parties have also found it difficult to articulate 'common values' that are British-specific and have often simply tended to counterpose more extreme forms of Muslim-based community values with those of the West (see, for example, Cameron, 2011). The development of local identities and belonging has therefore had a wide appeal and has been a mainstay of community cohesion programmes. This enables community cohesion to develop as a product of local relationships: it is about people being able to relate to one another in their everyday lives, in the street, in the newsagent, at the school gate and, particularly in ethnically mixed and diverse areas, where citizens from different backgrounds can feel they have something in common because they live in the same neighbourhood (Muir, 2007).

The development of predominantly local belonging campaigns undermines the position of critics like Burnett (2004) who attempted to present community cohesion as providing an adherence to a government-ordained set of values and mores, which could be used to forge a dominant cultural agenda and a 'them and us' discourse to encapsulate both national control and international exclusion. In fact, cohesion focused on a bottom-up local agenda which reflected diversity and promoted an 'all of us', or 'our shared future' concept, exemplified by the CIC report (2007).

The development of local identity and belonging campaigns to garner a sense of solidarity may also be a recognition of the new reality of national identity, suggested in earlier chapters. Whereas feelings of solidarity and common values could perhaps have been taken for granted in a period of ethnic and religious homogeneity, they now apparently have to be promoted more actively by the state to emphasise common citizenship (Kymlicka, 2003a, p. 195). This has even led to questions about whether we are now 'too diverse' and the promotion of solidarity and common values becomes difficult beyond a certain level of multiculturalism, and especially whether there can be a sufficient level of solidarity to maintain support for a national system of welfare benefits and health service (Goodhart, 2004). Local campaigns have side-stepped such concerns and are able to disregard contested ideas about nationality, and concentrate on more mundane ways of living together, while taking pride in a diverse local area. There have now been dozens of local 'belonging' campaigns covering every conceivable type of community in Britain, from Scotland's 'Many Cultures One Scotland' to highly localised town-specific 'one community' presentations (Cantle, 2008, p. 182), and more recently an 'I Love Hackney' campaign in London appealing to people's sense of civic pride and identification with the area, in order to deal with a number of problems that require collective effort and public participation, such as raising recycling levels and reducing antisocial behaviour, as well as promoting cohesion (Muir, 2007).

Muir (2007) has also pointed out that these campaigns have a number of spin-off benefits in that rates of local political participation are in part determined by the strength of attachment to local place, suggesting that by promoting local identities one can boost democratic engagement and the involvement of citizens in local civic affairs.

Belonging campaigns have a number of practical as well as conceptual advantages over those at the national level and present a new and positive picture of diversity without either attempting to define and institute a value system, nor raise questions about the contribution to national revenues and the use of expenditure programmes. Building belonging around local places may also be easier as it allows for more multifaceted identities, which reflect the present patterns of globalisation and super diversity. The concept of multiculturalism was unable to adapt to these new ideas about identity and remained rooted in the accommodation of migrants within host communities. Interculturalism is not limited in this way and can build upon the early work of community cohesion and provide a more international and dynamic view of identity which recognises that integration and solidarity can develop at a number of different levels.

The contribution of community cohesion has been profound and has challenged many of the shibboleths of old style multiculturalism, not because it was inherently wrong but simply because the defensive model it provided was appropriate for the 1960s and 1970s and it failed to adjust to the emerging era of super diversity and globalisation. Some early concern about the new concept of community cohesion was perhaps inevitable from those people steeped in an approach to race relations who saw any critique as another attack on minorities and diversity. In fact, it has proved to be exactly the opposite, promoting the value of diversity, encouraging a strong sense of inclusion and belonging, while continuing to tackle inequalities and injustices. It has challenged the host community to think about diversity in a more positive way and has improved tolerance, understanding and respect for difference. It has also recognised that 'difference' is no longer defined by simple black and white ideas about 'race' and is multifaceted and dynamic. More importantly, community cohesion programmes appear to have improved community relations at a time of considerable uncertainty and anxiety about 'others' at an international level and during a period of high levels of population change and churn. The levels of investment in community-based programmes have, however, fallen recently and local authorities and voluntary agencies are finding it difficult to sustain the programmes that have contributed to the building of capacity and confidence in communities and the local and professional bodies that provide services. Bearing in mind that the Far Right continue to champion a backward-looking agenda, capitalising on people's fear of change and difference, more investment will be needed to respond to an ever-changing world. We also need a new paradigm to underpin cohesive societies, and, whereas community cohesion has largely been a response to local divisions and tensions within nation-states, a new model of interculturalism will be necessary to replace our ideas about multiculturalism with a more outward focused and internationally orientated model in response to globalisation and super diversity.

6
Segregation and Integration – And Why They Matter

British multiculturalism was based, in principle at least, upon a policy of integration that emphasised the maintenance of immigrants' 'national characteristics and culture...in an atmosphere of mutual tolerance' (Jenkins, 1966). This statement was the only real attempt at any sort of vision for an emerging multicultural society and was made by the then Home Secretary in 1966. This version of integration provided reassurance to the UK's immigrant community who were frequently subject to harassment, intimidation and discrimination in a post-war Britain just beginning to come to terms with diversity. It was soon to be supported by strong anti-discrimination legislation and a number of positive action programmes to try to ensure some semblance of equal opportunities. Despite the problems, It stood in contrast to the approach of other European countries, notably France and Germany, which appeared to favour assimilation, in the case of France, or the 'guest worker' model in which long-term citizenship and rights were denied, as in the case of Germany. However, in common with France and Germany and many other countries, Britain is characterised by segregated areas that reflect the early patterns of settlement and reinforced by later inward migration.

Nevertheless, in many respects the UK policy has appeared to work well with falling levels of discrimination and growing tolerance (DCLG, 2011a) and some higher levels of integration, especially in the south of the country, and with a broader enjoyment of diversity in the form of intercultural activities, such as festivals, arts and music events and activities. This represents considerable progress since the report of the Community Cohesion Independent Review Team (Cantle, 2001) that followed the race riots in a number of northern towns and revealed that the acceptance of multiculturalism was far from universal and that relations between the migrant and host communities had become entrenched. White and Asian communities, in some areas at least, were found to be living in 'parallel lives' that:

> often do not seem to touch at any point, let alone promote any meaningful interchanges

and are based upon:

> separate educational arrangements, community and voluntary bodies, employment, places of worship, language, social and cultural networks.

The separation of communities had largely ensured a peaceful co-existence, though often with an entrenchment of inequalities, and the everyday experience of parallel lives meant that there were very few opportunities to develop trust, respect and understanding between communities. Consequently, it was relatively easy for any suggestion of a problem associated with either community to be turned into resentment, anger and violence – especially aided and abetted by Far Right groups. More generally, while the idea of multiculturalism did enjoy support at one level, it appeared that, for many, it had become associated with 'political correctness', with little real ownership and commitment and enforced by state-led political and cultural imperatives.

Since 2001, and particularly following the introduction of community cohesion programmes in the UK principally developed to improve the relations between different ethnic groups, the concept of 'difference' has been understood more widely and applied to a range of characteristics including sexual orientation, age, disability, faith and social class. Not all of these differences are entrenched in the form of 'parallel lives', but many do depend to some extent at least upon the notion of 'otherness' and the way in which the separation of social and cultural domains reinforce spatial differences in housing, education and employment. Segregation and integration, therefore, have to be understood in different ways to those simply based upon the visible distinctiveness of 'race'.

The domains of segregation and integration

There has been little by way of a serious attempt to define 'segregation' or 'integration' at a conceptual level or at a policy level. Early ideas about 'segregation' were devised purely on spatial analyses and focused almost entirely on the physical separation of communities in residential terms. These analyses did, at least, produce some clear measurements based upon indices, but were nevertheless conceptually limited. While the concept of 'parallel lives' introduced in 2001 (Cantle, 2001) fundamentally challenged that approach, it was not developed into a more formalised number of 'layers of separation' until 2005 (Cantle, 2008). There have also been a number of other attempts to move the debate on from the 'one or two dimensional lattice of spatial segregation' and to consider social forms (Fagiolo et al., 2007). There have been few attempts to promote integration at the spatial or any other level, except in the most general of terms, such as developing 'shared aspirations and values' and 'personal and social responsibility', and to 'take part, be heard' as in the most recent attempt at 'Creating the Conditions for Integration' (DCLG, 2012). The most notable of earlier and more meaningful attempts was the bussing of children to schools in the USA designed to enforce the mixing of children in the 1960s and 1970s. This was controversial and probably inhibited subsequent attempts to promote any other form of mixed community. Little else has been done to create more mixed environments, whether in housing, education, employment or leisure, with most governments around the world taking the view that these matters are best left to personal choice, even though it is clear that those personal choices are informed, or even determined, by a wide range of social and economic factors. Governments have also tended to put matters of integration in the 'too difficult' box, while some have been in denial about their countries actually being multicultural, let alone segregated.

Both 'segregation' and 'integration' are generally conceptualised in spatial or physical terms and therefore on a continuum from assimilation at one end of the scale, to the separate co-existence of communities, or 'parallel lives' at the other. This has severely inhibited the debate, which should be seen in much more multifaceted terms. Proposed domains of segregation and integration, based on the 'layers of segregation' (Cantle, 2008) are set out in Table 6.1, for further consideration below.

The nature and extent of segregation is not only conceptualised in relation to spatial divisions but is also generally only measured in these terms (and even then is contested, see below). Spatial segregation is rarely uniform across any country, or even within particular cities and regions. For example, the domain of 'spatial segregation' is most noticeable in the northern towns of England (between White

Table 6.1 The domains of segregation and integration

Domain	Characteristics
Spatial	Segregation of neighbourhoods, schools, workplaces and other institutions
Social and cultural	Segregation of social, recreational and cultural networks and activities
Functional	Equality of access to services, citizen/denizen rights and responsibilities, societal 'openness'
Values and norms	Observance and acceptance of shared values and behaviours, based on a common national identity or based on locally negotiated and accepted norms

and Asian communities) and in Northern Ireland (between Protestants and Catholics). Separation is less pronounced in English cities in the Midlands and least pronounced in the south, especially London. Nevertheless, both the Midlands and the south of England, including London, do have a number of highly segregated areas. There is a much richer literature on integration and segregation in the USA and a better understanding of residential preferences (Sampson and Sharkey, 2008), though the extent and nature of segregation is still a fundamental concern (the Eisenhower Foundation, 2008).

Patterns of spatial segregation and integration often dictate much of the cross-cultural contact in the other domains, perhaps especially 'social and cultural' and 'functional' areas. So, for example, school intakes, local employment arrangements, access to housing and recreational arrangements are often shaped by physical proximity (Johnston et al., 2006; the Eisenhower Foundation, 2008; Hiebert, 2009). These areas, in turn, often determine friendship patterns and much day to day interpersonal contact in the wider social and cultural sphere, but may be trumped by other forms of segregation.

The promotion of equal opportunities and positive action has had some impact in determining access to education and employment in particular, and in closing the performance gap between members of different communities. While this 'functional' approach has largely been on the basis of tackling exclusion, equality programmes have not only provided a greater level of fairness by rebalancing opportunities, they have also created many more opportunities for contact that bridge across levels of spatial separation. The presence of people from minority backgrounds alongside those from the majority in places of employment and educational institutions provides minorities with a higher level of 'linking' social capital and the opportunity for people who are different to build social and professional networks that transcend their difference. In this way, there is a symbiotic relationship between equality and interaction programmes.

Social and cultural networks have been seen as almost entirely a matter of personal choice and therefore beyond state interference, though, in Britain at least, private members' clubs have been subject to regulation to prevent discrimination on the basis of gender and ethnicity and this had led to a greater level of integration. However, the primary purpose of legislation has been to prevent discrimination, rather than to promote new patterns of interpersonal contact. The idea of segregation by 'value system' is very new and owes much to the present demonisation of Muslim communities, who have been depicted as living in one country while inhabiting a separate community dominated by internet and other virtual connections to extremist ideology. This view has been advanced, on a co-ordinated basis, by the leaders of France, Germany and the UK (Cameron, 2011; Merkel, 2011; Sarkozy, 2011). While this has undoubtedly been overstated, this concept does underline the limitations of considering 'integration' only at a national level and global communications are now so pervasive that strong and distinctive international and diaspora patterns of affinities have become much more evident and salient.

Spatial segregation and integration

There is still little agreement about what is meant by either 'segregation' or 'integration', even in a spatial sense. There is also little agreement about whether either is desirable, let alone what form they should take. After 50 years of multiculturalism, this lack of clarity and vision is surprising and perhaps reflects both the pace of population change within communities and the sensitivity with which these ideas have had to be addressed.

As the discussion of 'segregation' has largely revolved around the spatial domain, it has been conducted by geographers and demographers who have used a number of indices to plot spatial or physical separation of identifiable communities with very few attempts to relate this to other aspects of separation, nor to consider the concepts in more layered terms – for example, in respect of language, belief, education, employment, lifestyle and social structure, as set out in a previous study of community cohesion (Cantle, 2008). This is particularly true of academic reviews of the concept and complemented by a simplistic discussion of integration policy, which rarely addresses segregation in physical terms and tends to focus on very limited measures – for example, in terms of providing newer migrants with access to public services, or vaguer notions of values and cultural norms. There is also little by way of an evidence base to support linkage between the conceptual and practical development. This is a particularly serious and somewhat curious omission as remarked by Semyonov et al. (2007):

> Patterns of ethnic residential segregation, interethnic contacts and prejudice have been studied extensively for quite a long time. Consequently, the body of research on these topics has grown and has become substantial. Nevertheless, no-one has systematically examined yet the inter-relations between ethnic segregation, contact and prejudice. That is, no-one has examined whether, to what extent, and in what ways interethnic contacts mediate the relations between residential segregation and ethnic prejudice. This neglect is curious and somewhat unfortunate because the logic embodied in sociological writings on these issues leads us to expect that interethnic contacts would mediate the relations between residential segregation and prejudice.
>
> (p. 2)

However, even in spatial terms, there is little agreement about what levels of segregation (however this might be defined) is desirable in respect of any objective – for example, the provision of heritage support to a particular community, or the reduction of prejudice directed towards out-groups or the 'other'. The main focus of attention has been upon the number people from one or more minority communities within a given area, though it is axiomatic that the segregation of minorities depends upon the segregation of the majority community. Further, there is no accepted level of the percentage of one community within a given area that would justify the term 'segregated'. In the US a ghetto is generally taken to be an area with more than 90 per cent from the Black community. In the UK context, lower levels of 75 per cent have been used to define segregation by 'enclave' (Poulsen, 2005), perhaps as the number of areas with the USA's proportions would be small if limited to minority populations – but there are many majority White communities exceeding this level. However, as with all definitions of segregation, the size of the area used as a unit of measurement is crucial, as small areas, say just a few streets, are clearly likely to be more 'segregated' than a ward or a whole town or city.

Most Western societies have a significant degree of segregation, at least in the sense that visibly identifiable migrant communities tend to live in areas in which they predominate, or are heavily clustered. The USA appears to have the highest levels of concentrations of minorities, but also a high degree of neighbourhood segregation, in which 'members of ethnic and racial minorities tend to live in segregated-homogeneous and distinct neighborhoods and communities' (Semyonov et al., 2007). The 'universe of stable racial integration... (is) a small exceptional parallel to the dominant separatist universe that the majority of Americans experience' (Cashin, 2004, p. 43), with 'less than 4 per cent of Americans in stable integrated surroundings' (ibid., p. 42). Canada's segregation is also significant, with the population of visible minorities concentrated in the largest metropolitan areas of Montreal, Toronto and Vancouver (Hiebert, 2009).

European levels are generally lower than those of the USA (Semyonov et al., 2007) and while this is also true in relation to the UK (Iceland and Mateos, 2009) where Blacks are much less segregated than in the USA, for Asian groups, segregation tends to be lower in the USA (Iceland et al., 2011). However, residential segregation is substantial and widespread across European cities and the patterns of ethnic residential segregation in Europe and has been increasing over the years. The patterns are also quite similar to those observed in the USA with cities like London, Amsterdam, Frankfurt, Athens, Brussels, Paris, Lisbon and Stockholm, characterised by homogeneous and distinct ethnic neighbourhoods. For example, London has ethnically distinct segregated neighbourhoods populated mostly by Pakistani, Bangladeshi or Indian residents; Amsterdam has neighbourhoods inhabited by Surinamese and Moroccan; Athens has Albanian residential areas; Frankfurt has several Turkish neighbourhoods; and Paris and Brussels are characterised by a series districts and neighbourhoods inhabited mostly by immigrants of north-African origin (Semyonov et al., 2007, p. 5). Indeed, around 25 to 30 cities in Europe have set up their own network to consider how to develop local integration policies, especially where there is an absence of guidance, support and commitment for integration at a national level (Penninx, 2009).

There have been few attempts to measure the extent and nature of segregation across country boundaries. However, Johnston et al.

(2007) have developed a bespoke methodology to compare five English-speaking countries: Australia, Canada, New Zealand, the UK and the USA. This found segregation in all countries, with a number of common factors. It also showed that while the highest levels of segregation were found in the UK and the USA, Canada was also placed in this category. Australia and New Zealand also had significant levels of segregation, indicating that new patterns of migration had developed into segregation even in countries where the population is almost entirely migrant and not conditioned by colonial history in the same way. The different methods of calculating segregation produce different results and while segregation may be found, the levels to which it is represented varies according to the methodology adopted. Johnston et al. (2009), for example, illustrate this with regard to Pacific Islanders and Asians in New Zealand, where very different results are found under different measurement systems.

In the UK, there have been a number of measures adopted to assess the extent of spatial segregation. These use census data compiled on a ten-year cycle and are therefore unable to keep pace with population movement and change. However, there is a general agreement about the level of segregation, resulting first from the use of the Isolation Ratio which measures the probability of your neighbour being of Black or Minority Ethnic (BME) origin if you are BME yourself, and the probability of your neighbour being BME if you are White. The highest levels of segregation are thus found in the northern towns of England, such as Bolton, Bradford, Blackburn, Rochdale, Oldham and Burnley (three of which were subject of race riots in 2001). Some London boroughs, by contrast, exhibit the lowest levels of isolation. The Index of Dissimilarity (ID) measures the degree of separation between White and BME communities as a whole and the unevenness in distribution between two social groups – for example, a minority and a majority social group. The ID score – which varies from 0 to 100 – indicates the proportion of one group that would need to move for there to be an even spread of the two groups across the district. This produced similar results, with generally more segregated areas, by ethnicity, in the north of England, the lowest in the south and a medium level in the towns of the Midlands. However, pockets of segregation are found in all parts of England and the UK has a whole.

The principal debate in the UK has been as to whether the level of ethnic segregation is increasing, particularly following the intervention of the then chair of the Commission for Racial Equality who suggested that Britain was 'sleepwalking into segregation' (Phillips, 2005).

This has been hotly disputed, though there is certainly some evidence of an increase, in some areas. For example, Simpson (2003), using information from the last available census, found that the number of enumeration districts with over 75 per cent 'South Asian' population had increased from 29 in 1991 to 77 in 2001 and those with 25 per cent to 75 per cent 'mixed South Asian and others' increasing from 152 to 163 in Bradford. Poulsen (2005) concluded that, with regard to 16 UK major cities, Pakistani and Bangladeshi communities were increasingly separated and isolated and this will continue to increase over time. More worryingly, the one national database that can provide a more up to date assessment is that of school populations, which are monitored on an annual basis, and work by Johnston et al. (2006) found 'national patterns of both residential and school segregation, with the clear suggestion that the latter is greater than the former, especially among those of South Asian ethnicity'. There is also evidence that the diversity of some areas is increasing at the same time, particularly as BME communities expand out of their traditional areas into neighbouring predominantly White areas. What is less clear is whether those areas then become dominated by BME households as a result of their continuing in-movement and the subsequent outward movement of White households, perhaps for a number of reasons including that of 'White Flight'. The whole notion of White Flight has, however, also become hotly contested, with a number of academics appearing to fear that the acceptance of this term would tend to support the idea that multiculturalism has 'failed'. Prior to the Phillips' speech, White Flight was acknowledged (Cantle, 2008, pp. 60 and 80), but this is less likely to be the case now in academic circles for fear of appearing to endorse Phillips' views. However, the loss of White population from many cities between 1991 and 2001 certainly exceeds the losses attributable to the 'natural movement' resulting from births and deaths, with a net increase in the minority population of London approaching 1 million over the period (Cantle, 2008, p. 81). In Europe, too, the 'political correctness that praises multiculturalism...while turning a blind eye to de facto segregation' (Cuperus, 2011) has also inhibited open discussion.

White Flight is evident in countries beyond Europe and appears to be more readily acknowledged. In the USA, for example, the reluctance on the part of the White community to live in mixed neighbourhoods is well documented:

> Studies that examine residential preferences uniformly contend that most whites are reluctant to live in neighborhoods where blacks live,

and to a lesser extent, where Hispanics and Asians reside. Whether preferences for 'residential homogeneity' stem from prejudice or from fear of potential undesirable social and economic consequences or from a wish to live with your 'own kind' (ethnocentrism), the end outcome of these preferences leads to the persistence of ethnic residential segregation.

(Semyonov et al., 2007, p. 4)

Very specific studies in the USA, for example, in Chicago, have clearly indicated that the movement of population 'falls along racial and ethnic lines' (Sampson and Sharkey, 2008). Other non-UK studies of UK segregation have also been a little more forthright than studies from within and, for example, Iceland et al. (2011) found that segregation for Asian groups in Britain had not reduced, even in respect of more recent migrants (and the same was true for Blacks in the USA), with intergenerational minority disadvantage persisting, which perhaps also indicates that the 'separate but equal development' notion has failed to deliver.

The recent unwillingness by certain academics to acknowledge the existence of White Flight is compounded by a similar reluctance to acknowledge that segregation might be increasing, as this again might support the idea that multiculturalism has 'failed'. An attempt to refute the suggestion of the growth in the size and nature of segregation has been condemned by one academic as 'a political struggle for the correct position' (Carling, 2006), who also contests the idea that segregation is a 'myth' as suggested by Simpson (2003). More recently Simpson has co-authored a book (Finney and Simpson, 2009) to 'challenge the myths about race and migration' and any suggestion that segregation is growing, or that it constitutes a problem. He again bases his arguments on census data from 1991 to 2001, but to support his contention develops a rather spurious approach in which segregation is effectively redefined and based upon an assessment of certain types of population movement and the ignoring of the changes brought about by natural factors (birth and death rates). Tucked away on page 163, however, is the acknowledgement that 'segregation is increasing when measured by the size of minority populations'.

The unfortunate tendency to refuse to acknowledge the problems of diversity and to discuss them openly is understandable given the history of race relations in the UK, but now simply represents a continuation of the 'defensive' mode of multiculturalism referred to earlier. It is no longer necessary, British people are now capable of a more mature debate and, again as discussed earlier, are no longer vulnerable to the naked racist appeals of the past. And segregation is not the preserve, let alone the fault, of minority communities. Segregated minority communities go hand in hand with the segregation of the majority; indeed, they depend upon each other.

The debate over whether segregation exists and if it is increasing also deflects us from discussing the real nature of segregation, the typologies other than in respect of 'race' and the implications of relatively closed communities. It also deflects us from considering whether some degree of segregation (of whichever community type) may actually have beneficial effects. A degree of clustering of people from the same background, for example, will have multiple benefits in terms of proximity to specialist shops, particular places of worship and especially in terms of social and cultural capital and support (Cantle, 2008). There is a considerable difference between 'clustered communities', which are permeable and welcoming to others and where contact with people from different backgrounds operates at a number of levels, and those that are so dominated by one group that they create the 'parallel lives' found in 2001 (Cantle, 2001).

While there have been a number of studies in the UK charting social segregation (which often depends to some extent upon spatial separation), these are few and far between, but do show that the limited friendship patterns across ethnic groups is significant (Phillips, 2005), and the latest data in the UK indicates that 'for a majority of people, networks tended to be fairly homogenous' (DCLG, 2011). In other European studies this has been taken further with (Semyonov et al., 2007, p. 19) presenting findings that

> reveal, rather forcefully, that ethnic residential segregation decreases opportunities for the establishment of interethnic contacts and positive interethnic contacts, in turn, are likely to reduce negative attitudes and social distance between the majority population and ethnic minorities.

Similarly, in the USA there is a clear acceptance that the 'sorting' of neighbourhoods by race and ethnicity, especially Asians, Latinos, African Americans and Whites, is consistently determining residential decisions (Sampson and Sharkey, 2008).

Perhaps 30 or 40 years ago, locational factors would have determined all, or many, of our social and other networks; most people lived locally, went to school in their local area and worked nearby. And society was far less diverse than it is today. Social mobility is still limited, but more people do now work, and are educated, in different areas from where they live and have many more opportunities to form associations with people from different backgrounds. There is some evidence to suggest, however, that even where wider opportunities are available, social and friendship networks are not as diverse as the society in which people now move and that the culture of 'sticking to our own' still prevails not just within neighbourhoods but also within employment and education (see, for example, CRE, 2007; DCLG, 2011).

The social contacts within or between particular neighbourhoods has to be set alongside other spheres in which contact is likely to take place. As suggested earlier, the composition of schools and workplaces is likely to be determined to a significant extent by residency. This is as true in the USA (the Eisenhower Foundation, 2008) as it is in Britain, where there is considerable evidence that school intakes are shaped by residency (Burgess et al., 2004; Johnston et al., 2006). And even in London, one of the UK's least segregated cities, this also holds true particularly in respect of primary schools where the highest levels of segregation are to be found (Harris, 2011):

> Although about 75 per cent of the Black population were living in census neighbourhoods with a majority white population (in 2001), only 42 per cent of Black primary school pupils and 51 per cent of Black secondary pupils attended a school where the same was true. Similarly, though about 60 per cent of the South Asian population lived in white majority neighbourhoods, only 35 per cent of South Asian pupils were in white majority primary schools, and 46 per cent in white majority secondary schools. Overall the results of the study showed greater ethnic segregation in schools than in neighbourhoods, more so for primary schools than secondary schools, more so for Black and South Asian pupils, especially Pakistani ones, and generally more so in London than in other places.

The separation at school level will not only shape much of the early attitudinal development of the children themselves, but will also greatly contribute to the friendship patterns for both themselves and for their parents and carers. There is also evidence that these early separate educational experiences are carried on to university level with a number of universities having either very predominant White intakes or others with over-representative BME intakes (CRE, 2007). The large proportion of faith schools also exacerbates this trend and the UK government has recently developed new policies that have served to increase the number and range of faith schools.

For many people, their employment provides an opportunity to relate to others who are different from themselves and these professional relationships are generally conducted within codes of conduct and norms of behaviours that ensure respect for difference and require trust in each other's roles. Nevertheless, discrimination and harassment are still evident within some workplaces, despite legislation at the national level and at the European level for members of the EU. It is also the case that workplaces are segregated by ethnicity or nationality and also by gender. Such segregation is continuing at the present time, with Eastern European workers in particular finding themselves in low-skilled and low-paid roles in Western Europe. In Britain, such workers represent almost 100 per cent of the workforce of some of the businesses engaged in food picking, processing and packaging. A report by the Equality and Human Rights Commission (EHRC, 2010a) revealed that many workers in these industries were agency workers and most of these were migrants. Often, whole shifts or teams, or indeed whole production units, were of one nationality. If British workers were employed it would often be on a separate shift or team basis. The migrant workers had little chance of progression and were often treated poorly, especially in comparison to other workers. Moreover, these new migrant workers were often housed by the employer, or in accommodation found by them, which is separate from other housing. Needless to say, these workers are often regarded with suspicion and even hostility by local people who have little or no contact with them. The integration of ethnic minorities into many other forms of employment is also far from even, with, for example, many people of Pakistani and Bangladeshi origin to be found in the taxi, takeaway or market trading businesses. Many studies in the UK and in other parts of Europe have also found that minorities generally have lower paid and lower status employment and are more likely to be unemployed. This means that, whether in work or not, the separation of minorities from the host community and sometimes from each other, can be compounded by employment arrangements, rather than eased. Indeed, Hickman et al. (2008) have pointed out that work can be an obstacle to social cohesion where the effective segregation of immigrant workers was found at work, which gave rise to similarly segregated social lives.

Minorities are also much more likely to be victims of racial harassment and attack and to perceive that they are more likely to suffer in this way (DCLG, 2011a), and this means that they are less likely to feel safe in their neighbourhoods and wider environment and will be less willing to socialise more generally. This also bears upon the discussion of self-segregation in respect of minorities, as it often fails to reflect socio-economic realities. The most disadvantaged groups occupy the poorest section of the housing market, having generally lower levels of income, and where residency tends to follow established patterns of inward migration. While self-segregation may have a degree of choice, then, it is often constrained by socio-economic position, support systems, fears and anxieties about other areas and choices based upon familiarity. Indeed, housing choices are generally conservative and are sequential, based upon neighbourhoods close to their existing home (ALG, 2006).

There is, therefore, a vicious circle of segregation in which minority communities tend to live in distinct and separate areas, with newer migrants positioned by their socio-economic status and occupation. They also have greater concerns about their safety, are more dependent for support on their own community, as fearful of other communities as they are of them, and as likely to be conservative in their choice of new areas, preferring familiarity, with concomitant separation of educational opportunities and social and cultural networks.

The same vicious circle is evident for the host or majority community too (though they may see it as a 'virtuous circle', based upon economic advantage). They are less likely to live in predominantly minority areas, or even in significantly mixed areas, with greater choice afforded by a better socio-economic position and less concerns about their safety. They tend to be less dependent on support from their own community but are as fearful of other communities as they are of them, and just as likely to be conservative in their choice of new areas, preferring familiarity, moving to areas that have higher performing schools and ethnically distinct social and cultural networks.

It is therefore not appropriate to 'blame' any community for the preferences they exercise, but rather to understand that they are making rational choices in their particular circumstances. While interfering in personal preferences and choices has long been resisted by democratic states (and indeed, in the UK at least the choice agenda has been reaffirmed by the present and previous governments) it is extraordinary that little has been done to even counterbalance the negative factors and to facilitate a wider range of preferences, given that they depend, to some extent at least, upon inequalities and prejudices. In the USA, where there have been more studies of segregation and a greater recognition of its impact upon inequality and a generally more open level of discussion there have been a number of attempts at encouraging more mixed neighbourhoods. The limited basis and scale of these developments has, however, recently been lamented by the Eisenhower Foundation (2008) in their reflective report looking back on the 40 years since the civil disorders. They have therefore sought to re-energise the policy:

> To succeed with a comprehensive policy for stable, racially integrated neighborhoods, we need to promote the ability of racial minorities to move into White neighborhoods; encourage White families to move into minority neighborhoods; control market forces to insure that low income (especially minority) families are not pushed out of neighborhoods as a result of gentrification; and reduce racial discrimination by key players in the housing chain.
>
> (The Eisenhower Foundation, 2008)

There have been few attempts to promote mixed communities in the UK, though research has generally concluded that a higher degree of heterogeneity makes for more successful places (Tunstall and Fenton, 2006). For the most part in the UK, 'mixed' communities have also been more conceptualised in social class terms, with planning policies considered with a view to providing a range of housing and tenures and to preventing a concentration of deprivation in any given area (Berube, 2005), rather than one based upon ethnic integration. A number of minor initiatives have nevertheless been undertaken (see, for example, DCLG, 2009b), but there is no vision for mixed communities, little idea about what they should be like, in which way they should be mixed, nor yet why mixed communities and environments are seen to be desirable. Moreover, there is great reluctance to intervene and there are genuine concerns that any element of compulsion, along the lines of the bussing of children to schools to enforce mixing, is almost bound to be counterproductive. Given the increasing levels of diversity, it is unlikely that a policy of non-intervention will be sustainable, and it will be necessary to facilitate and incentivise change on an incremental basis. The fundamental problem is the lack of political will – and the inability to come to terms with the challenge of super diversity and globalisation.

However, in areas that are segregated by characteristics other than ethnicity, there has been a greater acceptance that 'parallel lives' (Cantle, 2001) create and reinforce stereotypes about who is different, and there is a willingness to provide alternatives. Indeed, the term 'segregation' has been seldom used in relation to other areas of difference despite the evident separation of a number of identifiable groups or communities that can only be thought of as 'segregated', that is occupied or used predominantly, or exclusively, by people from one background and where social contacts and networks are generally formed by the spatial separation inherent in the areas. These include:

- gated communities for wealthy people;
- Catholic and Protestant areas in Northern Ireland;
- White working-class social housing estates and areas;
- housing developments exclusively for older people;
- special housing provision for people with disabilities;
- separate care facilities for people with long-term mental health conditions;
- accommodation for asylum seekers and refugees; and
- traveller and gypsy sites.

The extent to which the above may create conditions that constitute 'parallel lives' is very variable. Certainly, the Catholic and Protestant areas in Northern Ireland are highly segregated with the separation in spatial terms, reinforced by separate faith schools, leisure facilities and activities and many other aspects of daily lives. This clearly constitutes 'parallel lives' and is seen as problematic, with the Northern Ireland First Minister calling for an end to segregation and more emphasis on shared futures as recently as 2011. While gated communities for wealthier families are also physically distinct, social networks and occupational patterns may be more variable. This may also be the case for White working-class social housing areas and estates, though the evidence suggests that this group is indeed more insular (Biggs and Knauss, 2011). Again, there have been a number of policy interventions to encourage more cross-cultural contacts, partly because they are seen to be vulnerable to the appeal of the Far Right (Goodwin, 2011b).

The same concerns exist with regard to traveller and gypsy sites, which are clearly distinct and the daily lives of travellers and gypsies are socially and culturally very separate, often reinforced by very different occupational structures. However, the concerns about this area of separation have been less about the insularity of these communities and more about the way in which they are seen and demonised by others. With the 'racism towards most ethnic minority groups now hidden', that towards 'Gypsies and Travellers is still common, frequently overt and seen as justified' and supported by 'abusive media coverage' which 'add to the ignorance and prejudice of many members of the settled population' (Cemlyn et al., 2009, p. v). This has been particularly true of the Roma community, who have become more prevalent and visible throughout Europe. The Roma community were, for example, attacked in Belfast in 2011 and homes set alight in an attempt to force them to leave. The European Commission (2011) had no hesitation in developing a Europe-wide integration strategy for this group, though whether this translates into anything very meaningful remains to be seen.

Intervening in other areas of segregation has also been more about trying to influence the way in which particular communities are seen negatively, and the way in which they see others, rather than a concern for their own insularity. This concern is true of new migrant groups in general, though especially of refugees and asylum seekers who have been persistently demonised in the press and media. The 'key challenges' for refugees in the UK include 'to prevent racial harassment faced by some refugees through creating better public awareness and community relations' and to 'to encourage alternative approaches to stereotyped and over-simplified portrayals of refugees, and better understanding of the issues they face' (Home Office, 2005b). There have been no qualms about proposing 'integration' even to the extent of developing a national programme to ensure the 'successful dispersal' of asylum seekers (Anie et al., 2005).

Similarly, the separation of people with disabilities, special needs and mental health problems, and in some cases older people, has been seen as problematic because these groups are stereotyped as 'other' and feared and misunderstood. There have been many attempts in the UK, often with considerable success, to provide more care within communities and to provide for integration into neighbourhoods, schools and workplaces. The successful desegregation of education previously separated on the basis of disability and learning difficulties has been a priority in the UK, where it has been seen as a 'crucial first step in helping to change discriminatory attitudes' (Cantle, 2008, p. 221). Similar programmes have been put in place, for the same reasons, to provide integrated care and support for people with mental health problems, who were formerly incarcerated in very separate institutions.

With regard to people with disabilities, it has also been widely recognised that the:

> Fear of difference can be exacerbated by the lack of contact that non-disabled people may have with disabled people, reflecting the history of institutionalisation and the lack of integration of disabled people in many aspects of society. Until relatively recently, many

disabled people lived in institutions, were educated in segregated schools and worked in segregated employment, cut off from contact with mainstream society, and literally in many cases, 'hidden away' from society. Over the last 20 years there have been welcome steps to enable more disabled people to live independent lives within the community. There have also been moves to reduce the level of segregation of disabled children within the education system, with fewer children educated in 'special' schools. [....] If we accept evidence that disability related harassment is linked to wider attitudes to disabled people, then public awareness campaigns have a role to play.

(EHRC, 2011, p. 164)

There is, then, acceptance in each case that these various forms of 'segregation' are to some extent at least problematic. These concerns fall into two categories: first that insular communities tend to have a more limited view of others, less engagement and interaction with people who are different from themselves and may therefore be more prejudiced towards them, and second that the separation of any particular group tends to lead to their stereotyping, and even demonisation, as there are few opportunities to engage with them and to develop mutual understanding and trust. However, the history of the development of multiculturalism, and especially its rooting in the 'defensive' phase discussed in Chapter 4, means that there is much more ambivalence towards the integration of those communities segregated on the basis of 'race' and ethnicity.

Social and cultural segregation and integration

The physical or spatial separation of people from different backgrounds is, then, clearly an important determinant of how they see each other but, as suggested above, this will depend upon the extent to which these spatial arrangements determine, or are supported by, social and cultural segregation. Indeed, social and cultural determinants can be more influential than residential patterns where they dominate social networks and many aspects of daily life, and fundamentally shape attitudes towards others. For example, people educated in private schools (who often board and live separately while at school) have been accused of segregation amounting to a form of 'social apartheid' (Adonis and Pollard, 1997). This emotive language has been used more recently by none other than the Master of Wellington College, who reinforced the notion of 'apartheid' by describing independent schools as 'detached from the mainstream national education system, thereby perpetuating the apartheid that has so dogged education and national life in Britain since the Second World War' (Seldon, 2008). And, in fact, there are very significant differences in the attitudes of those educated in private schools compared to those educated in the state sector and the way in which they view each other (British Social Attitudes, 2011).

Evans and Tilley (2011) remark upon the implications of having a very disproportionate number of privately educated among the UK's governing elite and sound 'warning bells' for 'separate development':

> In theory, social exclusivity need not result in unrepresentative government: a man can, in principle, share the concerns and values of a woman, just as a middle-class person can understand those of someone who is working class. But for this to work in practice there has to be some basis of shared values and experiences to allow a proper understanding of the lives and concerns of other people. If the education system – as the moulding social influence on the lives and minds of young people – enshrines the kind of separate development where the future leaders of society are educated apart from the people they will later govern or judge, then warning bells should probably sound.

In a similar vein, Members of Parliament in the UK have been accused of living in a form of parallel universe as part of the 'Westminster bubble', in which their separate cloistered existence is compounded by their 'self-confirming universe' of social contacts from the press and media and policy-making community of influencers and lobbyists (Cantle, 2010). Despite the adversarial nature of politics, the political community does possess strong 'bonding capital' and certainly the electorate often regards them as not being especially well connected to the real world, and in that sense possessing low 'bridging capital'.

More conventionally, but perhaps not unconnected, the existence of a strong male occupational culture is often held to be so unwelcoming and culturally distinct as to be exclusionary towards women. This is a common phenomenon across Europe with 'persistent segregation' that 'has to be reduced' at the same time as equal opportunities policies are introduced if either is to be effective (Kriemer, 2004). The occupational division between men and women is not replicated in residential segregation, but is reinforced in other social and cultural spheres and in modes or areas of education. The historical roots of labour market segregation underpin the cultural distinctions and, in some areas at least, have become the critical determinant of structural divisions.

Social and cultural segregation can also be virtual, made possible by the advent of global communications in many different forms – particularly the growth of the internet, satellite television, globalised media and social networks[1] that effortlessly cross borders and social and cultural boundaries.

In positive terms, it is therefore perfectly possible that people can be living and working in entirely segregated communities, but somehow manage to virtually and vicariously communicate with a variety of people from different backgrounds and build an understanding of and empathy for the 'other'. This may even be achieved, to some extent at least, through the medium of film and literature. However, meaningful interchanges are difficult to develop – and sustain – at an indirect and remote level. Moreover, positive messages and views are often contested and contradicted at many different levels and especially through the national press and media. Sustained and personal contact through everyday interaction is far more likely to change attitudes and to disconfirm stereotypes and create an empathy with others. Segregated schools, workplaces and local communities clearly militate against such regular contact. The use of virtual communications has also been viewed in a negative sense, in which they are used simply to reinforce existing subcultural norms and views, rather than engaging with a variety of different people in local communities. In recent years, there have been particular concerns about the fuelling of both Far Right and Muslim extremism through websites and virtual communities that promote terrorism and hatred. There is limited research as to whether the 'banal encounters' experienced through virtual contact have the same richness as those in local neighbourhoods, but it seems probable that, as the latter are more likely to be based upon chance, they will be less controlled and more varied.

Lesbian, Gay, Bi-Sexual, Transgender and Intersex (LGBTI) groups are not necessarily identifiable as 'communities' and are also unlikely to be spatially segregated, though there are a small number of distinct areas in cities around the world. There is more evidently, however, a cultural distinctiveness and this has become more prevalent as a result of rising levels of public acceptance, and it has been possible for these groups to become more prominent within the public sphere. The LGBTI communities are perhaps an interesting example of the 'layers of segregation' where being from an LGBTI background does not necessarily define communities, or the individuals themselves, and where this element of distinctiveness is countered by other areas of integration, for example in education, employment and various other social and cultural spheres – there are no gay schools or workplaces and there is no evidence that gay people only have other gay people as friends and acquaintances.

There is, then, an apparent agreement about the need to challenge segregation in communities that are defined by characteristics other than 'race' or ethnicity'. There is recognition that breaking down these boundaries, making communities more permeable and open to others and to change generally, is likely to result in a much greater acceptance and tolerance of difference. More open communities have the benefit of challenging not only the conception that those communities have of others but also the views that others have of those communities and, in both cases, disconfirming stereotypes. Segregated or insular communities can also be resistant to change and exhibit intolerance and even violence towards others. They have been found to be less welcoming to newcomers and in some cases aid extremist groups, notably the Far Right (Biggs and Knauss, 2011).

Despite this, there is a much greater difficulty in drawing any consensus on the need to tackle segregation in communities defined by 'race' or ethnicity and this is both political and conceptual. It is political in the sense that the 'defensive' form of multiculturalism referred to earlier is suspicious of any attempt to challenge minority communities, or even to challenge the exclusionary nature of White host communities (as in White Flight). This would be tantamount to accepting that multiculturalism has 'failed'. It is conceptual in that segregation is generally presented as a continuum between assimilation at one end of the spectrum and complete separation, or 'parallel lives', at the other. Both views are wrong. Moreover, both are inappropriate in an age of super diversity and globalisation.

Functional segregation and integration

Integration can also be considered at a functional level, where the language is more one based upon 'rights' and entitlement. This approach emphasises preventing exclusion, or promoting inclusion, rather than preventing segregation, or promoting integration. However, they amount to the same thing and have been used most readily in relation to more recent migrants as a means of ensuring that they obtain equal access to services like housing, education and health for themselves and their families; whether they have equal rights within the labour market; and whether they have similar rights to the majority population in respect of political participation, discrimination and the full equivalent benefits of citizenship.

The 'right to be included' turned the language of assimilation, which had tended to emphasise compulsion and requirement, on its head. The development of the European Inclusion Index (Leonard and Griffith, 2003) promoted a competitive approach to integration between members of the EU, in which 'laggards' would be subjected to 'overwhelming' peer pressure. This approach recognized from the outset, however, that it was based upon the development of a 'sense of integration' in at least some key areas, particularly 'access to education, political participation and freedom of movement' (ibid., in Foreword by Vitorino, p. 5).

Leonard and Griffith went on to distinguish what they described as 'thin and thick definitions of citizenship and inclusion', in which the 'thick' indicators were regarded as essential elements of a multicultural community and demonstrated that it was open to newcomers and 'allows' integration. This approach at last began to recognise the different domains of integration and segregation and has been supported, more recently, by the Migrant Integration Policy Index (MIPEX) (British Council and Migration Policy Group, 2011). This was produced as a reference guide and fully interactive tool to assess, compare and improve integration policy. It measures integration policies in 31 countries in Europe and North America. The MIPEX project is led by the British Council and the Migration Policy Group and is supported by 37 national-level organisations, including think-tanks, non-governmental organisations, foundations, universities, research institutes and equality bodies in 31 countries across Europe, Canada and the USA.

However, despite the support for international openness and the continuation of migration on a significant scale, further migration does not generally enjoy popular support and the issue has helped to garner votes for the Far Right (Goodwin, 2011); the levels of openness to newer migrants tend to be seen as a threat by the host or majority communities, including longer standing migrant communities, who feel that they may be undermined and unable to compete, especially in times of economic recession. Existing residents may also harbour some degree of prejudice towards newer communities for a variety of historical and other reasons and these may take some time to change. The concept of openness, however, does begin to recognise the importance of these perceptions and, moreover, represents a new way of understanding integration and supports the idea of a multi-dimensional concept, rather than the simplistic continuum of assimilation-to-separation model of the past.

The implication of the development of 'openness' is that, while it is not a guarantee of cohesion, it does at least set out the circumstances in which new migrants are able to quickly gain access to the labour market, take advantage of services and be able to join key parts of political and civil society, without losing their distinctiveness. In this sense, they are immediately more integrated and are less likely to be pushed into subservient roles, housed in poorer and separate areas, with fewer and less good services.

The more conventional forms of functional segregation and integration relate to ideas about 'rights' and, to a lesser extent, to 'responsibilities'. These revolve around a number of key areas:

- citizenship rights and participation;
- the labour market – employment rights and equal pay;
- access to public services, especially housing, health and education and welfare benefits; and
- the criminal justice system.

There has been a renewed interest in the 'citizenship agenda' often from the point of view of integration of newcomers but with restrictions imposed by many countries in respect of naturalisation (Cantle, 2008, pp. 162–170). Voting rights are usually dependent upon citizenship and a shared polity is rarely achieved very quickly. The Council of Europe (2011) have recently advocated the granting of early voting rights in local elections to newcomers, which begins to recognise that they do have an interest and commitment to local communities, as denizens, long before a formal incorporation into citizenship. Sandercock (2004, p. 20) recognises the importance of a shared political community:

> An intercultural political community cannot expect its members to develop a sense of belonging unless it equally values and cherishes them in all their diversity and reflects this in its structure, policies, conduct of public affairs, self-understanding and self-definition but no existing multicultural society can claim to have achieved this state of affairs yet.

While the polity is seen in terms of formal rights and responsibilities, it does then have an impact upon the sense of belonging and the development of a shared value system. Mason (2010) believes that integration into the polity is not only important, but perhaps the key dimension of integration and distinguishes it from the sharing of a national identity, which he believes is not contingent. Certainly, the new dynamics of globalisation and diversity, and particularly the emerging 'democratic deficit' inherent in national political systems, suggest that new political processes and rights might be necessary (this is discussed in later chapters).

In respect of access to, and equality in, the labour market, public services and criminal justice systems, governments have made strides to improve equality of opportunity and, to a lesser extent, equality of outcomes. This generally takes the form of specific and targeted programmes to ensure that providers are not discriminating against minorities and that they are actively encouraging and promoting their interests. For the most part, these programmes fall under the title of 'positive action' in which attempts are made to equalise opportunities (for example, to provide interview training for people who have not been in the job market previously) rather than 'positive discrimination' (for example, giving preference to an applicant on the basis of their background rather than their skills, though this is lawful and applied in some cases). These have had an impact, but in some cases have proved to be controversial and may have actually reinforced prejudices, because of the perception of special treatment. For a full discussion of the measures that have been adopted to 'promote equality and prevent discrimination' (see Cantle, 2008, pp. 174–178).

In most cases, equality and positive action programmes recognise 'the importance of ethnicity data', for example:

> Our strategy is underpinned by increasing efforts to collect and analyse data by ethnicity. This helps us to understand what is happening, for example whom and where, and then to check our progress in closing the gap.
>
> (DCLG, 2007, p. 13)

There is no doubt that 'ethnic monitoring' as it is known in the UK (where it has been increasingly extended to the monitoring of age, disability, faith and sexual orientation) has helped to focus on particular gaps and develop specific responses. However, it has also resulted in the continuous 'flagging' of specific identities, suggestive of difference, with little commensurate flagging of commonality. The very specific programmes have also been undertaken by ethno-centric programmes that again emphasise difference and are undertaken by providers who are from the same backgrounds and can empathise with the participants. The opportunities for bringing people together on a cross-cultural basis to share the problems and learn from each other are rarely taken. Further, 'single-identity funding', which has been used to support culturally distinct organisations, has institutionalised the arrangements. Suggestions that single-identity funding should be reduced or withdrawn (Cantle, 2001; CIC, 2007) have been resisted, partly because there remains a belief that it is necessary and partly to maintain and protect those organisations whose very existence, and influence, depends upon the funding.

While this is a very controversial area, ethnic monitoring and identity-specific programmes and funding, do require reconsideration in an era of super diversity, both in principle and in practical terms. The identification and targeting of whole ethnic, faith or other groups no longer makes sense when needs have themselves become so varied and diverse. And in practical terms, the sheer number of identity groups means that it is impractical to provide services on a separate basis, even if it were possible to avoid reinforcing the separation inherent in the process. However, it is also the case that inequalities do have to be recognised and addressed and this will require the development of new approaches, consistent with an intercultural policy.

Values and segregation and integration

Visible differences have seldom been enough to justify discriminatory attitudes and behaviours and have been underpinned by notions of the superior worth of one group over another. The recent demonisation of the Muslim communities in many parts of Europe has specifically linked the idea of separate and segregated communities contributing to, or even being responsible for, the development of distinct and separate 'values', which are inherently illiberal and anti-democratic.

For example, when UK Prime Minister David Cameron spoke to the Munich Conference in early 2011 (Cameron, 2011), he talked solely in terms of shared values, or the lack of them:

> We have even tolerated these segregated communities behaving in ways that run counter to our values.

and suggested that:

instead of encouraging people to live apart, we need a clear sense of shared national identity, open to everyone.

The reference to 'living apart' is not, though, to be taken literally, as there are no UK policy initiatives designed to promote interethnic or interfaith communities living together in a physical sense and David Cameron's speech only referred to bringing people together through shared values and identity. The UK government nevertheless believes that the development of anti-Western values is inculcated in the seg-regated environments of independent faith schools and mosques, and has proposed to tackle this by interventions that would provide a chal-lenge to them and to offer alternatives (HM Government, 2011). Across Europe, the Open Society Foundations have also found concerns about the 'segregation of media' that arises partly from the negative rep-resentations of Muslims in the domestic media and also because of language barriers. Again, interventions have been designed to develop more integration in this area, based on a wider value set, to try to change the reliance and dependence on these distinct and separate sources (Open Society Foundations, 2011, p. 149).

Initiatives in France, Belgium and other European countries to ban the wearing of a face veil in public places, and in Switzerland to refuse planning permission for the use of minarets on mosques, have gone somewhat further and they simply represent an attempt to outlaw visible expressions of separateness and to reduce the social distance of Muslim communities. As such they are proving to be much more controversial and are likely to be counter-productive. However, all inter-ventions in this area reflect the growing ability of diaspora communities to develop and sustain ideas and values that cross national boundaries, have some form of visible expression and are reinforced by social, cul-tural and faith networks in order to maintain their internal coherence. The state's new-found enthusiasm for the 'integration of the mind' pol-icy of today is a far cry from the enforced physical integration in the USA, through the bussing of children to break down the ethnic segrega-tion of schools. Further, it has been given new impetus by what the West sees as a more general threat from the Muslim communities, across the diaspora. This has been represented as a 'clash' of 'culture and cultural identities, which at the broadest levels are 'civilisation identities [...] shaping patterns of cohesion, disintegration and conflict' (Huntingdon, 2002, p. 20). Although the 'clash of civilisations' concept has been con-tested in academic and policy circles, it does seem to underlie some of the more recent political thinking (Cameron, 2011; Merkel, 2010; and

Sarkozy, 2011) and especially the growth of the Far Right across Europe, including the founding of the English Defence League and many similar anti-Muslim organisations in other countries. These views have gained popular support and Christian and Muslim relations are now often seen in these terms. Chek Wai Lau (2004) also believes that the 'clash of civilisations' is the 'logical conclusion' of the form of multiculturalism that celebrates various cultural achievements and their own histories, sharply defining the boundaries between cultures according to their perceived essences, in 'which battlefields are drawn between civilisations (cultures writ large)'.

The growth of virtual networks provides an opportunity for the reinforcement of single-identity diasporas, through internet, satellite TV and social networking. These were simply not possible just a couple of decades ago and many temporary and permanent migrants felt almost obliged to 'fit in' with their new community at all levels. Technological developments make it far easier to maintain diaspora connections, reinforcing the values of the 'homeland' irrespective of the day to day activities within the new community. But while this may provide for the reinforcement of like-minded views, the internet in particular has also opened up huge opportunities for the expansion of leisure, educational, business, political and social cross-cultural networks, which expand horizons and threaten the very existence of closed value and belief systems. The impact of cross-border travel and international studentships in particular has also expanded horizons and greatly increased the chances of intermarriage and new friendship patterns across national borders. And, as noted in earlier chapters, the state's ability to create and maintain an identity around itself is increasingly challenged.

The state has of course recognised these challenges and is resisting change and the loss of its power of influence over its people. The state supports its national cultural markers, for example, the insistence on the use of the French language in France (and in the French-speaking province of Quebec), the celebration of 'unifying' national events like the Queen's Diamond Jubilee in the UK, or the resistance to the availability and use of unapproved internet information sources in China. Similarly, states have attempted to protect the integrity of their borders against outsiders, through many new forms of immigration barriers and restrictions, and where immigrants have been allowed to settle they are increasingly subject to education programmes, citizenship tests and demands for expressions of loyalty (Cantle, 2008, pp. 162–167). It seems unlikely that the past sense of national identity can be protected and maintained in this new era of globalisation and super diversity, and, as discussed in earlier chapters, it is on the wane, but nation-states will no doubt continue to attempt to maintain their influence and sense of political and social solidarity.

National governments, however, have been peculiarly loathe to establish a proper basis for which newcomers might establish shared understandings and values and they have generally been denied the right to vote and participate in political processes. This is despite the fact that most migrants pay taxes in their country of domicile yet have no say in the way their taxes are spent at the national or local level, and are often encouraged to maintain links with their home countries and to vote in those elections. This is, in part, the maintenance of the view that migrants are a temporary phenomenon and will return home eventually, and partly reflects the general hostility towards migrants and the unwillingness to concede any rights to them. In fact, governments have high hurdles in respect of citizenship, which have increasingly been linked to values (Cantle, 2008, pp. 162–170), and the recent anti-migrant sentiment in Europe at least has seen the raising of the barriers. Participation in political debate, for example, in local elections, as advocated by the Council of Europe (2011) would enable a faster pace of integration, without compromising national identity. As Sandercock (2004, p. 20) argues, 'a sense of belonging must ultimately be political, based on a shared commitment to a political community'.

Local identity has been less problematic and it has been less bound up in what have become increasingly contested notions of national identity. Further, it would appear that the everyday and 'banal' encounters that people experience, together with the shared and more organised opportunities to play sport, observe wildlife, sing in a choir or worship, will develop into 'shared values'. These may not be codified, nor amount to a statement of rights and responsibilities for citizens, but simply a series of understandings about 'the way things work around here'. They may owe something to national norms, attitudes and behaviours, but are essentially local in nature, to accommodate different cultures and contexts, and are dynamic. Participation in local social and cultural networks also appears to lead to a greater sense of trust of others in local neighbourhoods, including people from different backgrounds, as well as a greater sense of belonging (DCLG, 2011).

In reality the 'national values' promulgated by Western governments (for example, see HM Government, 2011) are seldom peculiarly 'national', and the same ideas about 'freedom of expression', 'freedom of association', 'equality before the law' and 'respect for others' have been trotted out by most states – they are, in reality, universal (or Western) values. They do contribute at a very general level, however, to the idea of a 'shared society', though often with the implicit suggestion that what each nation has in common in this respect stops at the national border. The context for the concern with national identity is also important, and, as with the search for a shared society and common values, has been given new impetus by the level of migration and population movement – as it has become increasingly obvious that we no longer all look alike and share the same historical perspective, so it appears that we now need to work harder to create common bonds. This is understandable, though it is reactive and borne out of the 'defensive' mode of multiculturalism, rather than forward looking and based upon a vision that can sustain the impacts of globalisation and super diversity.

Concerns about segregation are real, and should not be avoided as though this discussion is somehow tantamount to an acceptance of the failure of multicultural societies – it is not. The notion of segregation, wrapped up in emotive language like 'ghettoes' and 'no-go areas', does imply the separate existence of communities held together by a strong internal allegiance, beyond society's regulation and control. Segregated and insular communities can thereby perpetuate stereotypes of themselves and they are themselves fearful of others and more resistant to change. They are more likely to fear others and to see them as a threat and, in particular, to be fearful of the changes inherent in the process of globalisation and super diversity.

7
Interculturalism: Conceptualisation

The concept of interculturalism

The concept of interculturality is not new and can be traced back to 1959, while European perspectives date from the 1980s and 1990s (James, 2008). In the UK, there has been little by way of academic development, or agreement over the term; neither has it been adopted in policy and practice to any great degree. In other countries, such as Germany, Greece, Russia and Spain, the term has been employed (Meer and Modood, 2011), though seemingly often in relation to education programmes. It has also been used in Canada (Bouchard, 2011) but in this context may be more properly regarded as a progressive variant of multiculturalism – adding to the confusion over an already contested term used in many different ways.

The concept and experience of 'multiculturalism' was explored earlier and it was noted that it no longer commands political or popular support. While the post-war period of mass migration was addressed through the lens of multiculturalism and 'race', the emphasis was almost inevitably upon dealing with the discrimination and intolerance of monocultural host communities who felt threatened by 'difference' and offended by what they saw as unacceptable social and cultural minority norms. This did eventually give rise to progressive anti-discrimination legislation and positive action programmes – though, unfortunately, often at the expense of a separation of communities to try to avoid tensions, and the accusation of 'special treatment', which also created a sense of unfairness. This approach also 'locked in' the notion of a binary racialised divide (Chek Wai Lau, 2004) within nations, in which 'accommodations' between majority and minorities became the key issue, rather than a developmental process for identity across all communities.

While interculturalism needs to break free from past concepts, there is the opportunity to build upon some elements of multiculturalism, particularly the framework of rights, equal treatment and non-discrimination. It is also able to draw upon the successes of community cohesion, discussed in Chapter 5, and to maintain the interaction and belonging programmes that have helped to confound the myths and stereotypes and to enable different communities to naturally develop relationships and break down the segregation and separation in workplaces, schools, neighbourhoods and social settings. Again, there is strong evidence – particularly in the UK, which pioneered this approach – that this had some effect on the attitudes and behaviours of majority and minority communities (DCLG, 2011).

Meer and Modood (2011) have tried to reach towards a concept of interculturalism, which they hope will protect their support for past multicultural models. In doing so, they rightly suggest that interculturalism is:

> first, as something greater than coexistence, in that interculturalism is allegedly more geared toward interaction and dialogue than multiculturalism. Second, that interculturalism is conceived as something less 'groupist' or more yielding of synthesis than multiculturalism. Third, that interculturalism is something more committed to a stronger sense of the whole, in terms of such things as societal cohesion and national citizenship. Finally, that where multiculturalism may be illiberal and relativistic, interculturalism is more likely to lead to criticism of illiberal cultural practices (as part of the process of intercultural dialogue).
>
> (2011)

However, they attempt to argue that these features were 'foundational' elements of multiculturalism all along and they even go as far as suggesting that they may support interculturalism when it develops to the point of offering a 'distinct perspective', noting that it cannot yet 'eclipse multiculturalism, and so should be considered as complementary to multiculturalism'. However, the perspective from which Meer and Modood opine is very much one where difference is fundamentally about 'race', and in which difference is contested within national borders, generally between minority and majority communities.

It is suggested later in this chapter that the concept of interculturalism is more about the creation of a culture of openness which effectively challenges the identity politics and entrenchment of separate communities, based upon any notion of 'otherness'. But, it is also a dynamic process in which there will be some tensions and conflicts, as a necessary part of societal change in which people are able to positively envision ideas for multicultural and multifaith societies and where diversity and globalisation are recognised as permanent features of society, to be embraced, rather than feared.

It will also require a new and fundamental change to our concepts of personal and collective identity and, in particular, the development of common bonds on the basis of a more universal conception of humankind, replacing multiculturalist conceptions of primordial and 'natural' distinctiveness and cultural fixity. In a new language of 'interculturalism', a number of words will become readily associated – 'interdependency', 'interaction', 'interconnectedness', 'internationalism', 'integration' – to form part of the policy and practice discourse. This may give rise to a less academic and more practically orientated definition of interculturalism, and in so doing may have to overcome some fears about whether interculturalism is somehow designed to create a 'melting pot' of population in which the distinctiveness (or purity) of cultures is lost. This is very far from the case, but will demand recognition that at least some of the present cultural barriers represent a level of protectionism that continue to carry overtones of racism and cultural superiority.

Interculturality and intercultural dialogue

Interculturality and intercultural dialogue (ICD) have wrongly been used synonymously, or expounded on the basis that the former depends almost entirely upon the latter (see, for example, Council of Europe, 2008). Intercultural dialogue has certainly helped to challenge 'otherness' in a spirit of openness, utilising processes of interaction, and is an important and instrumental part of interculturality. Whilst ICD fosters understanding and empathy with others, these beneficial connections between individuals do not necessarily result in a change in the general climate of community relations.

The concept of ICD has been little used as a framework for diversity and cohesion and the principal proponents have been the Council of Europe (CoE) (2008, 2011), and the European Commission (EC) which established the Year of Intercultural Dialogue (EYICD) in 2008. However, both the CoE and the EC have tended to promote a narrow view of ICD, in which the concept and programmes are largely configured in relation to dialogue between individuals at the interpersonal level (and the EYICD was generally limited to 'cultural' activities in the sense of the arts), rather than to give effect to broader processes of change.

There are now some signs that ICD is now beginning to be seen as a means of building understanding and improving relationships on a community, or national, level. Indeed, Chatham House, an independent think tank on international affairs based in the UK, has developed a more ambitious approach, to use ICD empathetically at an international level, in which there is a concerted effort to understand the position of other nations in cultural terms, rather than simply negotiate on the basis of political positions, and to understand the other by putting themselves into their position (Chatham House, 2011). They are leading this work through a two-year policy research project that seeks to bridge the cultural gaps between the Euro–Atlantic community and emerging powers such as China, Russia, India and Brazil in terms of understanding the way in which they define, interpret and manage security. Their ambitious aim is to provide the conditions for a cross-cultural dialogue on security and defence within the traditional Euro–Atlantic community, and beyond that community to its global partners and competitors. The Chatham House position is very much influenced by Philip Windsor's essay 'Cultural Dialogue in Human Rights', in which he argues that 'all cultures depend on translating certain underlying values into the norms of social behaviour' (Windsor, 2002, p. 86). This allows for an appreciation of values and, therefore, a broader understanding of what each party is trying to achieve and the drivers behind these policies, without necessarily implying that they will be accepted. It represents a step change from the entrenched positions under the present politics of international relations – and potentially, a step change in ideas about inter or cross-cultural dialogue.

In the UK generally, there has been a much lower level development of interculturalism with little in terms of practical application prior to the introduction of the iCoCo national Awards for Bridging Cultures (ABCs), supported by the Baring Foundation[1]. This built upon the ideas of community cohesion, which from its inception in 2001 had urged the development of 'strong and positive relationships between people of different backgrounds' (LGA, 2002) for which national guidance was gradually developed and codified on the basis of 'meaningful interaction' (DCLG, 2009a). The intervention of the Baring Foundation and iCoCo meant that the programmes for 'cross-cultural' interaction, gradually became analogous with intercultural dialogue. However, the terminology was often confused with the wider concept of interculturalism sometimes reduced to 'intergroup contact...intercultural dialogue and communication' (James, 2008).

The development of community cohesion had therefore stimulated a renewed interest in 'contact theory'. This theory is generally credited to Allport with his seminal work *The Nature of Prejudice* (Allport, 1954). His hypothesis was that bringing together the members of different groups, getting them working towards common goals on an equal footing, would lead to intergroup prejudice being reduced. More recently, contact theory has been developed and championed by Miles Hewstone et al. (2006, 2006a, 2007, 2008, 2008a) and this has clearly demonstrated that contact between groups does bring about positive (or at least less negative) attitudes, reduces prejudice and builds lasting friendships. The creation of intergroup friendships is seen as more important than simple cooperation. Hewstone maintains that the type of contact, and the conditions under which it occurs, are all important and warns that if these are not optimal they can lead to an increase in prejudice. He has applied this approach to ethnic divisions in the UK, as well as those based upon sectarian conflict in Northern Ireland (Hewstone et al., 2006, 2008).

The reduction of prejudice – which is clearly at the heart of ICD – can be simply defined as 'bias which devalues people because of their perceived membership of a social group' (Abrams, 2010). Again, it is to social psychology that we turn to provide a deeper understanding of the areas in which prejudice can negatively impact upon cohesion and social solidarity. Abrams (2010) suggests that there are four areas that need to be understood:

1. **The intergroup context**
    This refers to the ways that people in different social groups view members of other groups. Their views may relate to power differences, the precise nature of differences, and whether group members feel threatened by others. These intergroup perceptions provide the context within which people develop their attitudes and prejudices.
2. **The psychological bases for prejudice**
    These include: people's key values; the ways they see themselves and others; their sense of social identity, and social norms that define who is included in or excluded from social groups.

    Prejudice is more likely to develop and persist where groups have different or conflicting key values: others are seen as different; people see their identity in terms of belonging to particular groups; and their groups discriminate against others.

3. **Manifestations of prejudice**
   There are many ways in which prejudice can be expressed. Stereotypes can be positive or negative, and may be linked to a fear that other groups may pose a threat. Some apparently positive stereotypes (as sometimes expressed towards older people or women, for instance) may nonetheless be patronising and devalue those groups.

4. **The effect of experience**
   This has several dimensions. First, people's experiences do not always match others' views about the extent of prejudice. For instance, few people express negative prejudice towards older people, yet older people report high levels of prejudice towards them. Secondly contact between groups is likely to increase mutual understanding, though it needs to be close and meaningful contact. A third factor is the extent to which people wish to avoid being prejudiced. This is based on personal values, a wish to avoid disapproval, and wider social norms. Each of these offers a means for potentially preventing the expression of prejudice and discriminatory behaviour.

   (Abrams, 2010, p. 4)

This is a very different agenda from that presented by sociologists, who tend to view tensions and conflicts between different ethnic groups and communities as emanating from structural conditions, though research is gradually confirming the cohesion agenda in that 'it is necessary to address both relational and structural issues' (Hickman, 2008, p. ix) and that these have not, in practice, been disconnected (Thomas, 2011). However, the above framework does recognise that the 'intergroup context', will reflect the differences in power and other variables, and the possibility of out-group threat. These may well include national differences, the legacy of 'the science of racism' and socio-economic conditions (see Cantle, 2008, pp. 101–126 for further discussion). While community cohesion attempted to bring these different elements into a conceptual and practical framework (LGA, 2002), there have been few attempts to unite the two academic camps. However, Biggs and Knauss (2011) suggest that the 'enduring sociological theory' which depends on the majority's perception of threat from the minority to their social position is not so very far removed from 'the opposite prediction derived from a theory which is strongly supported by social psychology', in which contact theory holds that prejudice is reduced by social interaction. They conclude that 'contact and threat interact': and that what generates hostility is not just the perception of a threat (from the minority population), but also a high degree of segregation of the groups.

The idea of breaking down the barriers, real and imagined, through 'Intercultural Community Bridge Building' is supported by Law et al. (2008). This concept is based on the premise that everyone, individually and as a nation, benefits from knowing, experiencing and working with other cultures. In doing so, the focus is on what is held in common rather than any differences, and it is these commonalities that bind groups together.

A 'grassroots study' also gathered evidence in support of bridge building and

> found strong evidence that bridge building activities can increase understanding between individuals and groups. In the most powerful examples, increased understanding could also reduce prejudice and conflicts between people from different faiths, countries and ethnic backgrounds.
>
> (Harris and Young, 2009, p. 5)

This approach is also supported by Varshney's study *Ethnic Conflict and Civic Life*, which focuses on the very different context of India, but draws upon similar studies in Yugoslavia, Northern Ireland and the USA (Varshney, 2002). The 'steel bands and samosas' critique (Kaur-Stubbs, 2008), however, tries to undermine the value of intercultural dialogue, suggesting that they are superficial and cosy cultural experiences which do not deal with more profound differences. However, both Varshney (2002) and Harris and Young (2009) evidence the way in which dialogue can actually deal with real tensions and conflicts and do engage in very challenging experiences in difficult contexts. Comedia (2010) in commenting on their intercultural cities programme also confirm that 'the intercultural city is not always an easy place to be'. Confronting prejudice and deeply entrenched and stereotyped views about others, however skilfully done, is unlikely to be an easy process.

The idea that groups should be brought together and into direct contact with each other specifically for the purpose of improving relations, is nevertheless challenged by research from the Commission for Racial Equality (2007a). This indicated that interethnic interaction achieves the best results when interaction is the by-product of people coming together for another purpose rather a premeditated intercultural activity. This may well be the case, but there is considerable difficulty in facilitating any form of meaningful encounters in divided and segregated areas, where the opportunities to engage are limited. Further, the number of 'shared spaces' that are accessible and used by all sections of the community is also limited. Research by Lownsbrough and Beunderman (2007) has begun to explore the motivations for entering public spaces, and assessed their potential for interaction and the dimensions of public space involved. However, so limited is the research and understanding in this area, that 'it is uncertain if we know where, indeed how, to start' (ibid., p. 10).

A number of commentators have also sought to dismiss ICD in much the same way as they attacked community cohesion for failing to have sufficient regard to poverty and structural issues. As discussed in Chapter 5, deprivation clearly has some impact upon community relations, but this is not necessarily a determinant and some poorer areas also have high levels of cohesion. However, it is the obsession with 'race' difference, and the failure to acknowledge all forms of prejudice and the ways in which they turn into a range of hate crimes, which has been most problematic. These connections are belatedly having to be made by those 'front line' agencies responsible for safety within communities. For example, tackling disability, homophobic, racist, religious and transphobic hate incidents throughout North-East England has been subject to a review, which highlighted both an apparent lack of activity to tackle disability and transphobic hate incidents within more general aims to promote good relations between groups. They then encouraged joint working to tackle a shared problem, in which poverty was not seen as a main driver, and the aim became to promote understanding and cultural competency, especially among services providers to enable 'disablist hate crime' to be tackled more effectively (and particularly in respect of services for disabled people and trans people) (Balderston and Roebuck, 2010).

The level and nature of 'dialogue' is, of course, critical and the DCLG (2008) have emphasised that it has to be sustained over time to be effective and, building on the work of the CRE (2007) they identify four types of dialogue:

Grounding interactions are about consolidating one's identity and values, take place with people with whom one shares a history, and help to build individual self-confidence and pride.

Banal interactions are about consolidating one's external environment, and take place with people with whom one shares a community.

[They] are typically fairly superficial – saying hello in the street or exchanging chit-chat. They help develop a sense of belonging and contribute to good community relations.

Opportunity interactions are about broadening one's external environment, and take place with people with whom one shares potential benefits. Networks, self-help groups, campaigns and committees can bring people from different backgrounds together and open up new opportunities.

Growth interactions are about broadening one's identity and values, and take place with people with whom one shares curiosity. It is through growth interactions that people change the way they see themselves and others, and find new things in common.

(DCLG, 2008)

The above perhaps over-emphasises the importance of interpersonal dimensions of ICD, whereas cohesion has been built around those interventions that begin to change the outlook of whole communities (and therefore has to be supported by the other pillars of cohesion – see Chapter 5 – and was central to the second national review of community cohesion 'Our Shared Future' (CIC, 2007)). This same interpersonal emphasis is to be found in the EU's contribution to ICD which came some seven years after the introduction of community cohesion, with the EYICD in 2008. This took a particularly reductionist approach in which interculturality was equated to ICD. James (2008) explained that the European Commission understands interculturality to be 'about dialogue between different cultural groups [...] to enable European citizens to acquire the knowledge and aptitudes to enable them to deal with a more open and complex environment'. The Year, in any event, also had a very limited impact as it tended to focus on 'culture' in the artistic sense and also prioritised intra-EU integration, rather than using a wider variety of programmes that could support the local contexts.

Contact, perhaps even 'dialogue', is also insufficient in itself. As Varshney (2002, p. 10) explained, in many diverse areas in India, particularly in cities, people from different backgrounds do see each other and engage on an 'everyday' and superficial level at least, but this has not saved them from communal violence. He has found that 'sturdier' forms of association, at the institutional level, are necessary and that these have to be built and sustained over time. Many of the other studies previously referred to in this section (and all of the guidance issued in respect of community cohesion, see Chapter 5) emphasise the need for a broader level of engagement to create a more open and tolerant climate of opinion and to gain wider political, media, institutional and civic support. Individual and interpersonal contact needs to be underpinned and reinforced by more robust normative processes.

ICD activities, then, have been used for a number of purposes, with a varied level of emphasis on interpersonal and group processes, including:

- to disconfirm stereotypes, change attitudes and behaviours to 'others';
- to promote understanding and tolerance more generally (for example, as in interfaith dialogue);
- to create the conditions for peaceful co-existence, following conflict;
- to promote more positive views of nation-states and their citizens across national boundaries (as, for example, in the EYICD); and
- as a means of building social capital, neighbourliness, trust in local institutions and 'good citizenship'.

The British Council (BC) (British-based but with offices throughout the world and involved in the promotion of community relations) have also invested in exploring both the concept and practice of intercultural dialogue, and (with iCoCo) produced a 'toolkit' and resource guide to promote their ideas (BC/iCoCo, 2009). This has been developed as a means of tackling problems in many different contexts and therefore tends to present intercultural dialogue as an essentially remedial process, repairing damaged community relations, or intervening to avoid the building up of tensions and conflicts:

> Intercultural dialogue is necessary today to engage with the difference that we encounter in the world, not only because we are likely to regularly meet very diverse people, but also because this can help with addressing and unlocking some of the challenges of today's globalised world.
>
> Intercultural dialogue can:
>
> - provide an avenue, where communication has broken down;
> - provide a voice, where understanding has been rendered complicated;
> - open new channels of communication;
> - help break down judgemental views.

One of the most important aspects of intercultural dialogue is its ability to challenge stereotypes and prejudices. We often generalise about what we don't know. Stereotypes are usually exaggerated views of particular characteristics, which result from our own cultural frames of reference. This becomes a problem when these generalisations become prejudices that affect the way we act towards others.

(BC/iCoCo, 2009)

However, BC/iCoCo work also set out a more ambitious concept of ICD, in the following layered terms:

National

A dynamic process by which people from different cultures interact to learn about and question their own, and each other's, cultures. Over time this may lead to cultural change. It recognises the inequalities at work in society and the need to overcome these. It is a process which requires mutual respect and acknowledges human rights.

This definition highlights ICD as a process marked by change and learning.

International

Intercultural dialogue aims to equip individuals with the knowledge and skills – so-called 'intercultural competences' – to participate in increasingly diverse societies. Knowledge of democratic values, citizenship and civil rights are essential elements of dialogue.

This definition highlights ICD as a process of skills acquisition – to help individuals and organisations successfully participate socially and economically in modern-day life.

Global

The idea of 'intercultural dialogue' takes as its starting point the recognition of difference and multiplicity of the world in which we live. These differences of opinion, viewpoint, and values exist not only within each individual culture but also between cultures. 'Dialogue' seeks to approach these multiple viewpoints with a desire to understand and learn from those that do not see the world in the same way as ourselves.

This definition highlights the importance of addressing difference through intercultural dialogue.

In this sense the concept of ICD becomes much closer to ideas about interculturality and embraces much wider community-based processes of change. In particular, the idea of building 'intercultural competence' and continual learning as a necessary component of modern super-diverse and dynamic societies. This seems to point towards a new policy framework and is discussed in Chapter 8.

Perspectives of interculturalism

With some exceptions then, the concept and practice of ICD has largely been focused on interpersonal contact and has, with apparent growing success, sought to reduce prejudice and disconfirm stereotypes of others, among individuals. This does have some impact on whole commu-nity processes when on sufficient scale and embedded into institutional arrangements and civil society. Further, it can lead to more profound changes, perhaps enabling the perception of a threat to social position being reduced and leading to more open processes in socio-economic terms. While the perspective for interculturalism in conceptual terms is still far from settled and the consequential implications for policy and practice have been barely considered, it does offer the prospect of the development of a wider approach to instil a greater sense of openness in communities and to begin to see 'otherness' and difference as a poten-tially positive experience that can bring creative and entrepreneurial advantage to society as a whole.

In visionary terms Sondhi (2009) suggests it is fundamentally about a 'new kind of living dialogue':

> So what then is different about the new concept of interculturality? The basis of this approach lies in the creation of a new kind of living dialogue – creating the space and opportunity and the inclination for two different entities to know a little more about how to reassure and interest the other while also avoiding those things that might insult or alarm them, thus minimising the potential obstacles to the transaction. But it is more than just a tool of communication – it is a process of mutual learning and joint growth. This implies a pro-cess of acquiring, not only a set of basic facts and concepts about the other but also particular skills and competencies that will enable one to interact functionally with anyone different from oneself regardless of their origins. This implies a different way of reading situations, signs, symbols, and of communicating which we would describe as intercultural literacy. This indicates the acquisition of an intercultural

competence, a certain frame of mind, which in a diverse society, becomes as important a competency as basic numeracy and literacy. No child should leave school without it and no public official with responsibility for deciding on local policy and resources should be without it either.

However, it would seem that a state of interculturality would also depend upon a much clearer sense of justice and equality to enable the barriers associated with particular backgrounds to be overcome and for a spirit of belonging to be established. Community cohesion and more progressive forms of multiculturalism have begun to develop policies and practices that are less hidebound by rigid conceptions of identity and provide for new cultural competences. They have not yet, however, embraced and given effect to the idea of identity as a dynamic process that can accommodate the international and transnational impacts of globalisation and are still heavily focused around 'race'. Consideration also needs to be given to the ways in which 'cultural competences' can be underpinned by rights and responsibilities and the means by which grievances and inequalities addressed.

Gerard Bouchard (2011) also proposes that interculturalism should shape our ways of living together in the future and suggests this is:

> a search for balance and mediation between often-competing principles, values, and expectations. In this sense, it is a sustained effort aimed at connecting majorities and minorities, continuity and diversity, identity and rights, reminders of the past and visions of the future. It calls for new ways of coexisting within and beyond differences at all levels of collective life.

Bouchard draws upon the work of the CoE (2008) to define interculturalism as:

- the rejection of multiculturalism, which was associated with fragmentation and seen as harmful to social cohesion;
- the rejection of assimilation due to the violation of individual rights that it entails; and
- the choice of interculturalism as a middle path, as a model of balance and equity.

Viewing interculturalism as some sort of middle way between assimilation and separation, however, is not helpful. Bouchard appears to regard interculturalism as no more than a form of integration based on agreed accommodations. As discussed earlier, integration is not itself positioned on a simple linear path between these two extremes and there are several domains and many more layers of integration that can operate at different levels. In addition, the 'middle way' seems to suggest that this revolves around some form of mediation between the host community(ies) and newcomers, rather than a more dialectical view of the modern globalised world in which both national and international parameters are also changing.

Bouchard's view is very much coloured by the context of the French-speaking province of Canada and indeed draws upon his work for the government of Quebec (Bouchard and Taylor, 2008). This became known as the Bouchard–Taylor Report and was founded on the idea of a rejection of Canadian multiculturalism (what was seen as the vision imposed on French-speaking Canadians by English-speaking Canadians) and its replacement by 'interculturalism'. However, this alternative concept of interculturalism depended upon a view of integration that embedded the 'fundamental values' of Quebec society and these were presented as gender equality, secularism and the French language. Given that this also amounted to French being imposed upon new migrants, including those from English-speaking backgrounds whose children were required to attend schools where teaching is conducted in French and who are denied the choice of English-speaking schools in the same Province; and that English is generally not permitted in many aspects of the public sphere, including road signage and by retailers; this concept of interculturalism may therefore be seen as somewhat partial.

Bouchard's view of interculturalism does, however, raise a significant point in that he believes that integration is not a process in which migrants are assimilated into a host culture, nor that integration results in the adaptation by the host community to the extent that their fundamental nature is eroded:

> interculturalism concerns itself with the interests of the majority culture, whose desire to perpetuate and maintain itself is perfectly legitimate, as much as it does with the interests of minorities and immigrants – we thus find no reason to oppose either the defenders of the identity and traditions of the majority culture on one side, or the defenders of the rights of minorities and immigrants on the other; it is both possible and necessary to combine the majority's aspirations for identity with a pluralist mindset, making for a single process of belonging and development.
>
> (Bouchard, 2011)

In the same article, Bouchard also suggests that interculturalism 'must be combined with a symbolic element that helps foster identity, collective memory, and belonging'.

Many majority communities will, no doubt, find Bouchard's thesis very reassuring, as almost any form of change can be unsettling and threatening. However, the reality is that all communities are in a state of flux and ever more so in a period of globalisation. The arrival of migrants is only one part of the change – though often the most visible. As a result, they are often identified with the change and seen as the cause, rather than the consequence, of the underlying processes of globalisation which are much more pervasive – and inevitable. Trying to 'buck the market' of cultural change by holding on to a fixed conception of culture is a futile exercise – making some communities even more isolated from the real world and the likelihood that even greater change will be more sudden and difficult. Ironically, the concept of multiculturalism advanced by the Canadian government[2] and so soundly rejected by the Bouchard Taylor Report, may be somewhat nearer to more generally accepted ideas about interculturalism.

The pioneering work by the Comedia Group, assisted by funding from the Joseph Rowntree Foundation (Wood, 2004), has helped to develop a much broader concept of interculturalism and has subsequently led to a programme of 'intercultural cities' around the world, supported by the CoE. Cities participating in the CoE programme include Oslo, Dublin, Berlin, Limassol and Lisbon. A further 30 cities are participating in the CoE's index and intercultural cities network and these include Barcelona, Genoa, Mexico City, Montreal and Munich. This is beginning to result in new ideas and the development of best practice.

The CoE have high ambitions for their programme and believe that a 'genuine intercultural city cannot emerge from disconnected initiatives or small-scale policy changes. It can only be the result of a shared vision and the concerted efforts of a range of institutional and civil society stakeholders and the establishment of partnerships and alliances at national and international levels.'[3] The CoE also contrast this intercultural approach with previous frameworks in which they say diversity was ignored (as with guest-worker approaches), or denied (as with assimilationist approaches), or where diversity was overemphasised and thereby reinforced walls between culturally distinct groups (as with multiculturalism). For them, interculturalism is about explicitly recognising the value of diversity while doing everything possible to increase interaction, mixing and hybridisation between cultural communities, while also about addressing cultural conflict or tension (religious customs and requirements, communitarianism, women's rights and so on) openly though public debate. Bloomfield and Bianchini (2004) similarly argue that:

> The intercultural approach goes beyond equal opportunities and respect for existing cultural differences to the pluralist transformation of public space, institutions and civic culture. It does not recognise cultural boundaries as fixed but in a state of flux and remaking. An intercultural approach aims to facilitate dialogue, exchange and reciprocal understanding between people of different backgrounds.

The idea of interculturalism, 'providing a critique of multiculturalism' with a vision of more fluid and dynamic cultures was developed by the Baring Foundation (Sondhi, 2008). The explicit aim of the Baring Foundation was to 'promote interculturality' through a more user-friendly brand – the ABCs – and applicants were clearly told of the underlying philosophy of the scheme in the ABCs; guidance (ABCs at iCoCo, 2009). The guidance goes on to define interculturality in the following terms:

> a dynamic process by which people from different cultures interact to learn about and question their own and each other's cultures. Over time this may lead to cultural change. It recognises the inequalities at work in society and the need to overcome these. It is a process which requires mutual respect and acknowledges human rights.

The Baring Foundation commissioned a study by Malcolm James (2008) which was intended to support that critique and develop the new theoretical framework. This 'outlined a move away from models for post-colonial society based on sealed cultural groups towards a more multifaceted notion of interculturalism'. There is, however, little by way of an accepted body of academic opinion on the subject and it is notable that only 2 of the 26 references used by James in his 2008 paper (James, 2008) use the term in their title. There is even less by way of established policy and practice (though Chapter 8 proposes a number of areas for development). It is also far from clear whether there is real agreement that the underlying premise of interculturalism – that culture 'cannot be understood as static, eternally given, essentialist and that it is 'always evolving, dynamic and hybrid of necessity' (Sandercock, 2004, p. 18) – is really understood.

The CoE (2011) have recently set out the ways in which they believe 'peaceful co-existence' can be achieved. In rejecting the concept of 'multiculturalism', they set out 17 'guiding principles' for living together. These mainly revolve around legal rights, with an emphasis on citizenship and participation and the retention of distinctive cultural heritage, possibly hyphenated with nationality or faith. This does not necessarily imply a static view of 'culture', if culture is seen as multifaceted and able to operate on different levels. For example, they argue for early voting rights for migrants and for tolerant and respectful leadership and while there is little new in the report and much could be attributed to a 'progressive form of multiculturalism' referred to earlier, there is more emphasis on integration, particularly from the perspective that 'in order to live together in peace people need skills or "competences" which are not automatically acquired'.

This view of the need for intercultural skills and competences is supported by others, but Kymlicka (2003, p. 160) suggests that many people seem to prefer a form of global interculturalism, focused on learning about distant/world cultures, to local interculturalism. He believes that this preference for global over local forms is quite explicit in many countries and is a way of choosing particular relationships over others – for example, in Germany educational programmes promote interculturalism which is explicitly aimed at enabling Germans to interact with the citizens of other European countries, rather than enabling Germans to deal with their (sizeable) local minorities, such as the Turkish 'guest-workers'.

The concept of 'interculturalism', even as evolved to date, is much more demanding than 'intercultural dialogue' and involves wider community, structural and political processes. ICD has generally been developed as a process by which two or more individuals or communities with different identities interact and build trust and understanding, but it does, at its best, nevertheless contribute to wider processes of change and envisages a society in which people are at ease with difference and see it as an opportunity to engage and develop, rather than as a threat. This also supports the thesis that whereas multiculturality is concerned with respecting and acknowledging cultural diversity, allowing different cultures to co-exist, and in a sense reinforcing differences, the key feature of interculturality, and what differentiates it from multiculturality, is its sense of openness, dialogue and interaction between cultures leading to long-term change in both relational and institutional arrangements. Interculturalism is clearly aligned to community cohesion, which relied upon more deliberative programmes to tackle inequalities, promote diversity and belonging as well as developing trust and understanding through interaction. However, community cohesion has – at least in the UK's experience – been developed primarily at a local level (and has had some considerable success over the last decade, see Chapter 5), but has lacked a national and international metanarrative, in which to place the wider processes of super diversity and globalisation. Interculturalism can begin to eclipse the narrative of multiculturalism, which is still generally conceptualised as being about the relationships between majority and minority populations within nation-states and revolving around singular and binary concepts of racialised difference. The idea of 'an international society' has not yet developed to any great extent, though the concept of 'openness' (see below) points in that direction and is one that interculturalism will need to develop.

Interculturalism and openness

The concept of 'openness', which has been principally developed by the British Council and Migration Policy Group (2011) begins to move closer to interculturality in policy and practical terms. While it has focused on the ease of admission and treatment of new migrants in particular, the combination of objective and subjective dimensions would appear to allow for some transferability of ideas. Using no less than 148 policy indicators, the Migrant Integration Policy Index (MIPEX) creates a rich, multidimensional picture of migrants' opportunities to participate in society by assessing governments' commitment to integration. By measuring policies and their implementation it reveals whether all residents are guaranteed equal rights, responsibilities and opportunities.

For each of the seven policy areas – labour market mobility, family reunion, education, political participation, long-term residence, access to nationality and anti-discrimination – countries are then ranked in a way that MIPEX hopes will 'identify the highest European or international standards aimed at achieving equal rights, responsibilities and opportunities for all residents' (see Table 7.1).

This work is of some considerable value but, the main deficiency is that it provides few insights as to whether such 'rights, responsibilities and opportunities' are begrudged by the majority populations, or valued and willingly conceded – and even whether higher levels of openness improve perceptions of the value of diversity. This is partly because there is little by way of an assessment of whether these 'rights' are confined within separate spheres – on a 'separate but equal' basis – and with a continued separation in some or all of the four domains referred to earlier. It is therefore not clear whether these measures are integrative. There is

Table 7.1 Migration policy index III

Country rank order and score	
1 Sweden	83
2 Portugal	79
3 Canada	72
4 Finland	69
5 Netherlands	68
6 Belgium	67
7 Norway	66
8 Spain	63
9 USA	62
10 Italy	60
11 Luxembourg	59
12 Germany	57
= UK	57
14 Denmark	53
EU Average	*52*
15 France	51
16 Greece	49
= Ireland	49
18 Slovenia	48
19 Czech Republic	46
=Estonia	46
21 Hungary	45
= Romania	45
23 Switzerland	43
24 Austria	42
= Poland	42
26 Bulgaria	41
27 Lithuania	40
28 Malta	37
29 Slovakia	36
30 Cyprus	35
31 Latvia	31

Source: MIPEX (2011)

also little indication of whether there is a genuine understanding and empathy for each other within a spirit of mutual respect and goodwill. In other words, does this contribute to a 'shared society'?

A recent European comparison (European Commission's Directorate-General for Employment, Social Affairs and Equal Opportunities, 2010) appears to reinforce these concerns about the MIPEX approach, suggesting that access to services does not in itself lead to an identification with the country, nor necessarily create a sense of national solidarity. This study, based on a 'Eurobarometer', suggests that 'in the majority of countries most respondents feel that relations between people are good', but even where this view is most prevalent, in Luxembourg (71 per cent), Estonia (67 per cent), Finland (67 per cent), the UK and Latvia (both 64 per cent), Romania (62 per cent) and Spain (60 per cent), around 30 to 40 per cent of respondents did not apparently agree. Further, there are a number of countries where support for this view is below 50 per cent, like Croatia (49 per cent) and Turkey (38 per cent), and a number where the majority of citizens say relations between people are poor. Greece (60 per cent) has the highest incidence of citizens who say relations are poor, followed by the Czech Republic (56 per cent), Denmark (54 per cent), and Italy, Hungary and France (all 49 per cent). It is worth noting that Swedes are perfectly divided on the question.

These findings appear to challenge those set out in the Migration Policy Index – for example, Sweden having been presented as the most 'integrated' and open on the MIPEX scale, nevertheless scores badly on the 'Eurobarometer' and the reverse is true for Latvia, with a high score on the barometer and a low placement under MIPEX. The results could be interpreted in the opposite way to that intended for the Migration Policy Index – that is, the more open the country, the worse the internal relations, again suggestive of a 'paradox of diversity' (see Chapter 2). The real question remains whether the openness enjoyed by some groups is valued and owned by other groups; and whether that openness is seen as a strength or as a threat. This point was underlined by Wood and Landry (2007) who suggested that, although openness provides the setting for interculturalism to develop, it does not a guarantee that it will take place.

The results may also be at variance with individual country results and reflect subtle differences in the questions. For example, in the UK the principal question by which community cohesion has been judged has been by the perception that 'people from around here get on well with those from other backgrounds'. This has been tested by a number of Citizenship Surveys conducted by government and the results rose over time to 85 per cent affirmative in 2010 (DCLG, 2011). This figure is somewhat higher than the Eurobarometer, but may tend to reflect the experience of people in their own communities, rather than more generalised or national concerns.

Wood et al. (2006) have also attempted to assess the openness of cities through a series of indicators based upon four principal spheres of influence:

- the institutional framework;
- the business environment;

- civil society; and
- public space.

In their view, the 'openness of the institutional framework' is determined principally by the regulatory and legislative framework within national or local government. 'Easy access to citizenship' would, for them, be an indicator of this, and the means of measurement would include: the naturalisation rate; provision of language classes to learn the new language; or access to health and social welfare for refugees. This would also include policy areas such as 'intercultural/multicultural citizenship curriculum' in schools.

The 'openness of the business environment' refers to trade and industry, the job market and training. Indicators are drawn from the internal policy commitments of businesses on recruitment and training and to anti-discrimination/racial awareness monitoring and evaluation of outputs. At a national level the foreign trade of local companies and their diasporic links, the ownership of local businesses of various sizes, the recruitment of employees from the outside, and the diversity of the retail offer, is also suggested.

The 'openness of civil society' focuses on the extent to which 'the social fabric of a place is accessible and permeable', and in their view can be measured by the diversity of representation on health, welfare, education boards or management and community forums. The ethnic make-up of top management tiers and cross-cultural economic, social, cultural and civic networks and positive cultural representations or images of the 'other' in the media, is also regarded as indicators of openness.

Finally, in their 'social domain', Wood et al. (2006) suggest that the range includes incidents of racial assault or crimes against asylum seekers, and the treatment of refugees and the incidence of cross-cultural child adoption. The openness of public space relies on the extent to which people feel they have the 'freedom of the city' or whether there are spaces or whole neighbourhoods which feel closed or even hostile to one or more groups within the city. This includes the degree of mixing in housing and neighbourhoods; safety and mobility of ethnic minorities in all areas; the level of mixed use of city-centre libraries and sports centres; and the number of interfaith organisations/forums and meeting places to assess the level and density of contact between religions.

However, they also argue that it is necessary to understand the degree of openness and the dynamic relationship between elements of the social, economic, physical and institutional framework, in order to establish interculturalism, as these are 'the result of openness, both of organised intervention and voluntary effort, and so reflect the lived experience of an intercultural lifeworld'. This underlines that the ideas of openness are generally about access by other communities, rather than any sense of reciprocity from the host community, or their perceptions of the desirability and fairness associated with those processes, although Wood et al. clearly do support the need for a level of interaction and understanding between the host and arriving communities, based upon a mutually educative experience.

The BC have also produced a functionally orientated index through its OPENCities project (see Table 7.2),[4] built upon the work of Clark (2008). This provides an assessment of the 'openness' for around 30 cities, based again upon 'accessibility' in economic, regulatory, cultural and amenity frameworks, but it also includes a small number of perception indicators which attempt to assess the views of the host community. The result was a somewhat unwieldy index with over 50 indicators in 11 areas and included some questionable assumptions about what openness actually means, with most related to the position of international migrants in the labour market and the support and rights that they can obtain. Clark has made a powerful economic case for the openness of cities 'to attract and retain international populations'. Such populations, it is suggested, are not only seen to contribute to the labour force, but also to add enormously to the quality of life and the wider attractiveness of the city for international firms, events and investors (Clark, 2008, p. 16).

On the basis of the above factors, cities were ranked and this put London in first place with other super-diverse cities, such as New York and Toronto, following close behind. Cape Town, Sofia and Chongqing were placed at the bottom of the list of 26 cities.

The OPENCities project does represent a step forward in policy and practice as it aimed to identify the links between migration and cities' competitiveness, with particular emphasis on internationalisation and population strategies that can pose migration as a competitive advantage for cities. They suggest that the arrival of large numbers of new residents in many cities creates great opportunities for innovation and progress in social, economic and cultural development. While this also poses significant challenges for social cohesion and stability at a local level, it suggests that cities can play a significant role in helping the nationwide processes of integration and cohesion. Further, if cities are pursuing plans to be internationally connected, they may play an international role in transforming the global political economy, and the success criteria that the BC identified are the ability to attract talented and skilled people, and to build the balanced and cohesive human resources needed for the contemporary economy. This of course depends upon diverse communities being able to live together in some sense of safety and security. While some of the factors influencing openness are beyond the direct control of cities, many are within their competence or their immediate influence: the city's identity and character; its education, housing and cultural offer; the kind of local democracy it practices and the forms of participation it encourages.

The concept of openness has been particularly focused on the integration of new migrant arrivals and succeeded in making the case for more open cities and nations which can capture the creative and entrepreneurial advantage of diversity. It also avoids concerns about assimilation, as its concept of integration is built around rights and equality. While it does recognise the importance of leadership and creating a moral climate of opinion to support this openness, it remains to be seen whether the attitudes of residents of those countries and cities impacted by migration are less hostile to migrants and any less fearful of changes wrought by globalisation and super diversity. In fact, it would appear that one of the major concerns expressed by people across Europe at least, is precisely that they are 'too open' to migrants, with the Far Right building a platform on this basis (Goodwin, 2011) and both seeing migrants as a threat to the host community's economic position and with the cultural threat that migrants are seen to pose being of even greater concern (Goodwin, 2011c).

'Openness' in the sense of open borders, or the lack of any meaningful control over inward migration will, then, certainly be seen as politically and socially problematic – and the debate invariably returns to 'race', with migrants generally being associated with a non-White (and increasingly non-Christian) cultural threat to the continued assumption of largely White and Christian communities.

Interculturalism and difference

Multiculturalism was founded in a period which gave credence to what is now recognised as the outmoded concept of 'race' based upon spurious notions of physical distinctiveness. Multiculturalism later developed into a policy based on ethnic difference and faith divisions, some of which were identified as 'racial' groups for the purposes of public policy, and these became essentially viewed in much the same primordial sense. Progressive forms of multiculturalism went on to embrace ideas about hyphenated identities, often combining the country of origin or domicile with ethnicity and/or faith. However, these mixed, dual or multiple

164

Table 7.2 Indicators of city openness

Migration
Stock, inflow, composition and qualifications of international population; proportion of foreign-born retirees; perception of value of ethnic diversity, e.g. 'ethnic diversity enriches my life'

Freedom
Political rights and civil liberties; law enforcement and the application of civil law enforcement, e.g. in respect of racism; freedom of foreign investment; media: censorship, variety of international TV channels and international newspapers

Barriers of entry
Accessibility for migrants: ease of entry, integration and rights; ease of hiring foreign labour; access of foreigners to property market; foreign investment and ownership – prevalence and encouragement; public attitudes to migration

International events
International fairs and meetings: number and type

International presence
Number of embassies, international companies and organisations (including NGOs) and amount of foreign investment

Education
Proportion of international students; quality of universities and choice of educational possibilities for children of all ages

International flows
Tourist and visitor arrivals

Infrastructure
Internet availability and usage; telephone services; global accessibility, choice of direct international flights to major destinations on all continents

Quality of living
Quality of life factors: unemployment rates, differential unemployment between native and foreign-born population; crime levels, health and hospital services; perceptions: trust of another religion and nationalities

Standard of living
GDP per capita, average annual growth rates; cost of living, including rents and taxation

Diversity actions
Official websites with migration-specific information: welcome services and information, including ceremonies for new immigrants, specific community centres, events and consultative committees; interpretation: availability of services; language and/or integration courses and other actions to improve the sense of belonging

Source: British Council (2010)

identities also tended to become singular and fixed in much the same way as those based upon just one conception of identity.

Community cohesion programmes were established following a review of the race riots in a number of English northern towns in 2001 and went further still and cohesion activities quickly recognised the wider notion of difference, with programmes developed to tackle divisions and conflicts based on sexual orientation, disability, age, social class and other differences (Cantle, 2008). The widening of concern to all forms of difference was partly because of the practical arrangements in place at a local level. Local statutory agencies, including the police, local authorities and educational institutions, for example, now record and respond to all hate crimes and they are often supported by community organisations which encourage reporting and assist victims. All such agencies therefore have to be trained across the different strands and have developed common administrative systems and processes. Police forces in most parts of the UK have been collating data on some hate crimes, notably race, for many years, but since 1 April 2008 they have collected data for the five strands of hate crime (ACPO, 2010). The numbers vary by police area (generally organised on a county basis) dependent upon demographic characteristics. However, the variation also reflects the ease of reporting, trust in the police service and the extent to which each force encourages reporting.

Table 7.3 shows the hate crimes reported in England, Wales and Northern Ireland for 2009, and while they are dominated by 'race' around one-fifth are for other strands. Given the established practice in respect of reporting race hate crime, it is possible that the level of under-reporting in the other strands is much higher, as has been suggested in respect of disability (EHRC, 2011).

Second, the incidence of hate crimes across the strands is also causally connected, with insular and closed communities tending to be more fearful and resistant to all forms of difference. This is certainly the import of the studies of the 'authoritarian personality' stemming from the work of Adorno et al. (1950). The clear and strongly held prejudicial views of virtually all Far Right groups towards gays and lesbians, Black and ethnic minorities and non-Christians, and indeed the attempted annihilation of these and other groups in Nazi Germany, underlines this perspective. More recently, the segregation and isolation of individuals has been linked to the propensity to become members of the Far Right British National Party (Biggs and Knauss 2011). Further, Hewstone et al. (2008a) has demonstrated a more direct link between antipathy in

Table 7.3 Total recorded hate crime in England, Wales and Northern Ireland (2009)

Hate crime	Number
Race	43,426
Religion/Faith (of which anti-Semitic 703)	2083
Sexual orientation	4805
Transgender	312
Disability	1402
Total	52,028

Source: Association of Chief Police Officers (ACPO) (2010)

respect of one area of difference (sectarianism) to newer areas of diversity in Northern Ireland (racial and ethnic minorities):

> Although long concerned almost exclusively with cross-community relations, Northern Ireland like almost every other country in Europe is now having to think about diversity in a broader sense. We showed that neighbourhood contact had an indirect effect, via a change in how the other community was seen, on attitudes to other (racial and ethnic) minority groups. Hence successful efforts to promote cross-community contact can have positive implications for community relations generally, and the promotion of a truly inclusive, non-racist as well as non-sectarian Northern Ireland. Turning to indirect friendship, our data show that this mild, non-threatening form of contact helps to 'prepare' people for later, direct contact with outgroup members, and leads to an increase in direct contact at a later date.
>
> (Source: Hewstone, 2008a, p. 75)

The statutory duties enshrined in the UK's (single) Equality Act 2010 (HM Government, 2010) are also concerned with all areas of difference. Indeed, part of the rationale for creating a single equality body, the Equality and Human Rights Commission (EHRC), and the combining of legislation under the above Act, was to recognise that 'difference' encompasses everyone and should be responded to on a consistent basis. The conception and recognition of 'difference was therefore also extended under this Act with the designation of nine 'protected characteristics', as follows:

- age;
- disability;

- gender reassignment;
- marriage and civil partnership;
- pregnancy and maternity;
- race;
- religion or belief;
- sex; and
- sexual orientation.

Further, the Act created a duty upon public authorities to 'have due regard to the need to:

(a) eliminate discrimination, harassment, victimisation and any other conduct that is prohibited by or under this Act;
(b) advance equality of opportunity between persons who share a relevant protected characteristic and persons who do not share it;
(c) foster good relations between persons who share a relevant protected characteristic and persons who do not share it.

(Source: HM Government Equality Act, 2010, s149)

The need to 'foster good relations' across all forms of difference provides the opportunity to see the connectedness of different forms of prejudice and its genesis in insular and closed communities, separated by a range of socio-economic and cultural factors. Divisions between communities and the existence of hate crimes based upon a number of the 'protected characteristics' have, hitherto, been conceptualised and responded to on very different bases. For example, disability hate crime seems to be understood as the problem of 'deep seated animosity and prejudice' (EHRC, 2011, p. 163); hate crimes against religious minorities or against faiths and sects different to one's own are put down to sectarian rivalry; attacks on people with special needs are apparently because of 'ignorance' and the intimidation or attacks on the LGBTI community are seen as resulting from 'bigotry' and 'illiberalism'. However, in multicultural theory, attacks on people of a different ethnicity have often been regarded as being the function of poverty or the legacy of colonialism. Cleary, each of these areas has its own context, but there is a renewed interest in the reduction of all forms of stereotyping and prejudice and clear evidence of interaction programmes undermining the fear of 'difference' and changing both attitudes and behaviours across the strands. But seeing the linkages between all difference, let alone accepting that, as Sandercock (2004) suggests, the very nature of culture, and therefore of difference, has to be seen as dynamic and constantly renegotiated, depends upon a mind shift in conceptualising these issues. Such is the legacy of racism that the idea of 'culture' has become imbued with the same primordial sense of distinctiveness, that it has become defended with the same fervour with which the idea of 'race' was so rightly attacked. Linked to ideas about 'heritage', 'roots' and 'finding ourselves', the focus on culture has become a pretext for creating a strong sense of personal being with which then to negotiate against other identities, rather than to acknowledge that personal identities can only be understood in relation to, and with, those of others. Ironically, some commentators have also railed against the 'over-emphasising' of cultural factors because it turns the classic Marxist position of 'material and structural context' (McGhee, 2003) on its head, while recognising that 'race' is a social construct. Indeed, part of the problem of multiculturalism is that it failed to recognise that identity is no longer only seen through the lens of 'race', and that prejudice, discrimination, hate crimes, community tensions and conflicts, now reflect the many dimensions of difference.

There have been some attempts to develop programmes that encompass all difference. For example, the ABCs programme, referred to earlier (ABCs at iCoCo, 2009), was clearly focused around *cultural* difference and employed the language of 'interculturality' in the publicity and guidance for the scheme – but did succeed in attracting applicants for a wide range of 'differences' that are not generally regarded as 'cultural', for example, in respect of intergenerational, sectarian and disability differences. However, to be successful in an era of globalisation and super diversity, interculturalism would also have to be positioned to take this further, recognising the dynamic nature of difference and that it includes wider geo-political and international components. As discussed in earlier chapters, there is a sense of retrenchment by nation-states – and by regional and separatist movements within them – in the face of the perception of the loss of power and identity in an increasingly globalised world. The spirit of internationalism that began to emerge in the last century and that was so fervently pursued in the post-Second World War period, to recognise the common humanity between people and put an end to the terrible impacts of war just experienced, appears to have faded. This is exactly the reverse of what might have been expected in the light of this new era globalisation and super diversity. In fact, the current 'politics of identity' appear to be somewhat at odds with the aspirations that gave birth to the UN in 1945. The UN Charter (United Nations, 1945) set out its vision 'to develop friendly relations among nations based on respect for the principle of equal rights' and for 'international co-operation [...] without distinction as to race, sex, language, or religion'.

The Universal Declaration of Human Rights followed in 1948, which again arose out of the experience of the Second World War, with the international community vowing never again to allow atrocities like those they had just witnessed. World leaders decided to complement the UN Charter with a road map to guarantee the rights of every individual everywhere and this was written in the same aspirational style. This recognised 'the equal and inalienable rights of all members of the human family, is the foundation of freedom, justice and peace in the world:

> Everyone is entitled to all the rights and freedoms set forth in this Declaration, without distinction of any kind, such as race, colour, sex, language, religion, political or other opinion, national or social origin, property, birth or other status. Furthermore, no distinction shall be made on the basis of the political, jurisdictional or international status of the country or territory to which a person belongs, whether it be independent, trust, non-self-governing or under any other limitation of sovereignty.
>
> (UN, 1948)

The Charter set out 30 Articles proclaiming a wide range of liberties, rights and freedoms which should be underpinned by law. Particularly pertinent here are the 'the right to seek and to enjoy in other countries asylum from persecution' (Article 14), and the 'right to freedom of thought, conscience and religion; this right includes freedom to change his religion or belief' (Article 18).

The CoE was similarly established in 1949, with a view to promoting 'greater unity between its members', building on the Organisation for European Economic Co-operation (OEEC) which had been established in 1947 with the more urgent task of reconstruction, but again based upon co-operation. This soon developed into the Organisation for Co-operation and Economic Development (OECD) created in 1960 because 'European leaders realised that the best way to ensure lasting peace was to encourage co-operation and reconstruction'.[5]

What is striking, from this period, is the aspirational tone, with many nations working together. Globalisation might have been expected to bring nations even closer together by building upon these aspirations and giving effect to them but, rather, it seems our 'distinctions' have become more manifest and salient. Further, the focus appeared to shift, first towards the establishment of individual rights, for example, through the CoE and its oversight of the European Convention on Human Rights and the controversial task of balancing individual rights with those of the wider community. Second, the notion of international co-operation has been seen more in terms of agreement and stan-dardisation of regulatory conventions to facilitate trade across national boundaries and in respect of medicines, combating drug abuse, respond-ing to major hazards and natural and technological disasters. While very valuable, the focus has been upon institutional development, at a remote and supra-national level, with little attention to the original aspirations based upon the dignity of humankind.

The EU had the same post-war origins but was not based upon such lofty ideals – it grew out of the 1951 European Coal and Steel Com-munity (ECSC) and became the European Economic Community (EEC), formed in 1958. The EU then emerged and has grown in membership (27 nations), spawning a wide range of centralised institutions includ-ing the European Central Bank, the Court of Justice and the European Parliament. The EU has promoted a single market, with the emphasis on the free movement of capital, people, goods and services. The EU now controls much of agricultural and fisheries policies and supports many aspects of social and economic development on a regional basis. It has also ventured into security policy and has a new but limited role in respect of defence and external affairs. Notably, the Eurozone was established in 1999 and currently includes 19 nation-states.

The EU has enabled people to travel much more freely, without pass-port controls at every national border, with use of the euro in many states. Goods and services conform to the same standards and many aspects of daily life are now shared across borders. However, rather like the 'paradox of diversity', the growth of international institutions on this basis appears to drive people towards separate identities rather than a shared conception of themselves. Gary Younge (2010) explains this in relation to the introduction of the euro, which he believes has not only resulted in the ceding of national power over interest rates and economic sovereignty, but has also involved the loss of an important element of national identity through the much reduced symbolism and national markers that individually designed currency notes and coins provided.

As suggested earlier, the Far Right appear to understand the new dynamics better than centrist politicians, focusing on the divide between 'nationalism and globalisation' (Le Pen, 2011). Cuperus (2011) suggests that the 'neopopulist citizen's revolt in Europe must be understood as a sense of not represented in, but victimised by, the great transformation of our contemporary societies, in particular by the processes of globalisation/Europeanisation, post-industrialisation and multiculturalisation'. Younge (2010), who is no supporter of the Far Right, confirms this sense of disempowerment:

> But the truth is that, when it comes to identity, the global and the parochial have a symbiotic relationship. The smaller the world seems and the less control that we have over it, the more likely we are to retreat into the local spheres where we might have influence.

However, some global identities have emerged, particularly through the growth of more active faith-based diasporas, which have attempted to provide an 'alma mater' or spiritual home for migrant communities spread across the globe and often living in unfriendly or hostile states, or simply driven by geo-political forces. It may also be the case that we are beginning to see the growth of other forms of transnational affiliations, supported by global communications, which can transcend national boundaries. The use of social media in the Arab Spring enabled people to connect with others in their own country and to challenge the existing leaderships, but also to exchange ideas with other nationals across borders and create a more general movement for change. The anti-capitalist 'occupy' movement has similarly crossed national boundaries.

The response to globalisation and super diversity has generally been one of trying to reassert nationalistic concepts of identity and to strengthen national solidarity, with the credibility and influence of the political elite very much at stake. This has been understandable, and will no doubt continue while the nation-state is regarded as the only viable instrument of a political community. But the opposite is also needed – to prepare for the future of increasingly globalised identities – and not simply prop up a past conception of ourselves which will be increasingly subject to pressure and change in a globalised world. Globalised and national identities are not opposed and should be regarded as complementary.

Towards interculturalism

This section serves as a summary of the above discussion and the previous chapters, and presents a perspective for interculturalism. It is supported by the following chapter, which sets out a number of the policy and practical implications.

The legacy of multiculturalism is both good and bad. It did help to create a framework of rights for minorities during a hard-fought battle to overcome the racism inherent in the post-colonial era. It also established strong support for the concept of cultural pluralism and the need to maintain the heritage of distinct communities and to avoid the wiping away of identities through assimilation. But multiculturalism no longer enjoys either political or popular support, largely because it did not succeed in establishing the positive case for diverse societies, at least in the eyes of the host communities. Despite some evident improvement in community relations, particularly as a result of community cohesion and ICD programmes in the last ten years or so, fears about 'others' are still growing and the pace of globalisation and the accompanying movement of people on an unprecedented scale, means that people are generally ill-equipped for the new era and have become more fearful of change and have tended to retreat into traditional identity and support networks.

As any politician will attest, it is difficult to present a positive case for diversity, at least if they are expecting to get re-elected. But the case can be made – and in fact has to be made as the reality is that all societies are becoming more multicultural. People who live in multicultural communities are generally more supportive of diversity and have acquired some degree of multicultural competence, whereas the opposite is generally true in respect of people who live in insular communities with little meaningful experience of 'others'. However, while it is possible to change peoples' attitudes and behaviours towards others, the task is made much more difficult when the climate of opinion is working in the opposite direction. The role of leaders, particularly politicians, including the many minor so-called community leaders, who believe that they can only hold on to their power and influence by appealing to a particular constituency at the expense of the interests of others – and at the expense of community cohesion generally – is critical. But leadership also comes from civil society, business organisations, educationalists and others and there are signs of a growing movement among younger people, tired of the traditional battle lines and able to create more horizontal connections between people at a human level.

None of this will mean, however, that the tensions and conflicts between people from different backgrounds and with different interests will somehow magically disappear. Indeed, as the world becomes more multicultural so tensions and conflicts will increase and there will be constant negotiations and accommodations – these are the essence of change, which is both endemic and necessary. These include the present debates about the protection of particular languages and other cultural markers and nation-states should be expected to constantly debate what they stand for and how they wish to define themselves. One of the problems of multiculturalism was that it discouraged such debate, on the assumption that this again entailed disadvantaging minorities or 'giving oxygen' to the Far Right. The restrictive nature of the debate, however, meant that society as a whole found it difficult to come to terms with change and felt that the opportunity was being denied to them because of an underlying political agenda.

What has passed for a debate about multiculturalism was usually defined by migration. The pros and cons were generally discussed on the basis of economic considerations and couched in terms of curbing excesses and limiting numbers, all of which reinforced the notion of a threat to the livelihoods and social position of some of the existing populations. The Far Right have understood, however, that concerns about migration are more fundamental and now revolve around national identity and the sense of powerlessness of national governments to cope with global financial and commercial pressures. The concept of 'openness' is one response to this and attempts to make the case for diversity (particularly of cities), as the driver of entrepreneurialism and creativity. While this has some considerable support, the suggestion of more openness, particular of borders, is hardly likely to gain public support. Much of the debate has inevitably been set in a racial and xenophobic context, whereas there have been few attempts to locate it in broader population or economic strategies.

The perspective of interculturalism is, then, one that needs to be clearly separated from the past, and very much future-orientated, based upon a vision of what societal relationships we aspire to, but one that also recognises the concerns and fears that people have.

While it is accepted that 'race' is socially and politically constructed and that in biological terms there is but one human race, we must avoid falling into the trap of thinking that identities formed by ethnic, faith and other characteristics have a primordial basis. 'Culture' should also be regarded as a dynamic concept and it is constantly being made and remade, and the way individuals see their identity and the way particular groups and communities represent themselves will change over time. In the new era of multifaith and multicultural societies, the state must avoid privileging one over another. This is not to say that states should not invest in some forms of cultural preservation, but should be very wary of protectionism those attempts to hold back the evolutionary processes that transcend nation-states and intra-state dialogic community processes. Singular identities are no longer the norm – if they ever were – and choices do not have to be made between nation, faith, sexuality or other descriptor; it is perfectly possible to hold several conceptions of ourselves, perhaps not in equal measure, but certainly at the same time.

However, states do need to invest in the future as well as the past. The teaching of national history, the conception of national values built upon past successes (or failures) needs to be counter-balanced by international and global conceptions and to build cultural navigation skills to equip people for an increasingly globalised world. History needs to be taught in a way that enables us to learn from it, rather than be defined by it.

Most of all, a vision of a shared society and mixed communities is now needed. The history of migration has militated against this, as have the policies and practices of multiculturalism. A society that is clearly divided by race, ethnicity, social class or other demographic factor, will always struggle to build common bonds and to create a shared conception of fairness. This does not mean that policies should now lurch in the opposite direction with all communities designed on a 'melting pot' of mixing – indeed, some form of clustering helps to support cultural and social systems. But many countries in the West have high degrees of segregation which have led to impermeable and insular communities that perpetuate their own myths and stereotypes (and confirm them to others). Our concept of 'segregation' has been one of a continuum from assimilation on the one hand to ghettoes and 'no-go' areas on the other. This is out of step with the reality of societal divisions, and segregation (and integration) is possible on many different levels. It is also out of step with identities, which have become increasingly multifaceted, and people will now represent themselves in different ways and at different times, according to the context. Multicultural societies have been so preoccupied with race that they have also failed to recognise the growth of many forms of difference, particularly the emergence of faith and sexual orientation, within the public sphere.

Globalisation and super diversity have created even more profound challenges. The nation-state is under pressure as never before. It is increasingly difficult to control borders in a physical sense and the dramatic changes in international communications – real and virtual – mean far less state and identity-based control and influence over ideas, with a concomitant fluidity in emotional attachments and solidarities. At present, the response has been to try to tighten these controls, limit the influence of outsiders, or reinforce notions of the national story. These may have some impact in the short term, but need to be complemented by a very deliberative programme to increase cultural competence and confidence, to improve the competitiveness of individuals in a global market, and, in particular, to build confidence and reduce fear. More especially it is also essential to improve international co-operation and collaboration. The world is more global and diverse, but political systems and processes – both within and between countries – have remained almost unchanged. Interculturalism, then, will need to rediscover the spirit of internationalism from the middle of the last century and translate it into practice which can engage with populations on a multilevel basis.

8
Interculturalism: Policy and Practice

Much of the previous discussion points to the need for fundamental change and for the development of new ways in which we can learn to live together in an increasingly interconnected and interdependent world. Each society is of course different and the policies and practices of interculturalism need to reflect this. However, there are a number of common themes that would appear to offer a progressive and forward-looking agenda for change. Moreover, a successful transition to a new approach will depend upon the emergence of an international consensus, though this could build upon the work already undertaken by the Council of Europe, the British Council, the Comedia Group and others.

Leadership and vision

It almost goes without saying that the success of a new model of interculturalism – or any perspective about how we live together with others – will depend upon the development of a vision of a shared world and society in which people are encouraged to value the common humanity of all nations, faiths and ethnic groups. As discussed earlier, such a vision has only briefly flickered in the past and was perhaps at its strongest following the horror of the Second World War. Political leaders were then keen to emphasise the need to avoid future conflicts and to heal wounds and divisions, pledging to build trust and understanding and replace the bitter enmity of the past. And it has proved successful with peace in Europe at least for the longest ever period. Collaboration can soon give way to conflict, however, when the vision is dimmed over time and there are signs of new divisions emerging, partly as a consequence of globalisation, which will threaten the future peace.

Some see the divisions within and between nations as a natural phenomenon, borne out of man's innate competitiveness and tribalism. But this is nonsense. The divisions that we see as being important, or salient, change over time and in each different context: they are socially and politically defined, not primordial. Indeed, a great deal of political support is engineered on the basis of counterposing one set of interests against another. A threat to a nation's interest by another is soon conjured up or rediscovered, a faith group rallies its supporters by denouncing the practices or heresy of another, or one community creates a myth that it can only prosper if another is taken down a peg or two.

Such political differentiation has become even more sophisticated with the advent of opinion polling and more advanced communication strategies. Politicians now unashamedly talk about their 'core vote', which they then aim to retain with policies built around their particular interests and how they then need to woo additional voters with some new policy to reach the threshold necessary for power. The segmentation of the political community has become as normal as the segmentation of the consumer market place and political principles have given way to pragmatism dictated by the focus group, in which policies are decided on the basis of 'how it will play with' a particular section of the community.

There is, of course, nothing wrong with politicians engaging with their electorate, listening to concerns and proposing policies to tackle those concerns and scope out a better future. But the competitive process of party politics, generally on a knife edge in all Western states, and with coalitions and bilateral agreements to hold governments tenuously together, militates against inclusive government. This is 'what politics is about', getting the support of groups of citizens to have an impact on election results (Demirbag-Sten, 2011) – often much less than 50 per cent of the popular vote – to guarantee their party the power they crave. Consequently, a minor differentiation in approach, built around tentative incremental and nuanced policies, will be more than sufficient. They have chosen to ignore the most demonstrable expression of dissatisfaction from their citizens – voter registration and turnout is in decline in virtually every Western nation. In response, politicians bemoan the lack of interest and apathy, but have failed to recognise that political interest is in fact being channelled into single-issue politics which transcend the traditional party political arena. Civil society organisations have growing levels of membership, while party political membership is going in the opposite direction.

Ironically, they have perhaps become so accustomed to studying the electoral impact of the minor differentiation between parties, that they have also failed to notice that 'big' issues do matter to their citizens. This is underlined by a recent and rare glimpse of wider attitudes towards diversity, rather than the testing of comparative party advantage of this or that new restriction on migration, or targeted employment schemes. The key findings of the 'Fear and HOPE' report (SET, 2011) indicate the crucial role of political leadership in an era of globalisation and uncertainty. They suggest that a new politics of identity, culture and nation has grown out of the politics of race and immigration, and is increasingly the opinion driver in modern British politics (and is very likely to be the same in many other countries). The centre ground is now dominated by 'identity ambivalents' who are concerned about social change and security and, together with those expressing more strident views, represent around three-quarters of the population. But, interestingly, they also found 'a real appetite for a positive campaigning organisation that opposes political extremism through bringing communities together'; over two-thirds of the population would either 'definitely' or 'probably' support such a strategy.

It is undoubtedly the case, however, that the creation of a future vision would be better founded on a cross-party basis, with wider support from business and civil society. A wider climate of opinion, based upon a practical and moral case for change, outside of party political considerations, would enable the normal rivalries and the exploitation of genuine concerns for party political purposes to be put aside. Such cross-party political agreements in fact already exist at the local level in the UK, usually as part of a concerted strategy to head off the Far Right, which represent a threat to all centrist parties (Cantle, 2008, p. 181). They have also been developed into more positive statements and 'belonging', built around campaigns which create the aspiration of 'one community' that embraces all aspects of diversity (ibid., p. 182). Despite strong recent evidence that these local cohesion strategies, which are built on a united local leadership, have had some considerable success (DCLG, 2011), there is no equivalent approach at a national level.

Indeed, it has been found that 'countries divided along class and ethnic lines will place severe constraints on the attempts of even the boldest, civic-minded, and well-informed politician (or interest group) seeking to bring about policy reform' (Ritzen et al., 2000).

A key part of any national (and international) vision is to make it clear that multicultural societies are here to stay – there is no going back, the so-called 'guest workers' are now fellow citizens and migration is an ongoing an endemic process. Societies will inevitably become more multicultural – as 'we' go there, for trade, education and leisure, so 'they' will come here for reciprocal purposes and especially for employment. That does not mean that migration will be without controls, or that nations will no longer protect what they see as their interests, but it does mean an acceptance of growing interdependence and interconnectivity. People need to be told the truth, to bring to an end the pretence that somehow globalisation can be controlled on a national basis and at the same time, people need to be supported to acquire the skills and competence to have the confidence to face this future perspective.

Leadership is not, however, simply about the writing of a worthy 'vision statement'. It is about actively campaigning for change and embodying the vision in everyday actions and policies – even when they are neither conventional wisdoms, nor popular. Clark (2008, p. 17) suggests that a more open society depends upon a proactive leadership strategy that has a clear agenda to promote the benefits of diversity and tolerance, with a particular focus on the city level.

While the theme of city openness (British Council, OPENCities[1]) and the 'intercultural city' concept (Bloomfield and Bianchini, 2004) have begun to be explored, at present nation-states do little to encourage more outward-looking citizens. Clearly under pressure from the processes of globalisation and super diversity, they are desperately trying to reinforce partial and national conceptions. But championing ideas of internationalism and cosmopolitanism does not necessarily involve downgrading national identities – it is possible to have both, within wider patterns of identity.

Leadership is vital in an era of change. This may not, however, simply be exhibited in the traditional form of top-down and vertical structures. As noted earlier, the age of deference is over and respect has to be earned rather than taken. Vertical national power structures are also breaking down, perhaps most evidently in the countries of the 'Arab Spring' where the democratisation of information and virtual connectivity between people, within and across national boundaries, has fundamentally challenged repressive power structures. This is no less true, though generally less violent in outcome, in democracies where the personal and professional lives of politicians are exposed to constant scrutiny and information is no longer simply available through 'official channels'. The 'plummeting trust in politicians' (Curtice and Park, 2010) may have spurred on the present development of more horizontal and grass-roots forms of leadership, which are much more able to cross cultural and national boundaries than the established political parties and structures. This is already the case in respect of diaspora communities which inspire and galvanise people across the world, often on the basis of faith, but also on a cultural basis. Diasporas may, however, also find that their structures of power and influence are too vertically inclined and homogenising in conceptual terms to survive in their present forms, against the tide of globalisation.

The power structures at the international level are even more vertically inclined with little or nothing by way of grass roots democratic involvement and expression. To the extent that political leaders have acknowledged that they are no longer the in command of all social, economic and political forces within their realm, they have created international organisations in which the power elite come together in private meetings to try to agree how to influence, regulate and control global processes. Representative democracy has taken on a new meaning, in which the individual's contribution has been doubly removed from national level to supra-national bodies which are effectively answerable to no one. Indeed, national politicians, particularly in Europe are now seen to be accountable upwards to these bodies, rather than downwards to their electorates. This further enhances the feeling of powerlessness and creates a 'democratic deficit', accelerating the disenchantment with national and vertical structures.

In the current climate, it is possible that, rather than look outwards, national leaders will continue to try to shore up their own national support, which harks back to the past conceptions of identity and is generally based upon an exclusionary national story which identifies 'newcomers' as the (visible) threat to holding on to this national story. The Far Right across Europe have very much succeeded in this approach to date and centrist parties have tended to try to assuage these concerns by moving policies in their direction, rather than risking the offering of an alternative and progressive vision.

It is also possible that a new global movement, perhaps inspired through the burgeoning social networks, will develop through people who are frustrated by old divisions and anxious for greater global collaboration to secure changes on a global level, particularly climate change and to prevent and end conflicts. There is little to suggest that this is likely to be the case, though no one predicted the Arab Spring revolts in which millions of people emerged to provide new vision and leadership. One small and localised approach, which provides a hopeful indication of direction, is to be found in Luton, England, a town recently enveloped by racial and religious conflicts. The 'Luton in Harmony' campaign is based upon a pledge and invites local people to sign up and 'spread the word'.[2] Luton residents are asked to wear a badge, and sign a pledge card. This says that supporters will:

- wear the Luton in Harmony badge with pride – and tell people what it means;
- make friends with people from different backgrounds and life experiences – and learn about their values; and
- promote their own beliefs in a spirit of peace and harmony.

Astonishingly, over 65,000 people have signed the pledge and worn a 'Luton in Harmony' badge as a sign of their support – and perhaps a sign that hope can inspire more than hate.

It is, of course, also possible that the political class will themselves become emboldened to assert more strongly than ever before the idea of an interconnected and interdependent world in which the common humanity of people is regarded as fundamental. And that they will acknowledge the limitation of existing power structures and attempt to create democratic and international institutions, which can harness the power of technology to bring people together in new ways and in common cause. National borders and structures are in themselves very important but their influence has already been reduced by global processes and they will inevitably diminish, as globalisation ensures a much greater level of permeability across financial, business, recreational and social spheres. The question is how the transition will take place and whether it will be planned and eased, or involve more dramatic and sudden change.

The politics of identity

National identity is not only under threat from globalisation and the emergence of stronger diasporas but also challenged from below. While this is perhaps the inevitable consequence of migration flows and the advent of 'super diversity', the state has itself connived with this process. In a very legitimate attempt to address the disadvantage suffered by ethnic minorities in particular, the state has constantly 'flagged' separate identities through ethnic monitoring and created single identity programmes and budgets that have reinforced the salience of particular identities and created dependent separate organisations which constantly reaffirm their 'difference' in order to remain in receipt of this support. Further, government and public agencies have heightened, or essentialised, these separate identities (Jurado, 2011) through the privileging of access and by facilitating contributions to the decision-making processes.

This has even been the case where access and funding have been provided in order to challenge the influence of extreme views within particular communities. The Prevent programme in the UK (HM Government, 2008), which has been emulated by many countries around the world, has been almost exclusively focused on the Muslim communities and has consequently been judged to be counter-productive as a result of the homogenising identities within those communities and by counter-posing this conception of an identity with that of others (House of Commons Communities and Local Government Select Committee, 2010).

Again, it has to be recognised that the multicultural policy that gave birth to this approach was based on the best of motives, to tackle racism and disadvantage, but it failed to adapt and to recognise the way in which racism has been replaced by cultural and other conceptions of difference and the sense in which diversity has become the new normal. Rather than develop a more integrated conception of nation, this has resulted in further segmentation and 'hunkering down' of communities in many instances. It was also entrenched in ideas about difference which were rooted in each country and has not recognised the increasing conceptions of difference at an international level as a result of globalisation. States have generally stepped in very selectively to try to prop up particular forms of identity – for example, support has been given to the French language in Quebec Province in Canada, and to the Black community in the UK through the annual 'Black history month' project. Little has been done to promote more cosmopolitan forms of identity and, rather, they are often viewed as either as a threat to national identity or as a subtle assimilationist process (McGhee, 2005).

A cosmopolitan identity can, however, sit alongside national and local forms and complement, rather than threaten, each other. This is a crucial point as Cuperus (2011) points out that there is a great danger involved when a cosmopolitan post-national elite carelessly argue away the nation-state and national identity, just at the moment that the nation-state is for many the last straw of identification to cling to, a beacon of trust in a world in flux. There is also an important social class and age dimension to the development of a more cosmopolitan form of identity, as the pressures of adaptation to the new globalised world are particularly directed at those who do not fit into the new international knowledge-based economy – the unskilled and the low skilled (ibid., 2011). Younger people, in general, have found it easier to share much in common with youth globally (Mansouri, 2009), and second and third generation migrants in particular are able to express greater confidence in a multicultural future (Wood et al., 2006a).

Martell (2008) argues that globalisation has, in any event, created the conditions for the development of cosmopolitanism. First, nation-states have been undermined by internal problems such as the privatisation of state assets and sub-national fragmentation, and been overtaken by global processes in finance and communications. Second, the end of the cold war has ended the bipolar divide and created the many new alliances and multilayered relationships on a more global scale. Third, the nature and interconnectedness of problems like the proliferation of nuclear weapons, climate change and capital mobility have made the international institutions something of a necessity. But cosmopolitanism is also a way of seeing things, an entirely new outlook for a global era (Held, 2002), and an 'alternative imagination, an alternative imagination of ways of life and rationalities' (Beck, 2002). And like other forms of identity, cosmopolitan conceptions will be formed dialectically, as part of the process of forming attachments that are not simply situated in national ideas and prejudices.

Cosmopolitanism might be said to be underway through the everyday processes of international travel and communication, the integration of business, the development of transnational education markets, the social and cultural intermixing and the consequent emergence of multilayered affinities and identities. The real question is whether nation-states facilitate this transition, by developing wider understandings, trust and tolerance, or whether they constantly resist the process, expressing fear and concerns about the increasing incursions into national ways of life and institutions and have the opposite effect of exacerbating xenophobic tendencies. Creating a more global conception of ourselves is part of the development of cultural navigation skills and intercultural competence (see below) but is clearly linked to the vision each country has for itself in the future world. It should then be connected to very specific programmes like the teaching of a more cosmopolitan outlook in schools, as advocated by Shah (2008), but would also be found in every aspect of government policy, for example, in international aid and development, and with a high level of proactivity associated with multilateral processes and agreements.

Cosmopolitanism also offers the opportunity to resolve, or at least mitigate, the increasing segmentation of identities within nation-states and to offer a more encompassing and wider conception of ourselves which can positively augment, rather than threaten, particular heritage or regional identities. This is particularly the case in respect of 'mixed race' which is growing in all countries and yet remains outside most conceptions of identity, which are still bounded by notions of 'purity'. In academic and policy terms, the extent of mixed race, or interethnic and interfaith unions, are generally regarded positively as an indication of an integrated and open society (Wildsmith et al., 2003), but are often ignored, disapproved of, or discriminated against in many communities.

Barriers are usually particularly high among faith groups, despite the apparent support for idealised notions of common humanity. In the UK, for example, the overall rate among couples with partners from a different religious affiliation is 12 per cent but this varies from 5 per cent of Christian men, to around 10 per cent of Hindu, Sikh and Muslim men, rising to a third of Jewish men and over 40 per cent of men with no religion and for Buddhist men. Among women the variation is no less marked, with the lowest rate of partnership with a person of a different religion in Muslim women (3 per cent) followed by Sikh, Hindu and Christian women at around 7 to 9 per cent, followed by those with no religious affiliation (24 per cent) and Jewish women (30 per cent), rising to 62 per cent for Buddhist women (Platt, 2009).

Faith organisations should be encouraged to recognise that they are holding back the process of change and that they are fostering identity politics. Their disapproval of interfaith unions is hard for them to sustain in terms of their own religious beliefs and ideals and they therefore tend to raise practical barriers, over such issues as how to sanctify the marriage, or over the way that children are to be brought up in one of these faiths (and rarely in both). The practice of punishing apostasy also supports this rigidity and denies free choice. Though interfaith unions are inevitably increasing, governments have been reluctant to challenge these restrictive practices, despite Article 18 of the Universal Declaration of Human Rights, which states:

> Everyone has the right to freedom of thought, conscience and religion; this right includes freedom to change his religion or belief, and freedom, either alone or in community with others and in public or private, to manifest his religion or belief in teaching, practice, worship and observance.
>
> (United Nations, 1948)

The state support for faith groups, especially the formal establishment of one particular faith into the institutions of the state, as in the UK and many other countries, helps to promote the notion of the superiority of that faith (or faiths) over others. Faiths need little help in creating an almost primordial and superior distinctiveness for their particular belief system, and state endorsement certainly helps to consolidate their defensive position.

While faiths are self-governing, their rigidity and conceptions of 'identity purity' are often tacitly and explicitly supported by nation-states in other ways too. Support is given to faith-based groups for educational purposes, for example (and as discussed in earlier chapters), in relation to faith-based school systems. This has attracted particular criticism. Kymlicka (2003) suggests that:

> the proliferation of separate religious schools is regrettable, particularly when they will be controlled by conservative religious leaders who preach that their group is the chosen people, that people outside the church are evil and damned, that inter-marriage is a sin, etc. These schools may in fact generate precisely the sort of fear of 'otherness' that our conceptions of intercultural citizenship were intended to overcome.
>
> (p. 162)

Gallagher (2004) has also pointed out that the mere fact of separation sent implicit messages to young people that they were different.

However, faiths have also been supported financially in relation to the delivery of services to their communities. This 'single-identity funding' has been previously contested by independent reviews in England (Cantle, 2001; CIC, 2007) and though now reduced, still remains in many areas. While single-identity funding has been supported on the basis of the targeting of support to disadvantaged groups (McGhee, 2008), it has a more insidious effect of a state-sponsored programme of 'branding' for particular identities. Single-identity funding has also been applied in other areas, in particular to ethnic groups, where again it represents a state reinforcement of socially constructed identities (or 'state multiculturalism' (Cameron, 2011)). In the UK, until very recently, the state also appeared to support the idea of both ethnic and religious 'identity purity', by supporting adoption practices and agencies that would only allow adoption within the same ethnic or faith group.

Ethnic, faith and other sub-national and supra-national identities are not about to disappear. The same is also true of national identity, despite the weakening processes discussed in earlier chapters and the fact that, even for White groups in the UK, it is surprisingly low (SET, 2011). The pull of national identity should never be underestimated (Cantle,

2008, p. 140). English (2011), for example, has recently considered the rise of English nationalism and believes that it 'resonates with many of humanity's deepest instincts and needs: towards survival, security, protection and safety; towards the fulfilment of practical economic and other needs; and towards belonging, particularly to stable, coherent, meaningful, lastingly special and distinctive groups'. English, however, appears to see this as an 'attachment to our own special place', whereas the modern reality is that many people now have a number of special places, from the local to the global – and these need not be in any way mutually exclusive.

Separate and exclusive forms of state-sponsored community leadership have also underpinned homogeneous and privileged forms of identity. It has been convenient for states, at a local and national level, to delegate their engagement of those communities that they do not understand, through a series of community leaders, who may be self-appointed or representative of only a small section of their identity group. Such leaders may well receive funding which bolsters and institutionalises their role. They then have considerable autonomy and create the impression within their community that they are regarded as one group with one upward channel of communication. These leaders have been dubbed 'gatekeepers' (Cantle, 2008, p. 184) and can be contrasted with 'gateway leaders' (ibid.) who see their role to empower every section of their community to speak for themselves and develop a multiplicity of engagements. 'Gatekeepers', however, appear to have been the preferred model as they make it easy for public agencies to communicate with a particular community and dispense with all of the messy intracommunity politics. One dominant view is much easier to manage politically. It also makes it easier to negotiate political deals in which community leaders agree to deliver the votes from most members of that community. The promise of continuing funding, a new project, or community centre may well be enough.

The support for single-identity groups, especially in respect of schools, the privileging of one or more faith or community groups in representational and political terms, and the constant flagging of separate and spurious forms of 'pure' identity, all point in the wrong direction. It is, unfortunately, unlikely that these arrangements are part of what has been called 'state multiculturalism' (Cameron, 2011) and appear to actually remain valued by many political parties. As a minimum they do at least need to be counter-balanced by support for wider cosmopolitan conceptions of identities.

In the emerging world of interculturalism, the continuing development of social identities may well define the next decade. This is a highly contested area but states must be prepared to facilitate more multifaceted and dynamic identities that mirror the changes in financial, commercial and technological processes, and reflect this in the development of new democratic institutions.

There are some signs that a new pattern of social identities is already emerging, especially among younger people, and that the growth of mixed race or dual heritage identities is beginning to expose, in the most personal of terms, how present identities have become contrived and meaningless. Further, the development of complex hybrid or multiple identities will serve only to illustrate the commonalities rather than the differences between people.

None of this is to suggest that it is not important for people to want to hang on to their heritage (though there is a significant question about whether the state should have a role in this), but, rather, that there is an overwhelming need to invest more heavily in the development of identities that transcend national, faith and ethnic boundaries. We perhaps also need to take more radical steps. Richard Dawkins (2011), as part of his thesis 'The Tyranny of the Discontinuous Mind', suggests that perhaps now is the time that 'when an official invites us to tick a "race" or "ethnicity" box, I recommend crossing it out and writing "human" '. One could add that now is the time to cross out the many different choices coupled with the identities of origin, domicile and place and simply write 'global citizen'. This may be far-fetched in the current climate, but surely it is a legitimate aspiration and should form part of the vision of political and community leaders.

There is now a huge multiplicity of single identity groups (and the even greater number of mixed race/religion combinations) within what are now super diverse societies. Many of these are not recognised within the present ethnic monitoring arrangements with a whole series of generic groups, such as 'White', 'Muslim', 'Asian' or 'British' tending to dominate, with perhaps a 'write-in' category for the now many other identities. The huge variation of social and economic circumstance within such groups means that it no longer provides the most effective means of targeting disadvantage in practical terms. The process of ethnic monitoring (and flagging) of separate identities now need to be replaced with some new processes, which recognise the heterogeneity within communities and give rise to programmes that can tackle problems on a common and cross-cutting basis.

Secularism and governance in multifaith societies

Secularism is a key component of interculturalism. Diverse societies are also multifaith societies and the privileging of one faith group over another, or over people of non-faith, is clearly at odds with equality. However, secularism does not demand a society without religion. The visibility of faith and its presence in the public sphere is both an inevitable and desirable aspect of plural communities. Secularism, then, simply entails the separation of church and state institutions so that the system of governance, and especially the decision-making processes, in no way relies upon, nor privileges, faith-based views.

However, there is no absolute agreement about what is meant by 'secularism', with most definitions revolving around a separation of church and state, without any real clarity about the nature of that division. It is generally accepted that a secular society is one in which culture has become detached from religious doctrine and influence (see, for example, Berger, 1969), and Parekh (2009) reminds us of the early usages of the term, which relied upon the notion of the contrast between the 'immanency and time-boundedness of the modern world with the atemporality and eternal nature of the heavenly'. But Modood's attempts (2009) at a 'doctrine of separation' with more nuanced divisions based on 'radical' and 'moderate' models, is confused and confusing. And, the notion of a separation of state and church, in which 'citizens have full freedom to pursue their different values or practices in private, while in the public sphere all citizens would be treated as political equals whatever the differences in their private lives' (Malik, 2002), is too simplistic.

There is also no clear and accepted definition of what is meant by 'faith in the public realm' and a recent book devoted to the subject (Dinham et al., 2009) recognises its many different components, but does not offer a definitive view. Ratcliffe (2004) relates this to the way in which faith 'transcends the public–private divide, being intrinsic to the way people live their lives'. However, the notion of 'faith in the public realm' seems to owe more to its surprising 'political revitalisation' (Habermas, 2007), at a time when its decline seemed inevitable and science and rationality becoming ever more dominant parts of democratic debate. This 'political revitalisation' of faith is particularly evident in a number of Christian countries, especially the USA and also in many Muslim countries from Africa to the Far East, but the emergence of faith into the public realm is also apparent in many other countries, in Europe and elsewhere, even though religious beliefs and the extent of the practice of worship are in decline. This is the result of geo-political and other trends and especially the West's perception of a global threat posed by the Muslim community.

It is unfortunately true that a number of states, swept up in a tide of Islamophobic sentiment, have also compounded this perception and further confused the notion of a public/private divide by seeking to ban displays of faith from the public realm, especially those associated with Islam. This simplistic interpretation of the public nature of faith is based upon whether faith is 'visible', through the display of religious symbols. This might include the wearing of the cross or skull cap, or the various forms of head and face coverings for women. This is perhaps the most obvious form of public manifestation, but it is hardly central to the real issue of secularism and governance. The UK has long since taken a different view of such symbols to countries like France – in the UK they are generally valued as expressions of diversity and seen as part of culture and heritage alongside other forms of traditional dress, at least until the recent demonisation of Muslim minorities. In fact, the protection of religious dress in the public sphere was brought into legislation to accommodate minorities as long ago as 1976 when Sikhs were allowed to wear their turbans, rather than crash helmets, when riding a motorcycle. Of course, in some recent and perhaps exceptional cases, dress codes are a basis for division, and bans have been introduced on particular forms of clothing or accessories in the apparent interests of safety and/or communications. However, the target is not so much the emblems themselves as the oppositional views that they appear to represent.

It is therefore suggested, then, that what really matters, in terms of 'faith in the public realm' in the current context, is whether and how faith-based views are advanced, and contested, as part of the broader political dialogue. In a plural society, they form part of a more general and public discourse about national and international policies, as well as domestic and local issues. In one sense this is unproblematic and it is surely to be welcomed that people generally take an active interest in the public and political life of their community. It is almost inevitable that this activity will be supported by a greater display of the emblems of faith, and while these are generally only of personal and cultural significance, it is perhaps also inevitable that they then take on a political significance and are contested as part of that wider debate.

The real difficulty arises from the dissonance between faith-based views and expectations and the limited significance they obtain in the political realm. The reality is that Western democracies, which are now almost all multifaith societies, find it very difficult to take any account of faith-based arguments, let alone make decisions on such a basis. This is because to do so would, first, privilege one or more faiths over the views of other faiths or non-faiths, and, second, because the systems of governance in modern democracies increasingly have to justify the legitimacy of decision-making processes by reference to rational and legal processes with clear evidential standards which *no* belief system can hope to meet, whether or not faith-based.

The decision-making process is also impacted by the institutional arrangements in many states, which have often protected the dominant faith in some way. They have generally been protected by their historic position, often being granted formal status and constitutional privileges as well as becoming embedded into the social and cultural life of all citizens – for example, through institutional involvement in public ceremonies and the timing of holiday periods. Many of these remnants of a monocultural age are slowly disappearing but still give rise to accusations of preferential and privileged positions by other faiths.

The emergence of multifaith societies does not, however, create entirely new problems as a number of states have had to deal with long-standing divisions and conflicts between at least two principal faiths and have generally devised some form of pragmatic accommodation. In the UK, the division between Catholics and Protestants has been evident for 500 years and while this was to some extent resolved by pushing faith firmly into the private realm, it also entailed Anglicans retaining a limited privileged position over Catholics in relation to the governance system, which has lasted until the present day. This is of a relatively minor nature – royal lineage, representation in the House of Lords and so on – with discrimination in employment and other fields largely being dealt with some time ago. But the inherent unfairness and obvious injustice nevertheless remain a source of complaint and are only now being addressed.

The political salience of faith has come to the fore, at least in part due to globalisation, particularly as a result of the rise of diaspora communities. These are not entirely new (Soysal, 2000) and the UK, in common with many other European countries, has had a Jewish community – perhaps the longest-standing diaspora – for at least 800 years. But as Jonathan Sachs (2007) has pointed out, the modern diaspora communities have far more significance and find it easier to sustain themselves than ever before, largely because of the ease of modern transnational communications (Cantle, 2004). Any modern system of governance, then, has to take account of intrasociety pressures from faith and cultural groups and also from diaspora communities who transcend national boundaries and command support at many different levels. In other words, even those societies that have relatively small faith-based minorities, and where the majority faith is clearly predominant in the public sphere, are still potentially influenced by a multifaith world society.

The presence of faith in the public and political discourse does, however, give rise to some very particular problems. In the first instance, many faith beliefs have been protected by blasphemy laws and by cultural taboos. The emphasis therefore shifts to a dialogue based upon respect and understanding rather than one of contestation. This is inherent in those types of policies that emphasise the co-existence of faiths, as in the guidance created by the UK government, following consultation with faith and other bodies in 'Side by Side' (DCLG, 2008). However, the inevitable consequence of being more prominently in the public sphere is that faith arguments and the very foundations of those belief systems will increasingly have to accept a higher level of contestation, challenge and even ridicule – a price which faith organisations seem very reluctant to presently accept.

The central issue for democracies is, then, whether the system of governance is based upon any form of belief system, rather than clear and transparent empirical evidence and science. This is irrespective of whether the belief system is one that is faith-based, or based upon another form of moral or ethical code, or the particular beliefs of an individual leader or group. In a modern multifaith society, governmental decisions require a rational basis and this inevitably militates against those dictated by one or more faiths. This is partly because any decision based upon a particular belief system will potentially conflict with the beliefs of other faiths and groups who have adopted different moral and ethical codes and also because an evidence-based decision is the only means of ensuring equality of power and influence. And while the belief system of one group (usually the majority group) could be selected over that of others, the effect would clearly be to disenfranchise those of others and become the cause of tensions and conflict. Further, simply expressing, and acting upon, a belief that one course of action is preferred to another is no longer an acceptable justification for a decision. In a modern bureaucratic state, decisions are open to public and legal challenge if they have not been able to demonstrate a legitimatising process and a reasonable evidential standard. For example, they must show that the relevant consultations have taken place and been taken into account, that expected impacts have been considered, and that the evidence forms the basis of the decision. Nowhere is this more certain than in the criminal justice system, where to assert a belief that a person is guilty of a particular crime would be literally laughed out of court, and generally followed by a writ for slander. While the standards expected in the criminal justice system are higher and clearer, those obtaining in the political system are not far behind and are gradually being extended (largely through the judicial review and challenge).

None of this is to say that decisions cannot be based upon some notion of right and wrong and that this notion may have been influenced by religious beliefs. But in the first place, morality is not the sole preserve of the faith communities and second, few governmental decisions can now expect to be unchallenged if they simply assert that they wish to pursue a policy because they believe it to be right and will still require some assessment of impacts in more tangible forms. Other points of view will clearly have a different perspective of what is 'right' and some form of justification, based upon reason and evidence, will inevitably be necessary. For example, a prohibition of abortion based upon religious or moral rectitude would be contested by people of other faiths and no faith and, in order to arbitrate between such competing arguments and to avoid accusations of 'privileging', governments have to fall back on rational arguments. In this case, this might be based upon the age at which babies can survive outside the womb, the evidence of health impacts on the mother, or other documented benefits and disbenefits – in other words, an evidential and objective basis.

A modern multifaith society will inevitably develop notions of universal rights and responsibilities that transcend all faith and belief systems and often as a means of mediating between them. Faith and belief systems have given rise to many moral and ethical standards and have long since been incorporated into legal systems. The adoption of moral values based upon a notion of right and wrong that coincides with the beliefs of one or more faiths is not in itself problematic, providing that there is a consensus that can ensure some form of wider acceptability and that it has a rational basis – in other words, is not simply an 'act of faith'.

Our system of governance, of course, also extends to regional and local agencies, including local authorities. And faith bodies have a number of roles, which are connected to government but not necessarily a part of the governance arrangements. For example, many such bodies are funded to deliver public services and are thought to be able to offer higher standards in this respect as they can utilise committed volunteers and empathise with and understand the cultural sensitivities of their group. However, while this has been questioned as part of the criticism of 'single group funding' (CIC, 2007), there is a distinction between a service delivery role and that of policy-maker, albeit a fine one. This is perhaps most evident in the provision of faith schools, discussed earlier. They are generally charged with implementing education policy rather than making it – and are funded and regulated on this basis. However, at the margins they are able to determine a number of processes, particularly with regard to admissions and to providing religious instruction to students drawn largely from that faith community, as well as influencing the general ethos of the school. Church schools provided the first system of formal education in the UK and have been part of the state education system ever since; indeed, the state merely filled the gaps in their provision (Howard, 1987). They have since been continued without any serious thought, and have been extended to minority faiths because it would be clearly discriminatory not to do so rather than because of any political or popular support. They have come under pressure to widen access and to promote respect for other faiths (Cantle, 2001; Runnymede Trust, 2008) and have also been made subject to the duty to promote community cohesion (DCSF, 2007). However, their continued existence remains incompatible with a secular system of governance.

The debate about 'faith in the public sphere' should, therefore, revolve around the extent and nature of faith in our system of governance at all levels, in terms of either the reliance on belief systems as a justification for particular decisions, or whether one or more faiths has a privileged access to, or influence over, the organs of government as compared to other faiths or those of no faith. In a multifaith society no single faith or group of faiths should have a constitutional or practical advantage over another. Inevitably, any principal church will have to be disestablished, but the mere fact of establishment should not be taken to imply a continuing and wholly unacceptable level of advantage, given historic accommodations over time and ongoing reform. Similarly, modern democracies are built upon rational-legal decision-making processes and as this is set to become more and more manifest so policy-makers will find it increasingly difficult to cite value laden belief systems for justification and will have to be able to demonstrate an empirical and scientific evidence basis for decisions.

The right to hold and express religious views and to worship in accordance with that faith is a fundamental human right and is not under any threat from secularism. In this way – and judging from the continued and rising levels of faith in some parts of the world – it should remain in the public sphere and be part of the political and social discourse with visible emblems welcomed as another valued component of diversity. In this sense alone, no modern democracy can now ever be thought of as 'secular' society. Secularism of the political community, however, is a necessary component of interculturalism.

Responding to segregation and integration

As discussed in Chapter 6, segregation contributes to the entrenchment of attitudes and the intolerance and fear of the 'other'. But our notion of a segregated community has been too simplistic and has generally only been discussed in residential terms. The concept of parallel lives that emerged in 2001 (Cantle, 2001) began to change that approach and emphasised the compound effect of segregation in residential and other spheres. However, though there have been a number of attempts to describe a more nuanced approach through the 'layers of separation' in 2005 (Cantle, 2008), and a move away from 'the one or two dimensional lattice of spatial structures' towards considering the segregation in social environments (Fagiolo et al., 2007), there are very few measures or indicators which explore the various interrelationships between individuals and communities. For the most part, the studies have generally been highly localised and reactive and take little account of the new patterns of diversity. They also tend to focus on 'race', even though segregation can be identified at different levels for communities, based upon age, disability, faith, sexual orientation and social class (see Chapter 6).

Only in exceptional circumstances, and where community relations have broken down to the extent that tensions are manifest and conflict has resulted, has government intervened. A small number of measures have thus been taken to reduce segregation in the USA, the UK and other countries, but there has been a general presumption against intervention, based largely on the view that to promote integration would interfere with personal preferences and social and economic market forces. There is, therefore, little by way of established practice and professional competence. Where people live – and the nature of their neighbourhoods – does matter, even for national governments, which tend to be far removed from the local scale (Hiebert, 2009).

However, there is also no real positive vision for any form of mixed communities, in which people are still able to maintain their own heritage and support systems, perhaps with a significant degree of clustering, but in which the many different groups develop meaningful relationships, build understanding and avoid tensions and conflicts from emerging. The pretence that segregation is a natural phenomenon, resulting from the exercise of free choice, is untenable. The choice of housing is severely constrained by price, by concerns about safety and social and cultural acceptance. The choice of school is also determined by socio-economic position and by neighbourhood, and whether the governance is linked to specific communities. The workplace and occupation are also heavily influenced by social class and skill level, and in some instances by discrimination. Further, social and cultural networks are bounded by historic, faith, class and heritage positions.

Even if it were the case that choices were freely exercised, the state should surely be concerned about the underlying tendencies that motivate communities to associate exclusively, or mainly, with people from the same background. It simply serves to indicate a divided nation, based upon insular and fearful communities that neither wish, nor want, to relate to each other.

The focus of segregation has also been on minority communities, although it is clearly the case that more mixed communities are also dependent on the integration of White or majority areas. This has hardly received any attention, except in so far as some concern has been expressed about 'White Flight', though even the term has been challenged as it is, for some, suggestive of a 'failure of multiculturalism' (see Chapter 4). Any attempt at promoting more mixed communities – whether in educational, employment, cultural or residential terms – must involve all communities to gain a real commitment to creating diverse environments.

The scale of the task has been illustrated by Chair of the Equality and Human Rights Commission (EHRC) in relation to the development objectives for the London Thames Gateway area:

> Here we are, about to build one million homes in the South East without a clue as to what creates a mixed community. High density housing is increasing and there is evidence of increased segregation and different groups becoming more exclusive.
>
> (Phillips, 2006)

For the development of new communities, it might be expected that the plan would set some objectives and use a number of policy instruments, but it is clear that not only is there no real vision behind this, no serious thought has even been given to the idea. There is little by way of established practice or professional skills to assist in the process of creating a mixed development based upon a very specific understanding of the nature, design and use of shared spaces, let alone the social processes involved. But this is the challenge that lies ahead, as 'learning to live together' requires some degree of interaction and exchange and it is an iterative process where confidence is built upon successful experience and experimentation.

Once again 'race' has confounded sensible discussion and has played no part in a vision for more mixed communities, despite a clear understanding of the need for 'mixing' in relation to class. Cole and Goodchild (2001) point out that the notion of achieving 'mix' is hardly new and that the pursuit of 'social balance' featured prominently in earlier planning visions, such as Joseph Rowntree's New Earswick Village in York, Ebenezer Howard's Garden City movement and George Cadbury's Bourneville Village outside Birmingham. Moreover, in 1949 the health and housing minister, Aneurin Bevan, was only too willing to promote the idea that new post-war council housing should include a diverse mix of workers:

> ... it is entirely undesirable that on modern housing estates only one type of citizen should live. If we are to enable citizens to lead a full life, if they are each to be aware of the problems of their neighbours, then they should all be drawn from different sections of the community. We should try to introduce what was always the lovely feature of English and Welsh villages, where the doctor, the grocer, the butcher and the farm labourer all lived in the same street ... the living tapestry of a mixed community.
>
> (Aneurin Bevan, 1949, cited in Cole and Goodchild, 2001)

The 'mixed communities' of social class have been promoted in social housing development ever since (Berube, 2005) and have also featured in private owner-occupied housing estates, where planning policies have secured the inclusion of rented units. In respect of class, then, mixed communities are a legitimate aspiration, but in relation to 'race', no such vision has yet emerged, and the current *laissez faire* approach represents 'turning a blind eye to de facto segregation' (Cuperus, 2011).

The link between mixed communities and the equalities agenda is also generally ignored. While there is recognition that the 'fairest societies are those in which people share experiences and common ambitions whatever their racial, religious or cultural backgrounds ... to reassert the need for a society based on solidarity in which everyone's life chances are unaffected by what or where they were born' (Lownsbrough and Beunderman, 2007, p. 3), the absence of mixed communities clearly limits the possibilities for sharing of experiences. This does not simply depend upon the design of shared spaces, but also requires that they are used by all sections of the community as part of everyday experiences. The more equal the society, the more likely that people from different backgrounds will find themselves in the same factories and offices, places of learning, social and community centres and public spaces. Comparable levels of income will enable people from different backgrounds to buy or rent similar properties in the same area, participate in the same social and recreational activities and utilise the same employment and educational networks. There is then also a likelihood that social capital will be built around these more mixed networks. As Robert Putnam (2000) has outlined, shared places and spaces can play an important role in building strong community ties and networks of social support and reciprocity and while the debate about social capital in this context rightly emphasises 'bridging' social capital between different groups, it is the 'linking' social capital which connects individuals to wider opportunities and is more crucial for equalising life opportunities.

As Varshney (2002) has pointed out, interaction is not sufficient if this simply entails people from different backgrounds passing each other in the street, using the same public transport, or frequenting the same shops. This is superficially a mixed community, in which a process of engineering more meaningful dialogue would need to be devised in order to break down the barriers between communities and build up the necessary trust and understanding. Similarly, with regard to Helsinki, Comedia (2010) have pointed out that too many people in that city who consider themselves to be open to diversity regard 'tolerance' between citizens of different ethnic background to be a satisfactory and ultimate goal, but 'such "benign indifference" is simply not good enough'.

A process of ongoing evaluation of relationships is required to provide pointers to the way in which people currently relate and to provide interesting and enticing opportunities to enable them to engage. This has to be done at different levels to reflect the domains of segregation and integration suggested earlier (see Chapter 6) and, while it is not in itself a difficult task, few societies have deemed it necessary to consider interpersonal and intercommunal relationships in this depth and there is little by way of development of the necessary professional skills. Further, the scale and nature of the interventions will be contextualised, with some benefiting from structural changes, for example, to challenge the segregation in schools and workplaces, rather than continuing with manufactured programmes of engagement on a long-term basis to compensate for the lack of interaction which might be expected in more mixed communities.

Reviews of the use of public spaces are also rare and there is again little by way of established practice and professional competence to draw upon.

The Intercultural City project, established by Comedia and supported by the Joseph Rowntree Foundation (Wood, 2004) has led, however, to the development of a number of pilot projects and reports, and, in particular, tries to reflect the connection between spaces and intercultural activity:

> The intercultural city concept is based on the premise that in the multicultural city we acknowledge and ideally celebrate our differing cultures. In the intercultural city we move one step beyond and focus on what we can do together as diverse cultures in shared space to create greater wellbeing and prosperity.
>
> (Auckland City Council, 2006)

However, another approach is to develop interaction around the various nodes or points of communication and to ensure that access and interaction take place within them. Lownsbrough and Beunderman (2007) suggest that the 'search for spaces of comfort in relatively homogeneous microcommunities is becoming increasingly popular' and, in common with the way in which nation-states have come under pressure from separatist movements suggest that at a local level there is a similar retreat from the shared realms of the community. They also suggest that the number of public spaces is dwindling because of the reduced role of the public sector and that many public spaces now have implicit barriers to entry that diminish their truly public character. Even if these spaces are 'public' they may not be 'civil' and are not conducive to lingering and exchange.

Lownsbrough and Beunderman's research focuses on the potentiality of these spaces and has identified eight main types, which cut across each other as they are defined by the activity taking place within them. Their proposed categorisation of public spaces is:

- Exchange spaces – for people to interact in their local area, during the pursuit of their everyday needs.
- Productive spaces – used by people engaged in activities to create, or grow, products and goods for everyday use.
- Spaces of service provision – for services run both by the state and the voluntary and community sectors.

- Activity spaces – for the provision of leisure activities for different age groups, which can be another point of contact.
- Democratic/participative spaces – for engagement and participative activities in any aspect of governance and citizenship.
- Staged spaces – which can emphasise the symbolism and public culture.
- In-between spaces – which are between segregated and bounded areas, which can be brought back into shared use.
- Virtual spaces – which can be developed into more meaningful exchanges than the general impersonal use of the internet and global communications.

(Lownsbrough and Beunderman, 2007)

The categories of space do present a range of opportunities for positive interactions ranging from 'everyday and banal' encounters, to functional engagement and to celebratory and participative interaction. But the central aim, according to Lownsbrough and Beunderman, is to understand how they work as trusted spaces and that interaction is 'fostered' rather than promoted within them – in other words using an indirect approach that embraces innovation and creativity.

The Helsinki 'intercultural city' report (Comedia, 2010) provides details of the varied ways in which some of these cities have developed their own intercultural programmes:

London Borough of Lewisham, England

This project focused on local development studies and master planning techniques from an intercultural perspective, exploring ways that intercultural thinking can enhance and develop the public realm in order to better meet the needs of an increasingly diverse community. In recognition of its rich and evolving cultural diversity Lewisham wishes to develop a new intercultural sense of place through more culturally appropriate processes of consultation and planning. The study explored consultation strategies and techniques to engage new partnerships and intermediaries in order to improve Council's understanding of its diverse communities.

Oslo, Norway

The case study in Oslo, Norway, investigated the critical success-factors for the contribution of ethnic diversity to economic development and the creation of value. The research explored areas of current economic activity to establish where there was intercultural innovation and to what extent local intercultural agents and networks have the capacity to support an intercultural creative milieu.

Brammen, Norway

Also in Norway a case study was commissioned in the city of Brammen to explore ethnic diversity and entrepreneurship. The aim was to develop a better understanding of the social, economic and cultural capital of immigrants and examine how the immigrants' potential for innovation and entrepreneurship may be developed and brought to use in the community.

Logan, Australia

In the Queensland city of Logan the major focus of the *Intercultural City* case study was on the spatial, social and economic dynamics of settlement and population distribution across the suburbs of Logan. The study considered to what extent intercultural mixing rather than clustering assists or hinders the development of a sense of belonging in Logan by ethnic minorities. The study also sought to understand what the conditions are that have encouraged migrants to settle throughout Logan rather than gather in geographic/cultural clusters.

Auckland, New Zealand

The aim of this study was to better understand how an intercultural approach contributes to economic, cultural, and social wellbeing. In economic terms this means considering how diversity contributes to innovation, creativity and entrepreneurship. In social and cultural terms the study investigated how diversity influences the conditions that encourage intercultural networks, the benefits of cross-cultural activity and how an intercultural approach can sit alongside the bicultural approach.

(Comedia, 2010)

And in respect of the Helsinki Report:

It finds that Helsinki has been highly successful in some aspects of international competitiveness and attractiveness (its technological assimilation and innovation, tolerance, good governance, education, public services and business environment); but lags behind international good practice in other regards (language barrier, insularity of the labour market and of professional and social networks, an excessively functional and sanitized physical environment and a lack of diversity of lifestyles and opportunities).

It warns that the city cannot afford to be complacent. The freshness and optimism that the city's new diversity now engenders could, in a generation or less, degrade into a sullen stand-off between mutually uncomprehending groups and could see Helsinki marginalised in the network of competitive and cosmopolitan cities.

(Comedia, 2010)

In more functional, though no less important, terms a great deal can be done to remove the barriers to the different levels of integration. These largely revolve around the institutional arrangements referred to in Chapter 6, particularly in the spheres of education, employment, criminal justice and polity. These are more generally seen in terms of the rights agenda and are inextricably tied to the prevention of discrimination and the promotion of equality of opportunity. It is not intended to rehearse all such measures here (discussed in Cantle, 2008, pp. 174–178), other than to emphasise the need for a clear framework of rights which is shared by both the majority and minority communities and to suggest some further priorities.

In particular, and as suggested by Mason (2010), access to and use of the polity is a key area of entitlement and the exercising of rights and responsibilities can only be done as part of a dialogue with others, directly or indirectly. Newcomers should be given the right to vote in local elections as a means of recognising their de facto local citizenship. They pay local taxes as part of their rent, or as a local property tax, incur energy and other charges for utilities and enjoy the same use of local facilities, such as local parks and schools for their children. They are, in effect, in the same position as existing service users and do not need a broader understanding of national history or institutions to contribute. Voting in national elections would remain as a condition of citizenship. Taking part in political and civic discussions would help with the process of developing a common understanding and contribute to shared values. It would also encourage people to act as individuals, rather than come to rely upon 'gatekeeper' community leaders.

The promotion of a common language, or languages, is also a key issue. A common language is essential to political integration and also to equality of opportunity within the labour market. Languages also help to provide cultural integration, through the use of idioms and humour and the common enjoyment of literature, television and film. A common language does not require the elimination of minority languages and there is no reason why their continuation should not be encouraged and fostered as part of a broader programme to celebrate and promote diversity. The common language, like a common identity, can augment rather than undermine other ideas about identity. When the suggestion of a common language requirement was first mooted in the UK as part of a broader programme of community cohesion in 2001 (Cantle, 2001) it was contentious, but soon gained support and is now generally accepted. Nevertheless, the programmes for 'English for Speakers of Overseas Languages' (ESOL), which were introduced to help people to learn English, have remained under-funded and fragmented.

Insistence on a particular language, though, may be controversial in some contexts. For example, in francophone Quebec Province it has proved difficult as a significant minority of citizens are in fact native English speakers and form part of a broader English-speaking majority in Canada as a whole. Following a provincial government review (Bouchard and Taylor, 2008), the 'institution of French as a common public language' has been judged as a 'legitimate contextual precedence' by its supporters (Bouchard, 2011). However, this could easily be regarded as assimilationist, rather than accommodating, given that all migrants, even those that are English speakers, are required to send their children to the French-speaking schools, rather than use available places in English-speaking schools.

This gives rise to consideration of a more general principle of whether it is justified for a predominant or majority culture to protect its own cultural interests and history, through its institutional arrangements. This may be particularly topical in relation to newer migrant groups, but is also relevant to many states where the privileging of the majority community over established and long-standing minority communities has subsisted for many hundreds of years. These matters generally revolve around language, history and faith – especially how faith is expressed and recognised.

Bouchard (2011) ponders how to preserve the present French culture in Quebec in the face of the wider and pervasive anglophone Canadian culture by which Quebec residents are clearly also influenced, and the variety and number of newer migrants who bring their own cultures, and have a more universal cultural expression. In considering what aspects of French culture can be 'legitimately' preserved and protected, he suggests the following:

- the institution of French as the common public language;
- allocating a prominent place to the teaching of the francophone past in history courses, or, in other words, a national memory that is inclusive but gives predominance to the majority narrative;
- the current priority position given to the presentation of Christian religions in the new course on ethics and religious culture;
- the official burials of heads of state in Catholic churches;
- keeping the cross on the Quebec flag (which has already been subject to challenges);
- laying Christmas decorations in public squares or buildings; and
- the sounding of bells in Catholic churches at various moments throughout the day.

On the other hand, he considers the following to be 'abusive extensions of the principle of ad hoc precedence' for the majority culture:

- keeping a cross on the wall of the National Assembly and in public courtrooms;
- the recitation of prayers at municipal council meetings;
- the funding of chaplain or Catholic pastoral care positions in public hospitals with state funds, to the exclusion of other religions;
- the general prohibition against wearing religious signs for all employees in the public and semi-public sectors;
- the reference to the supremacy of God in the preamble of the *Canadian Charter of Rights and Freedoms*;
- including articles or clauses in a charter that establish a formal hierarchy between the cultural majority and minorities; and
- the prohibition against wearing a burka in streets and public places (except for security or other compelling reasons).

In many ways this is a very prosaic list, though these dimensions of language, faith and history are clearly tantamount to 'core values' and can come to represent some fundamental concerns about the loss of identity and culture. Very similar issues to those described by Bouchard, which again touch upon underlying and more fundamental concerns, could be created in most other Western nations, though the precise nature of issues will vary from country to country. The 'negotiations' over legitimacy and entitlement are, however, situated in the context of majority nations attempting to cling to some semblance of their past and present

conceptions of themselves, faced with the 'threat' of change from globalisation in general and their migrants, in particular, who embody that
change. The starting point is, therefore, not one which is forward-
looking, nor based upon questions like 'how can we live together in
a increasingly interdependent and interconnected world?' And it is not
positioned around 'how can we make this work for us?', but rather, 'how
can we hold back the forces of change?'

There is also some irony in Bouchard's list as it continues to invoke
faith (and the cultural expression of faith) as a dividing line between
majority and minority communities, even though this has changed
profoundly in recent years and the majority's religious observance has
continued to decline significantly. Language has suddenly become the
new cultural marker to which the majority are advised to cling, and
is overtaking that of faith – an evolutionary process that could not be
stopped by governmental lines in the sand. Change has affected all
communities and a model of interculturalism needs to recognise that
cultural developments are not simply based upon an iterative process
between majority and minority, nor are they confined to changes within
the borders of any one country. Clinging to a static concept of culture is
not an option in a globalised world.

Much of the more recent discussion about segregation has been based
upon a perception of distinct and separate values for each community
and, generally, the perception of the failure of the minority community
to integrate and accept national values (Cameron, 2011; Merkel, 2010;
Sarkozy, 2011), and is a view strongly promulgated by the Far Right who
now seek to emphasise cultural distinctiveness (Goodwin, 2011a). This
has been given new impetus by the counter-terrorism work in many
countries which have focused on their Muslim communities and, unfortunately, both hardened internal Muslim identities and created a wider
perception of their 'otherness' (House of Commons Communities and
Local Government Select Committee, 2010). However, the promotion
of 'common values' has also featured in a number of previous proposals to create a shared identity (Denham, 2001) and has been a feature
of those national identity campaigns that have attempted to create a
strong sense of nationhood and to undermine separatist movements,
for example, with regard to 'Britishness' and Scottish independence.

However, as noted earlier, the state is itself sometimes responsible
for the creating and sustaining of separate identities (which might be
termed 'state multiculturalism', after Cameron (2011)), where specific
funding regimes and privileged representation have heightened these
differences and created more rigid identities that are resistant to change.

Unfortunately, the state has also had great difficulty in promoting any real sense of common values, partly because there is no real agreement about what they actually are and values such as 'freedom of speech', 'equality before the law' and the 'belief in tolerance and fairness' are universal, rather than country-specific, values. Community cohesion programmes have had more success in developing a 'common vision' and a 'sense of belonging' (Cantle, 2008, pp. 178–186), but this has been heavily based upon localised approaches, and an understanding about everyday 'ways of doing things around here'.

Even less has been done to promote common values at an international level, or to try to create a sense of global citizenship. As with any set of national common values, a top-down process may well prove to be difficult to sustain, but there are signs of a growing voluntary and bottom-up process which is sponsoring horizontal forms of leadership and identity. In an era of the democratisation of knowledge through the internet and global communications and the emergence of transnational social media, national boundaries may come to mean very little, as the recent events of the 'Arab Spring' and the *indignados* in the Europe protest movement has clearly shown. The Public Interest Research Centre (2010) which is supported by a number of influential NGOs, including Oxfam, World Wildlife Fund and Action for Children, are beginning to provide new approaches. They suggest that the 'prioritising of intrinsic values, such as freedom, creativity and self-respect, or equality and unity with nature, concern about social justice, environmentally-friendly behaviours, and lower levels of prejudice' is more beneficial than 'extrinsic values – such as wealth, or preservation of public image' – as they tend to undermine levels of personal wellbeing.

The Think Global (2011) organisation, which is supported by 230 groups, mainly NGOs and educational bodies, believe that new global values will emerge as a result of citizens from different countries working on common and pressing issues:

We live in an interdependent and globalised world. Collectively we face a range of challenges – inequality and poverty; climate change; racial and religious intolerance. And the future poses new issues that we cannot yet predict.

We will meet these challenges through the power and creativity of an engaged public which is open to learning new ways of thinking and responding to a changing world. Change will not come about solely through the efforts of a government or non-governmental organisations. Catalysing this citizen movement requires us to learn about the global challenges we face, our interdependence and our power to effect change.

(Development Education Association, 2010)

Other organisations, like Playing for Change,[3] are also trying to effect more global connectivity. It is a multimedia movement created to inspire, connect and bring peace to the world through music, and is based on a belief that: 'no matter whether people come from different geographic, political, economic, spiritual or ideological backgrounds, music has the universal power to transcend and unite us as one human race'. However, these are small scale and limited initiatives.

Segregation and integration have to be given new and more nuanced understandings. Breaking down segregation, or promoting integration, can be advanced in many different ways and at different levels, without endangering existing conceptions of ourselves. This enables new identities to be added to existing ones, creating layers and multifaceted forms which will also continue to change and evolve over time and in different contexts. However, in an intercultural world, these have to be seen in an entirely new global context in which transnational connectivity will begin to describe global values. But change does have to be facilitated, made stimulating and exciting at best and non-threatening, at worst. It has to be developed positively and proactively to counter the impact of globalisation which is often perceived as a threat to insular communities, who are encouraged to believe that it is possible to gain some protection by a further 'hunkering down' and putting up of barriers to others.

The development of cultural navigational skills and intercultural competences

In order to cope with the fear of difference and to begin to regard diversity as an opportunity rather than a threat, people need time to adjust and to benefit from educational and experiential learning opportunities. This activity is, in any case, a constant and everyday experience to some degree. 'Others' are either observed or viewed through the TV, internet and other communication channels, or learned about in schools, through literature and film media. In more mixed areas there are many more possibilities through everyday banal contact in the streets, shops and transport, in integrated workplaces and schools. This may only represent 'benign indifference and not necessarily entail an intercultural experience' (Comedia, 2010) and as Varshney (2002) has warned this may be of little value if communal tensions increase. Also, contact theorists have noted, the circumstances in which exchange takes place must be conducive to the building of reciprocity and trust, or relationships might decline rather than improve.

In wider society, a great deal can be done by government agencies and NGOs to develop an appreciation of other nations, ethnic groups and faiths. This can take the form of 'openness' as suggested by Clark (2008), in which there is a constant effort to provide international festivals and events and to try to create an investment framework that is not antipathetic to foreigners. The general climate of opinion can, of course, be influenced by political leaders and bellicose and nationalistic statements may 'play well' with particular sections of the majority community, though these are hardly conducive to the wider unity of nations and run contrary to the style of leadership advocated above. The World Bank has concluded, 'from an extensive body research on social capital', that:

> Social cohesion manifests in individuals who are willing and able to work together to address common needs, overcome constraints, and consider diverse interests. They are able to resolve differences in a civil, non-confrontational way.
>
> (The World Bank, 2010)

Globalisation and super diversity represents a real challenge to the way that populations now relate to each other and that will continue to change as the composition and movement of people continues to evolve. The development of another layer of identity – in the form of a cosmopolitan, or global citizenship conception – must now be gradually added to the already growing complexity of personal identity, if further tensions and conflicts are to be minimised. Nations need to begin to invest in the development of cultural navigation skills to enable citizens to acquire the ability to explore other identities and build the ability to understand and embrace other cultures.

There is a particular and evident need to target younger people who will also need such skills to compete in an ever more competitive employment and business market:

> What global companies look for are people who we think can take a global perspective. Students are well placed to do this if they have taken opportunities to widen their cultural perspective. The people

that succeed can work in multi-disciplinary, multi-cultural and multi-locational teams. If students have demonstrated they can work with other cultures and teams, that's a big plus for us as we need students to be intellectually curious and culturally agile if they are going to work in a global context.

(Sonja Stockton, Director, Talent, PricewaterhouseCoopers;
British Council and Think Global, 2010)

Indeed, opinion polls of business leaders suggest that they are more likely to recognise the growing need in this respect and believe that governments have been too slow to respond and have failed to prepare young people in the UK for our globalised world. Three-quarters of board and director level executives and CEOs think that young people 'are in danger of being left behind by emerging countries unless they learn to think more globally' and a similar proportion are 'worried that many young people's horizons are not broad enough to operate in a globalised and multicultural economy'. Further, they believe that the UK will be 'left behind by fast growing emerging countries such as China, India and Brazil unless young people learn to think more globally' (British Council and Think Global, 2010). Employability skills are vital in business success and as the economy becomes ever more globalised, global employability skills will be one of the crucial determinants of business success and economic growth.

More general internationally orientated educational and experiential learning opportunities are vital and the curriculum of schools is in urgent need of reform to reflect this. Unfortunately the current trend is very much in the opposite direction in the UK at least, with a greater focus on national history and the 'national story' to try to engender a stronger sense of national identity and solidarity. This may well be desirable, but on its own is an inappropriate response to globalisation. National identity is not challenged by an additional and global conception of the nation or ourselves, they are complementary. This suggests that the emphasis of formal education should be on the building of an understanding of common world history and culture – and on the building of a common world future – rather than on narrow nationalism. The essential task here is not simply learning sympathetically about others, but, as Gundara (2000) suggests, it is about 'how education can help in the task of developing cohesive civil societies by turning notions of singular identities into those of multiple ones, and by developing a shared and common value system and public culture'.

The UK government is apparently out of step with more general public opinion and polls suggest that as many as 86 per cent of the public believe that young people should learn about global issues in schools, according to research conducted by Ipsos MORI (Think Global, 2011). In fact, the public has generally been supportive of intercultural learning programmes, which to date have often been small-scale, underfunded and time-limited, usually implemented only in response to some form of tension or conflict. The emerging practice in the UK has largely been led by voluntary organisations, most of whom are very localised and small (ABCs at iCoCo, 2009). Many of the public-service providers have failed to include intercultural learning programmes or 'bridging' within their main programmes and do not position this activity as part of their corporate strategy and targets, even though it is clearly fundamental to service delivery and equality work.

As with the development of interaction competences, professional bodies generally lack the necessary skills and have had insufficient training to overcome the reluctance to engage in what is a relatively new area of expertise. While some voluntary organisations have gradually extended their work and built expertise in this area, possibly as a simple development of their everyday work within their community, professional bodies have been slow to respond to the new agenda. A review of professional development in 143 organisations, mainly connected to the built environment, found that knowledge and skills development in respect of cohesion and sustainability was 'disappointing' (iCoCo, 2007). This notion of 'cultural literacy' is seen as a 'vital skill', especially for those in the planning and built environment professions, but while methodologies for development have been set out (Brecknock, 2006), these have not yet filtered through to practice. More worrying, those professions specifically charged with 'promoting community cohesion' through learning processes are also under-equipped, with the teaching profession generally failing to equip new teachers, let alone existing ones, with the confidence to teach in multicultural schools (Ajegbo, 2007). Indeed, as Gundara (2001) has noted, education systems in most parts of the world have not come to terms with the educational implications of the reality of the range of heterogeneity in societies.

Some resistance is also apparent in voluntary agencies, particularly those single-identity groups who are themselves reluctant to engage with others, as they see it as a threat to their own identity and argue that building confidence in one's own identity is a prerequisite of learning about others. This often amounts to no more than creating a defensive boundary around a narrow conception of that identity and is based on a predetermined and traditional back-to-our-roots type process which positions the exploration of other identities as oppositional. Identities are, in any event, only formed by others – we define ourselves by what we are not, not by what we are, simply because the salient points of our own identity are socially defined and 'historically contingent and inherently relational' (Sandercock, 2004). The point of exploration of other identities is to change and to develop empathy with others, which can only be done if we embrace some part of their identity in addition, rather than as an alternative, to our own.

A number of communities have already erected strong cultural barriers and are not only unwilling to engage in intercultural exchange, but advise their members against everyday contact and experiences. The patterns of leadership may also militate against interaction and depend upon a high level of identity politics. However, the strongest cultural barrier is generally towards intermarriage and can be fiercely opposed, sometimes by barely legitimate means. The opposition to intermarriage is such that there is a fear of any form of intercultural contact, lest it develop into a more permanent relationship.

The practice of voluntary agencies, like that of the main public service providers, will also need to be developed and a higher level of confidence and competence is essential. Impact assessments are still rudimentary and while some intercultural work is now properly measured, programmes often rely upon anecdotal evidence and the views of other stakeholders, such as the police or faith and community leaders. The impacts cited are often of a general nature in relation to quality of life issues, such as crime and anti-social behaviour and making people feel more comfortable or good about their local area, rather than specific prejudice reduction measures. Public agencies and voluntary organisations also often seem to operate in isolation, perhaps confined to one area or based upon one community, without alignment with other groups and to wider initiatives. As a consequence, they may deal with one area of division without establishing a wider acceptance of difference. For example, a scheme based on race or faith difference may ignore sexual orientation, or those that focus on young people in schools may be undone by other more negative forces among parents and the wider community. In this sense, they could not be said to be promoting interculturality despite a clear process based on ICD principles. Many schemes are also not connected to a wider strategy and may fail to promote a sense of belonging, tackle inequalities or promote the value of diversity more generally. These difficulties have been recognised in practice:

Cities that wish to realise the full advantage of openness and diversity need to pursue a dynamic policy agenda based upon active engagement and cooperation between people in education, neighbourhoods, public space and the economy.

These trends will have powerful impacts on the desirable qualities in individuals and on the culture of organizations and how they need to work affecting the private and community sectors and public administrations alike. The mental dispositions and skills required to be successful and rising to the fore more strongly include communication ability, collaborative interdisciplinary working, cultural literacy and lateral and holistic thinking. These require openness. In organizational terms it means far more integrated working, the capacity to value the combined insights of different disciplines and the need to operate as task oriented teams as distinct from operating in silos.

(Comedia, 2010)

The development of intercultural competence is, then, at an early stage, though some initial programmes have had good, clear measurable impacts. The nature and scale of what is now required, however, is at a significantly higher level. People need to be encouraged to learn about others, within their local, national and international communities. Practices which seek to hold this back and promote static and singular forms of identity need to be challenged. Schools, colleges, workplaces and community organisations should promote intercultural dialogue and a wider societal interculturalism, based on inclusion and openness. Opportunities need to be made available, in particular, for insular, segregated and closed communities and they need to be resourced on a disproportionate basis. Professional development should be facilitated for public agencies, voluntary organisations and employers, to give them the technical skills and the confidence to be able to promote an intercultural environment. However, they cannot succeed without the support of a style of leadership which encourages more cosmopolitan forms of identity, and constantly search for wider engagement with, and a better understanding of, others. Similarly, this will require the support of an independent and secular system of governance that permits freedom of faith and expression in the public sphere and values and promotes belonging for the many dimensions diversity. Most of all, the development of intercultural competences will need to be part of a wider culture of openness which welcome those dynamic forms of identity that can constantly remake themselves in response to the ongoing process of globalisation.

Interculturalism, is more than a simple set of policies and pro-grammes. As one of the 'intercultural city' reports points out 'it is about changing mindsets, creating new opportunities across cultures [...] to support intercultural activity [...] it's about thinking, planning and acting interculturally' (Auckland City Council, 2006). Perhaps, more importantly still, it is about envisioning the world as we want it to be, rather than determined by our separate past histories.

Notes

2 Globalisation and 'Super Diversity'

1. On 15 October 2011 the *'indignados'* inspired an international day of protest, with demonstrations in around 90 countries to promote global change to combat the way in which 'the ruling powers work for the benefit of just a few, ignoring the will of the vast majority and the human and environmental price we all have to pay … it is up to us, the people, to decide our future. We are not goods in the hands of politicians and bankers who do not represent us' (http://15october.net/).
2. 'Labour' refers to the British Labour Party.
3. Tariq Ramadan published his 'Manifesto for a new "we"' as 'an appeal to the Western Muslims and their fellow citizens' on 7 July 2006.

3 Reforming the Notion of Identity

1. The song *Melting Pot* was released in the UK in 1969 and performed by Blue Mink and later by Culture Club.
2. The Prevent programme has been revised over the years; this version sets out the programme prior to the changes discussed in this chapter.

4 The 'Failure' of Multiculturalism

1. This approach is still evident as a 'knee jerk' reaction to communal politics, for example the response to a further outbreak of Scottish sectarianism in April 2011 resulted in an attempt to ban internet hate messages, rather than deal with underlying causes of intolerance and conflict.
2. See http://www.cic.gc.ca/english/multiculturalism/citizenship.asp.
3. Alastair Campbell, Prime Minister Blair's director of strategy and communications, intervened in an interview with *Vanity Fair* magazine to prevent the prime minister from answering a question about his Christianity. 'We don't do God,' Mr Campbell said (May, 2003). In February 2012, however, Sayeeda Warsi, a minister in the Cameron government has suggested that her government does 'do God' in a speech in the Vatican City.
4. For a full discussion of the development, policy and practice of community cohesion see Cantle (2008).
5. Margaret Thatcher famously used the word 'swamping' in 1978 and so too did David Blunkett, the then Labour home secretary, in 2002. More recently David Cameron's reference to the 'failure of multiculturalism' was claimed as support for the EDL who were mounting a protest on the day following his announcement at the Munich conference in February 2011.

5   The Contribution of 'Community Cohesion'

1. This duty was introduced by the Education and Inspections Act 2006 and became operational in 2007.
2. For a full discussion of 'the journey to community cohesion', see Cantle (2008). Revised and updated edition 2008.
3. In the first official report into the UK riots in August 2011 (Riots, Communities and Victims Panel, 2011), a 'link between deprivation and rioting' was only established in the sense that 'Our unique analysis shows that 70 per cent of those brought before the courts were living in the 30 per cent most deprived postcodes in the country.' (However, those 'brought before the courts' may have not been the same as those taking part in the riots, as the police were more likely to arrest people who were already known to them.)
4. The early Race Relations legislation did include duties to promote 'good relations', particularly between immigrants and the host community, but these were largely ignored – see Cantle (2008), pp. 38–40.

6   Segregation and Integration – And Why They Matter

1. Facebook alone apparently has over 700 million members, with suggestions that it could reach 1 billion in a few years.

7   Interculturalism: Conceptualisation

1. View programme at www.bridgingcultures.org.uk.
2. http://www.cic.gc.ca/english/multiculturalism/citizenship.asp.
3. http://www.coe.int/interculturalcities.
4. http://opencities.britishcouncil.org/web/index.php?home_en.
5. http://www.oecd.org/document/25/0,3746,en_36734052_36761863_369524 73_1_1_1_1,00.html.

8   Interculturalism: Policy and Practice

1. http://opencities.britishcouncil.org/web/index.php?home_en.
2. http://www.luton.gov.uk/harmony.
3. http://playingforchange.com/.

Bibliography

ABCS at iCoCo (2009) *Guidance for Applicants* (Coventry: iCoCo).

Abrams, D. (2010) *Processes of Prejudice: Theory, Evidence and Intervention* (London: EHRC).

Adler, R.D. (2008) *Counting on the Middle Class* (Santa Barbara, CA: Miller-McCune).

Adonis, A. and Pollard, S. (1997) *A Class Act: The Myth of Britain's Classless Society* (London: Hamish Hamilton).

Adorno, T.W. *et al.* (1950) *The Authoritarian Personality* (New York: Harper and Row).

Agg, C. (2006) *Trends in Government Support for Non-Governmental Organizations: Is the "Golden Age" of the NGO Behind Us? Civil Society and Social Movements Programme* (Geneva: This United Nations Research Institute for Social Development (UNRISD)).

Ajegbo, Sir K. (2007) *Diversity and Citizenship* (London: Department for Education and Skills).

Ali, S. (2003) *Mixed-Race, Post-Race: Gender, New Ethnicities and Cultural Practices* (New York: Berg Publishers).

Alibhai-Brown, Y. (2009) 'Writing' *The Independent*, Saturday, 22 August 2009.

Allport, G. W. (1954) *The Nature of Prejudice* (Cambridge, MA: Addison Wesley).

Anie, A., Daniel, N., Tah, C. and Petruckevitch, A. (2005) *An Exploration of Factors Affecting the Successful Dispersal of Asylum Seekers* (London: On Line Report for the Home Office).

Association of Chief Police Officers (2010) *Total of Recorded Hate Crime from Regional Forces in England, Wales and Northern Ireland During the Calendar Year 2009*. Available online at: www.acpo.police.uk/asp/policies/Data/084a_Recorded_Hate_Crime_-_January_to_December_2009.pdf.

Association of London Government (ALG) (2006) *Choice Based Lettings and Pan-London Mobility: The Aspirations of Tenants and Applicants, and Their Impact for Marketing Choice Based Lettings and Mobility* (London: ALG).

Auckland City Council (2006) *Intercultural City – Making the Most of Diversity. Auckland Case Study* (Auckland: Auckland City Council).

Balderston, S. and Roebuck, E. (2010) *Empowering People to Tackle Hate Crime* (London: EHRC).

Baldwin, C., Chapman, C. and Gray, Z. (2007) *Minority Rights: The Key to Conflict Prevention* (London: Minority Rights Group International).

Bartlett, J., Birdwell, J. and King, M. (2010) *The Edge of Violence* (London: Demos).

Beck, U. (2002) 'The Cosmopolitan Society and Its Enemies' *Theory, Culture & Society*, 19(1–2), 17–44.

Bell, D. (1987) 'The World and the United States in 2013' *Daedalus*, 116(3), 1–31.

Berger, P. (1969) *The Social Reality of Religion* (London: Faber and Faber).

Berube, A. (2005) *Mixed Communities in England: A US Perspective on Evidence and Policy Prospects* (York: Joseph Rowntree Foundation).

Biggs, M. and Knauss, S. (2011) 'Explaining Membership in the British National Party: A Multilevel Analysis of Contact and Threat' *European Sociological Review* Forthcoming (Oxford: OUP).

Billig, M. (1995) *Banal Nationalism* (London: Sage).

Blackaby, B. (2004) *Community Cohesion and Housing. A Good Practice Guide* (Coventry: Chartered Institute of Housing and the Housing Corporation).

Bloomfield, J. and Bianchini, F. (2004) *Planning for the Intercultural City* (Stroud: Comedia).

Blunkett, D. (2004) *New Challenges for the Race Equality and Community Cohesion in the 21 Century, Speech to the Institute of Public Policy Research, 7 July 2004* (London: Home Office).

Bouchard, G. (2011) 'What Is Interculturalism?' *McGill Law Journal* 56(2), 435–468.

Bouchard, G. and Taylor, C. (2008) *Building the Future: A Time for Reconciliation*, Report of the Consultation Commission on Accommodation Practices Related to Cultural Differences (Quebec: Gouvernement, du Québec).

Brah, A. (1996) *Cartographies of Diaspora: Contesting Identities* (London: Routledge).

Brah, A. (2007) 'Non-Binarized Identities of Similarity and Difference' in *Identity, Ethnic Diversity and Community Cohesion*. Wetherell M., Lafleche M. and Berkeley R., Eds (London: Sage).

Brecknock, R. (2006) *More Than Just a Bridge: Planning and Designing Culturally* (Bournes Green: Comedia).

British Council (2010) http://opencities.britishcouncil.org/web/index.php?home_en

British Council (BC)/Institute of Community Cohesion (iCoCo) (2009) *Intercultural Dialogue Resource Guide*. Available online at: http://www.cohesioninstitute.org.uk/Resources/Toolkits/InterculturalDialogue.

British Council and Migration Policy Group (2011) *Migrant Integration Policy Index (MIPEX)* (Brussels: British Council and Migration Policy Group).

British Council and Think Global (2010) *The Global Skills Gap – Preparing Young People for the New Global Economy* (London: British Council and Think Global).

British Social Attitudes No. 28 (2011) *Private Schools and Public Divisions: The Influence of Fee-Paying Education on Social Attitudes* (London: National Centre for Social Research).

Brynin, M., Longhi, S. and Martinez Perez, A. (2008) 'The Social Significance of Homogamy' in *Changing Relationships*. Ermisch J. and Brynin M., Eds. (London: Routledge), 73–90.

Burgess, S., Wilson, D. and Lupton, R. (2004) *Parallel Lives and Ethnic Segregation in the Playground and the Neighbourhood*, CMPO Working Paper No 04/094 (Bristol: CMPO).

Burnett, J. (2004) 'Community Cohesion and the State' *Race & Class*, 45(3) 1–18.

Burnett, J. (2006) 'Book Review of 'Community Cohesion: A New Framework for Race and Diversity' *Race & Class*, 48(4), 115–118.

Cameron, D. (2011) Speech to the Munich Conference, 5 February. Canadian Government. Available online at: http://www.cic.gc.ca/english/multiculturalism/citizenship.asp.

Cantle, T. (2001) *Community Cohesion: A Report of the Independent Review Team* (London: Home Office).

Cantle, T. (2004) *The End of Parallel Lives? Final Report of the Community Cohesion Panel* (London: Home Office).

Cantle, T. (2008) *Community Cohesion: A New Framework for Race and Diversity* (Basingstoke: Palgrave Macmillan).

Cantle, T. (2010) *'Reconnecting the Political Class' in Cohesion and Society* (Coventry: Institute of Community Cohesion).

Cantle, T. (2011) *The Far Right: Rumours about Their Death Are Premature.* Parliamentary Affairs 2011; doi: 10.1093/pa/gsr058.

Carling, A. (2006) *What Myth? Racial and Ethnic Segregation, the Index Wars and the Future of Bradford* (Bradford: Bradford University).

Cashin, S. (2004) *(The Failures of) Integration: How Race and Class are Undermining the American Dream* (New York: Public Affairs).

Castells, M. (1997) *The Power of Identity: The Information Age, Economy, Society and Culture.* Revised Edition 2010 (Chichester: Wiley-Blackwell).

Castells, M. (2006) 'Globalisation and Identity: A Comparative Perspective' *Transfer, Journal of Contemporary Culture,* Number 1, 55–67, 2006.

Catholic Education Service for England and Wales (2010) *Value Added: The Distinctive Contribution of Catholic Schools and Colleges in England* (London: CES).

Cemlyn, S., Greenfields, M., Burnett, S., Matthews, Z. and Whitwell, C. (2009) *Inequalities Experienced by Gypsy and Traveller Communities: A Review* (London: EHRC).

Cheesman, D. and Khanum, N. (2009) 'Soft Segregation: Muslim Identity, British Secularism and Inequality' in *Faith in the Public Realm.* Dinham, A., Furbey, R. and Lowndes, V., Eds (Bristol: Policy Press).

Chek Wai, L.E. (2004) 'The Ownership of Cultural Hybrids' in *Interculturalism: Exploring Critical Issues.* Powell, D. and Sze, F., Eds (Oxford: The Inter-Disciplinary Press).

Christian Aid (2007) *Report Human Tide: The Real Migration Crisis* (London: Christian Aid).

Clark, G. (2008) *Towards Open Cities* (Madrid: British Council).

Clarke, T. (2001) *Burnley Speaks, Who Listens?* (Burnley: Burnley Borough Council).

Cole, I. and Goodchild, B. (2001) 'Special Mix and the 'Balanced Community' in British Housing Policy – a Tale of Two Epochs' *GeoJournal,* 51, 351–360.

Comedia (2010) *Helsinki Is an Open and Intercultural City* (Stroud: Comedia).

Commission on Integration and Cohesion (CIC) (2007) *Our Shared Future* (London: CIC).

Commission on Integration and Cohesion (CIC) (2007a) *'What Works' in Community Cohesion* (London: CIC).

Commission on Integration and Cohesion (CIC) (2007b) *Integration and Cohesion Case Studies* (London: CIC).

Commission for Racial Equality (CRE) (2007) *A Lot Done, a Lot to Do; Our Vision for an Integrated Britain* (London: CRE).

Commission for Racial Equality (2007a) *Promoting Interaction Between People From Different Ethnic Backgrounds: A Research Project for the Commission for Racial Equality* (London: Commission for Racial Equality).

Coombes, A. and Brah, A., Eds. (2000) *Hybridity and Its Discontents: Politics, Science, Culture* (Florence, KY: Routledge).

The Communitarian Network (2002) *Diversity Within Unity: A Communitarian Network Position Paper* (Washington, DC: The Communitarian Network).

Copsey, N. and Macklin, G., Eds (2011) *The British National Party Contemporary Perspectives* (London: Routledge).

Copsey, N. and Macklin, G. (2011a) 'The Media = Lies, Lies, Lies: The BNP and the Media in Contemporay Britain' in *The British National Party Contemporary Perspectives*. Copsey, N. and Macklin, G., Eds (London: Routledge 2011).

Council Of Europe (2008) *White Paper on Intercultural Dialogue – Living Together as Equals in Dignity* (Strasbourg: Council of Europe).

Council Of Europe (2011) *Living Together – Combining Diversity and Freedom in 21st Century Europe*. Available online at: www.coe.int.

Crystal, D. (2003) *English as a Global Language*, 2nd Edition (Cambridge: Cambridge University Press).

Cuperus, R. (2011) 'The Populist Revolt Against Cosmopolitanism' in *Exploring the Cultural Challenges to Social Democracy*. Michael, McTernan. Ed. (London: Policy Network).

Curtice, J. and Park, A. (2010) 'A Tale of Two Crises: Banks, the MPs' Expenses Scandal and Public Opinion' in *British Social Attitudes: The 27th Report – Exploring Labour's Legacy*. Park, A., Curtice, J., Clery, E. and Bryson, C., Eds (London: Sage Publications).

Davies, N. (2011) *Vanished Kingdoms – the History of Half-Forgotten Europe* (London: Allen Lane).

Dawkins, R. (2011) 'The Tyranny of the Discontinuous Mind' in *New Statesman*. 19 December (London: New Statesman).

Demirbag-Sten, D. (2011) 'Social Democracy and the Fall-Out From Multicultural Collectivisation' in *Exploring the Cultural Challenges to Social Democracy*. Michael, McTern, Ed. (London: Policy Network).

Denham, J. (2001) *Building Cohesive Communities: A Report of the Ministerial Group on Public Order and Community Cohesion* (London: Home Office).

Denham, J. (2010) Speech to the PVE National Conference.

Development Education Association (DEA) (2010) *DEA Global Learning Charter* (DEA: London).

Department for Children, Schools and Families (2007) *Guidance on the Duty to Promote Community Cohesion* (London: DCSF).

Department for Children, Schools and Families, (2008) *The Composition of Schools in England* Statistical Bulletin (London: DCSF).

Department for Communities and Local Government (DCLG) (2007) *Improving Opportunity, Strengthening Society: One Year on – A Progress Report on the Government's Strategy to Increase Race Equality and Community Cohesion* (London: DCLG).

Department for Communities and Local Government (DCLG) (2008) *Cohesion Guidance for Funders: Summary of Responses* (London: DCLG).

Department for Communities and Local Government (DCLG) (2008a) *The Government's Response to the Commission on Integration and Cohesion* (London: DCLG).

Department for Communities and Local Government (DCLG) (2009) *Place Survey 2008, England* (London: DCLG).

Department for Communities and Local Government (DCLG) (2009a) *Guidance on Meaningful Interaction – How Encouraging Positive Relationships Between People Can Help Build Community Cohesion* (London: DCLG).

Department for Communities and Local Government (DCLG) (2009b) *Delivering Mixed Communities – Learning the Lessons From Existing Programmes* (London: DCLG).

Department for Communities and Local Government (DCLG) (2011) *2009–2010 Citizenship Survey: Community Spirit Topic Report, England* (London: DCLG).

Department for Communities and Local Government (DCLG) (2011a) *2009–2010 Citizenship Survey: Race, Religion and Equalities Topic Group, England* (London: DCLG).

Department for Communities and Local Government (DCLG) (2012) *Creating the Conditions for Integration* (London: DCLG).

Dinham, A., Furbey, R. and Lowndes, V., Eds. (2009) *Faith in the Public Realm* (Bristol: The Policy Press).

Dinham, A., and Lowndes, V. (2009) 'Faith and the Public Realm' in *Faith in the Public Realm*. Dinham, A., Furbey, R. and Lowndes, V., Eds. (Bristol: Policy Press).

Economist (1999) 'The Non-Governmental Order: Will NGOs Democratize, or Merely Disrupt, Global Governance?' *The Economist*, 11–17 December 1999.

The Eisenhower Foundation (2008) *What Together We Can Do: A Forty Year Update of the National Advisory Commission on Civil Disorders* (Washington, DC: The Eisenhower Foundation).

English, R. (2011) *Is There an English Nationalism?* (London: IPPR).

Equality and Human Rights Commission (EHRC) (2010) *How Fair Is Britain? Equality, Human Rights and Good Relations in 2010* (London: EHRC).

Equality and Human Rights Commission (EHRC) (2010a) *Inquiry Into the Recruitment and Employment in the Meat and Poultry Processing Sector* (London: EHRC).

Equality and Human Rights Commission (EHRC) (2011) *Inquiry Into Disability-Related Hate Crime* (London: EHRC).

Etzioni, A. (2002) *Diversity Within Unity: A Communitarian Network Position Paper* (Washington, DC: The Communitarian Network).

European Commission (2011) *An EU Framework for National Roma Integration Strategies up to 2020* (Brussels: European Commission).

European Commission's Directorate-General for Employment, Social Affairs and Equal Opportunities (2010) *Eurobarometer: Social Climate Full Report.* (Brussels: European Commission 2010).

Evans, G. and Tilley, J. (2011) In British Social Attitudes No. 28 (2011) *Private Schools and Public Divisions: The Influence of Fee-Paying Education on Social Attitudes.* (London: National Centre for Social Research).

Fagiolo, G., Valente, M. and Vriend, N. (2007) *Dynamic Models of Segregation in Small-World Networks.* Working Paper 589, March 2007 (London: Queen Mary College, University of London).

Fanshawe, S. and Sriskandarajah, D. (2010) *You Can't Put Me in a Box: Super Diversity and the End of Identity Politics* (London: Institute for Public Policy Research).

Farrell, D. (2009) Quoted in *The Economist*, 12th February 2009.

Finney, N. and Simpson, L. (2009) *'Sleepwalking Into Segregation': Challenging Myths About Race and Migration* (Bristol: Policy Press).

Fukuyama, F. (2005) *State Building: Governance and World Oder in the 21st Century* (London: Profile Books).

Gale, R. and O'Toole, T. (2009) 'Young People and Faith Activism' in *Faith in the Public Realm: Controversies, Policies and Practices*. Dinham, A., Furbey, R. and Lowndes, V., Eds (Bristol: Policy Press).

Gallagher, T. (2004) 'Intercultural Education in a Divided School System' in *Interculturalism: Exploring Critical Issues*. Powell, D. and Sze, F., Eds (Oxford: The Inter-Disciplinary Press).

Giddens, A. (1991) *Modernity and Self-Identity* (Cambridge: Polity Press).

Giddens, A. (2002) *Runaway World. How Globalisation is ReShaping Our Lives.* (London: Profile Books).

Gilroy, P. (2002) *There Ain't No Black in the Union Jack: The Cultural Politics of Race and Nation* (London: Routledge).

Glasman, M., *et al.* Eds (2011) *The Labour Tradition and the Politics of Paradox* (Oxford and London: The Oxford London Seminars).

Goodhart, D. (2004) 'Too Diverse?' in *Prospect Magazine*, February 2004 (London).

Goodwin, M. (2011) *New British Fascism – The Rise of the British National Party* (London: Routledge).

Goodwin, M. (2011a) *Right Response – Understanding and Countering Popular Extremism in Europe* (London: Chatham House).

Goodwin, M. (2011b, June) *The Angry White Men and Their Motives* (London: Policy Network).

Goodwin, M., (2011c) 'Europe's Radical Right: Support and Potential', *Political Insight*, December 2011. Published by Political Studies Association of the United Kingdom.

Goodwin, M., Ford, R. and Cutts, D. (2011) *From Euroscepticism to Islamophobia: The Changing Face of UKIP.* University of Nottingham Research Briefing (Nottingham: University of Nottingham).

Griffin, R. (2011) 'Alien Influence? the International Context of the BNP's Modernisation' in *The British National Party Contemporary Perspectives*. Copsey, N. and Macklin, G., Eds (London: Routledge 2011).

Gundara, J. (2000) *Interculturalism, Education and Inclusion* (London: Sage Publications).

Gundara, J. (2001) 'Multiculturalism in Canada, Britain and Australia: The Role of Intercultural Education.' *London: Journal of Canadian Studies*, 17, 40–59.

Habermas, J. (2007) *Religion in the Public Sphere*. Unpublished Lecture. Available online at: www.sandiego.edu.

Hall, S. (1992) 'The Question of Cultural Identity' in *Modernity and It's Future*. Hall, S., Held, D. and McGrew, T., Eds (Cambridge: Polity Press) 274–316.

Hammer, L. (2004) 'Interculturalism and Migrant Workers in Israel' in *Interculturalism: Exploring Critical Issues*. Powell, D. and Sze, F., Eds (Oxford: The Inter-Disciplinary Press).

Hansen, P. (2009) 'Post-national Europe – Without Cosmopolitan Guarantees.' *Race & Class*, 50(4), 20–37.

Harris, J. (2008) *The Dialectics of Globalization: Economic and Political Conflict in a Transnational World* (Newcastle: Cambridge Scholars Publishing).

Harris, R. (2011) *'Sleepwalking Towards Johannesburg'? Local Measures of Ethnic Segregation Between London's Secondary Schools, 2003–2008/9*. Centre for Market and Public Organisation Working Paper No. 11/275 (Bristol: Bristol University).

Harris, M. and Young, P. (2009) *Bridging Community Divides* (London: IVAR).

Harrison, H. (2005) 'From Community Cohesion to an Inclusion and Co-Operation Agenda' in *Housing, Race and Community Cohesion*. Harrison, H., *et al*. Eds (Oxford: Chartered Institute of Housing).

Hasan, R. (2010) *Multiculturalism, Some Inconvenient Truths* (Chippenham: Politico's).

Held, D. (1989) 'The Decline of the Nation State' in *New Times*. Hall S. and Jacques M., Eds (London: Lawrence & Wishart).

Held, D. (2002) 'Cosmopolitanism and Globalisation' *Logos*, 1(3), 1–17.

Hewstone, M., Cairns, E., Voci, A., Hamberger, J. and Neins, U (2006) 'Intergroup Contact, Forgiveness and Experience of the Troubles in Northern Ireland' *Journal of Social Issues*, 62(1), 99–120.

Hewstone, M., Paolini, S., Cairns, E., Voci, A. and Harwood, J. (2006a) 'Intergroup Contact and the Promotion of Intergroup Harmony' in *Social Identities: Motivational, Emotional, Cultural Influences*. Brown, R. J. and Capozza, D., Eds (Hove, England: Psychology Press).

Hewstone, M., Tausch, N., Hughes, J. and Cairns, C. (2007) 'Prejudice, Intergroup Contact Andidentity: Do Neighbourhoods Matter?' in *Identity, Ethnic Diversity and Community Cohesion*. Wetherell, M., Lafleche, M. and Berkeley, R., Eds (London: Sage).

Hewstone, M., Kenworthy, J., Cairns, E., Tausch, N., Hughes, J., Voci, A., von Hecker, U., Tam, T. and Pinder, C. (2008) 'Stepping Stones to Reconciliation in Northern Ireland: Intergroup Contact, Forgiveness and Trust' in *The Social Psychology of Inter-Group Reconciliation*. Fisher, J.D., *et al*. Eds (Oxford: Oxford University Press).

Hewstone, M., Cairns, E., Tausch, N. and Hughes, J. (2008a) 'Can Contact Promote Better Relations? Evidence From Mixed and Segregated Areas of Belfast' *Report to the Community Relations Unit, Northern Ireland*. Available online at: http://www.ofmdfmni.gov.uk/gr-pubs.

Hickman, M., Crowley, H. and Mai, N. (2008) *Immigration and Social Cohesion in the UK: The Rhythms and Realities of Everyday Life* (York: Joseph Rowntree Foundation).

Hiebert, D. (2009) *Exploring Minority Enclave Areas in Montréal, Toronto, and Vancouver* (Ottowa: Citizen and Immigration Canada).

Hillyard, P. (1993) *Suspect Community: People's Experience of the Prevention of Terrorism Acts in Britain* (London: Pluto Press).

HM Government (2008) *Preventing Violent Extremism – a Strategy for Delivery* (London: HM Government).

HM Government (2009) *The United Kingdom's Strategy for Countering International Terrorism* Cmnd 7547 (London: HM Government).

HM Government (2010) *Equality Act, 2010* (London: The Stationery Office).

HM Government (2011) *Prevent Strategy* Cm 8092 (London: The Stationery Office).

Home Office *et al*. (2003) *Building a Picture of Community Cohesion* (London: Home Office).

Home Office and Office of the Deputy Prime Minister (2004) *Building Community Cohesion Into Area Based Initiatives* (London: Home Office).

Home Office (2004a) *Community Cohesion Standards for Schools* (London: Home Office).

Home Office (2005) *Improving Opportunity, Strengthening Society: The Government's Strategy to Increase Race Equality and Community Cohesion* (London: Home Office).

Home Office (2005a) *Community Cohesion: Seven Steps* (London: Home Office).

Home Office (2005b) *Integration Matters: A National Strategy for Refugee Integration* (London: Home Office).

Home Office (2006) *Improving Opportunity, Strengthening Society: The Government's Strategy to Increase Race Equality and Community Cohesion* (London: Home Office).

Hooson D. Ed. (1994) *Geography and National Identity* (Oxford: Blackwell).

House, C. (2011) *Cross Cultural Dialogue in Euro-Atlantic Security and Defence* (London: Chatham House).

House of Commons (2003) ODPM: Housing, Planning, Local Government and the Regions Committee, *The Effectiveness of Government Regeneration Initiatives, Vol. 2* (London: The Stationery Office Ltd).

House of Commons (2004) ODPM: Housing, Planning, Local Government and the Regions Committee, *Social Cohesion, Sixth Report of Session 2003–04, Vol. 2* (London: The Stationery Office Ltd).

House of Commons (2004a) ODPM: Housing, Planning, Local Government and the Regions Committee, *Social Cohesion, Sixth Report of Session, Vol. 1* (London: The Stationery Office Ltd).

House of Commons Communities and Local Government Select Committee (2010) *Preventing Violent Extremism, Sixth Report of Session 16th March 2010.* (London: House of Commons).

Howard, A. (1987) *RAB: The Life of R. A. Butler* (London: Jonathan Cape).

Huntingdon, S.P. (2002) *The Clash of Civilisations and the Making of the World Order* (London: Simon & Schuster).

Hussain, A., Law, B. and Haq, T. (2007) *The Intercultural State: Citizenship and National Security* (Leicester: East Midlands Economic Network).

Iceland, J. and Mateos, P. (2009) *Racial and Ethnic Segregation in the United Kingdom and the United States.* Paper to the Population Association of America 2010 in Dallas Texas. 16 April.

Iceland, J., Mateos, P. and Sharp, G. (2011) 'Ethnic Residential Segregation by Nativity in the United Kingdom and the United States' *Journal of Urban Affairs,* 33(4), 409–429.

Improvement and Development Agency for Local Government (IDeA) (2002) *Taking Forward Community Cohesion in Leicester* (London: IDeA).

Information Centre about Asylum and Refugees in the UK (ICAR) (2004) *Understanding the Stranger* (London: ICAR).

Inglehart, R. (2008) 'Changing Values Among Western Publics 1970 to 2006' *West European Politics,* 31(1–2), 130–146.

Institute of Community Cohesion (iCoCo) (2006) *The Power of Sport – Policy and Practice: Sport and Cohesion* (Coventry: iCoCo).

Institute of Community Cohesion (iCoCo) (2006a) *A Sense of Belonging, the Communications Toolkit* (Coventry: iCoCo).

Institute of Community Cohesion (iCoCo) (2006b) *Cohesion Mapping of Community Dynamics (COHDMAP)* (Coventry: iCoCo).

Institute of Community Cohesion (iCoCo) (2006c) *Challenging Communities to Change: A Review of Community Cohesion in Oldham* (Coventry: iCoCo).

Institute of Community Cohesion (iCoCo) (2007) *Understanding and Monitoring Tension in Local Communities* (London: Local Government Association).

Institute of Community Cohesion (iCoCo) (2007a) *Promoting Sustainable Communities and Community Cohesion* (Leeds: Academy for Sustainable Communities).

Institute of Community Cohesion (iCoCo) (2007b) *New European Migration, a Good Practice Guide for Local Authorities* (London: Improvement and Development Agency for Local Government).

Institute of Community Cohesion (iCoCo) (2008) *Understanding and Appreciating Muslim Diversity: Towards Better Engagement and Participation* (Coventry: iCoCo).

Institute of Community Cohesion (iCoCo) (2011) *Far Right Electoral and Other Activity: The Challenge for Community Cohesion* (Coventry: iCoCo).

International Organisation for Migration (2010) *World Migration Report 2010* (Geneva: IOM).

Ipsos MORI/Geographical Association Survey (2009) (London: Ipsos-MORI/Geographical Association Survey).

James, M. (2008) *Interculturalism: Theory and Policy* (London: Barings Foundation).

Jenkins, R. Speech to the Meeting of Voluntary Liaison Committees, London, 23 May 1966.

Johnston, R., Burgess, S., Wilson, D. and Harris, R., (2006) 'School and Residential Ethnic Segregation: An Analysis of Variations Across England's Local Education Authorities'. CMPO paper 06/145 (Bristol: Bristol University).

Johnston, R., Poulsen, M. and Forrest, J. (2007) 'The Geography of Ethnic Residential Segregation: A Comparative Study of Five Countries' *Annals of the Association of American Geographers*, 97(4), 713–738.

Johnston, R., Poulsen, M. and Forrest, R. (2009) '*Measuring Ethnic Segregation: Putting Some More Geography*' *Urban Geography*, 30(1), 91–109.

Jurado, E. (2011) 'Progressive Multiculturalism: A Social Democratic Response to Cultural Diversity?' in *Exploring the Cultural Challenges to Social Democracy.* Michael McTernan, Ed. (London: Policy Network).

Kaur-Stubbs, S. (2008) 'Poverty and Solidarity' in *Citizenship, Cohesion and Solidarity.* Johnson, N., Ed. (London: Smith Institute).

Kenichi, O. (1995) *The End of the Nation State: The Rise of Regional Economies* (London: Harper Collins).

Khan, K. (2009) *Preventing Violent Extremism and Prevent – a Response Form the Muslim Community* (London: An-Nisa Society).

Kharas, H. (2010) *The Emerging Middle Class in Developing Countries.* OECD Development Centre Working Paper 285, January 2010 (Paris: OECD).

Korten, D. (1995) *When Corporations Rule the World* (Virginia: Kumarian Press).

Kriemer M. (2004) 'Labour Market Segregation and Gender-Based Division Labour' in *European Journal of Womens' Studies.* May 2004 11: 223–246.

Kundnani, A. (2002) *An Unholy Alliance? Racism, Religion and Communalism* (London: IRR).

Kundnani, A. (2002a) *The Death of Multiculturalism?* (London: IRR).

Kundnani, A. (2009) *Spooked* (London: Institute of Race Relations).

Kymlicka, W. (2003) 'Multicultural States and Intercultural Citizens' *Theory and Research in Education*, 1(2), 147–169.

Kymlicka, W. (2003a) 'Immigration and the Politics of National Opinion' in *The Politics of Migration.* Spencer, S., Ed. (Oxford: Blackwell).

Latchford, P. (2007) *Lozells Disturbances: Summary Report* (Birmingham: Black Radley).

Laurence, J. and Heath, A. (2008) *Predictors of Community Cohesion: Multi-Level Modelling of the 2005 Citizenship Survey* (London: DCLG).

Law, B., Haq, T. and Greaves, B. (2008) *Building Intercultural Bridges Between Diverse Communities* (Leicester: East Midlands Economic Network).

Lederach, J.P. (1993) *Pacifism in Contemporary Conflict: A Christian Perspective*, Paper to the U.S. Institute of Peace, 1993.

Lederach, J.P. (1997) *Building Peace: Sustainable Reconciliation in Divided Societies* (Washington, DC: Institute of Peace).

Legrain, P. (2011) 'Progressives Should Embrace Diversity' in *Exploring the Cultural Challenges to Social Democracy.* Michael, McTernan, Ed. (London: Policy Network).

Lentin, A. and Titley, G. (2011) *The Crises of Multiculturalism: Racism in a Neo-Liberal Age* (London: Zed Books).

Leonard, M. and Griffith, P. (2003) *The European Inclusion Index: Is Europe Really Ready for the Globalisation of People?* (London: The Foreign Policy Centre and British Council).

Le Pen, Marine (2011) Interviewed in *The Guardian* 22 March.

Local Government Association *et al.* (LGA) (2002) *Guidance on Community Cohesion* (London: LGA).

Local Government Association (LGA), Home Office, ODPM, CRE, The Audit Commission, The IDeA, The Inter-Faith Network (2004) *Community Cohesion—an Action Guide* (London: LGA Publications).

Local Government Association (LGA), Improvement and Development Agency (IDeA), the Home Office, Audit Commission and Office of the Deputy Prime Minister (2006) *Leading Cohesive Communities: A Guide for Local Authority Leaders and Chief Executives* (London: LGA).

Local Government Information Unit (LGIU) (2005) *Scrutiny of Community Cohesion Issues* (London: LGIU).

Local Government Information Unit (LGIU) (2006) *Countering Myths and Misinformation During Election Periods* (London: LGIU).

Lockwood, D. (1966) 'Sources of Variation in Working-Class Images of Society' *Sociological Review*, 14, 249–267.

Lownsbrough, H. and Beunderman, J. (2007) *Equally Spaced? Public Space and Interaction between Diverse Communities*, a Report for the Commission for Racial Equality (London: Demos).

Mahrouse, G. (2010) 'Reasonable Accommodation in Québec: The Limits of Participation and Dialogue' *Race & Class*, 52(1), 85–96.

Malik, K. (2002) 'Against Multiculturalism', *New Humanist*, Summer 2002 (London: Rationalist Press Association).

Mansouri, F. (2009) *Youth Identity and Migration: Culture, Values and Social Connectedness* (Champaign, Illinois: Common Ground Publishing).

Martell, L. (2008) 'Beck's Cosmopolitan Politics' *Contemporary Politics*, 14(2),129–143.

Mason, A. (2010) 'Integration, Cohesion and National Identity: Theoretical Reflections on Recent British Policy' *British Journal of Political Science*, 40, 857–874.

McGann, J. and Johnstone, M. (2006) 'The Power Shift and NGO Credibility Crisis' *The International Journal of Not for Profit Law*, 8(2), 65–77.

McGhee, D. (2003) 'Moving to "Our" Common Ground – A Critical Examination of Community Cohesion Discourse in Twenty First Century Britain' *Sociological Review*, 51(3), 383–411.

McGhee, D. (2005) *Intolerant Britain? Hate, Citizenship and Difference* (Maidenhead: McGraw-Hill Education).

McGhee, D. (2008) ' "A Past Built on Difference, a Future Which is Shared" – a Critical Examination of the Recommendations Made by the Commission on Integration and Community Cohesion' *People, Place & Policy Online*, 2/2, 48–64.

McLuhan, M. (1962) *The Gutenberg Galaxy: The Making of Typographic Man* (Toronto: University of Toronto Press).

Meer, N. and Modood, T. (2008) 'The Multicultural State We're in: Muslims, 'Multiculture' and the 'Civic Re-Balancing' of British Multiculturalism' *Political Studies*, 57, 473–497. doi: 10.1111/j.1467–9248.2008.00745.x.

Meer, N. and Modood, T. (2011) 'How Does Interculturalism Contrast With Multiculturalism?' *Journal of Intercultural Studies*, 33(2), 175–196.

Merkel, A. (2010) Speech to Potsdam Conference, 17 October.

Messina, A. (2011) 'Assessing the Political Relevance of Anti-Immigrant Parties: The BNP in Comparative European Perspective' in *The British National Party Contemporary Perspectives*. Copsey, N. and Macklin, G., Eds. (London: Routledge).

Miah, R. (2004) In Evidence to the House of Commons Select Committee on Social Cohesion, *Sixth Report of Session 2003–2004, Vol. 2* (London: The Stationery Office Limited).

Minkenberg, M. (2011) 'The Radical Right in Europe Today: Trends and Patterns in East and West' in *Is Europe on the 'Right' Path? Right-Wing Extremism and Right-Wing Populism in Europe*. Langenbacher N. and Schellenberg, B., Eds (Berlin: Friedrich Ebert Stiftung).

Mirza, M. (2010) 'Rethinking Race' *Prospect Magazine*. October 2010, 31–37.

Modood, T. (1988) ' "Black", Racial Equality and Asian Identity' *New Community*, 14(3), 397–404.

Modood, T. (2005) *Multicultural Politics: Racism, Ethnicity and Muslims in Britain* (Minneapolis, MN: University of Minneapolis Press).

Modood, T. (2009) 'Civic Recognition and Respect for Religion in Britain's Moderate Secularism'. Lecture 21 January, London.

Modood, T. (2011) 'Secularism and Democracy, Some Responses to Ted Cantle and Sunder Katwala' in *British Secularism and Religion*. Birt, Y., Hussain, D. and Siddiqui, A., Eds (Leicestershire: Kube 2011).

Moore, K., Mason, P. and Lewis, J. (2008) *Images of Islam in the UK – the Representation of British Muslims in theNational Print News Media 2000–2008* (Cardiff: Cardiff University).

Muir, R. (2007) *The New Identity Politics* (London: IPPR).

Neville-Jones, P. (2010) Speaking on Islam TV Channel, 21 May.

Norris, P. (2011) *Democratic Deficit: Critical Citizens Revisited* (Cambridge: Cambridge University Press).

Northern Ireland Council for Voluntary Action (NICVA) (2004) House of Commons Select Committee on Social Cohesion, *Sixth Report of Session Vol. 2* (London: The Stationery Office Ltd).

Office of National Statistics (ONS) (2011) Statistical Bulletin: Population Estimates by Ethnic Group 2002–2009, 18 May (Newport: ONS).

Open Society Foundations (2011) *At Home in Europe: Living Together* (London, New York, Budapest: Open Society Foundations).

Osler, A. (2007) *Faith Schools and Community Cohesion: Observations on Community Consultations* (Runnymede Trust Interim Report. London: The Runnymede Trust).

Ouseley, H. (2001) *Community Pride Not Prejudice* (Bradford: Bradford Vision).

Ouseley, H. (2004) *The Guardian*, 10 April 2004.

Page B. (2004) 'The Death of Liberal England?', *Local Government Chronicle*, 9 September 2004.

Parekh, B. (2000) *The Future of Multi-Ethnic Britain*. Revised edition 2002 (London: Profile Books).

Parekh, B. (2000a) *Rethinking Multiculturalism: Cultural Diversity and Political Theory* (Basingstoke: Palgrave Macmillan).

Parekh, B. (2009) 'Foreword' in *Faith in the Public Sphere*. Dinham *et al.* Eds (Bristol: The Policy Press).

Penninx, R. (2009) *Decentralising Integration Policies* (London: Policy Network).

Phillips, D. (2005) 'Housing Achievements, Diversity and Constraints' in *Housing, Race and Community Cohesion*. Harrison *et al.* (Oxford: Chartered Institute of Housing).

Phillips, T. (2005) Speech to the Manchester Community Relations Council, 22 September 2005.

Phillips, T. (2006) Quoted in *Building Design*, 3 November 2006.

Platt, L. (2009) *Ethnicity and Family Relationships Within and Between Ethnic Groups: An Analysis Using the Labour Force Survey* (London: Institute for Social & Economic Research and University of Essex).

Poulsen, M. (2005) *The 'New Geography' of Ethnicity in Britain?* Paper to the Royal Geographic Society in London, 31 August 2005.

Powell, D. (2004) 'Living Souvenirs: Intercultural Memory, Longing and Nostalgia' in *Interculturalism: Exploring Critical Issues*. Powell, D. and Sze, F., Eds (Oxford: The Inter-Disciplinary Press).

Public Interest Research Centre (PIRC) (2010) *The Common Cause Handbook* (Machynlleth, Wales: PIRC).

Putnam, R.D. (2000) *Bowling Alone: The Collapse and Revival of American Community* (New York: Simon & Schuster).

Putnam, R.D. (2007) 'E Pluribus Unum: Diversity and Community in the Twenty First Century. The 2006 Johan Skytte Prize Lecture' *Scandinavian Political Studies Journal*, 30(2), 137–174.

Ratcliffe, P. (2004) *'Race', Ethnicity and Difference: Imagining the Inclusive Society* (Berkshire: OUP).

Riots, Communities and Victims Panel (2011) *5 Days in August. An Interim Report on the 2011 English Riots* (London: Dept. of Communities)

Ritchie, D. (2001) *Oldham Independent Review: One Oldham, One Future* (Manchester: Government Office for the North West).

Ritzen, J., Easterly, W. and Woolcock, M. (2000) *On 'Good' Politicians and 'Bad' Policies*. Policy Research Paper 2448 (Washington DC: The World Bank).

Runnymede Trust (2008) *The Right to Divide? Faith Schools and Community Cohesion* (London: Runnymede Trust).

Runnymede Trust (2009) *Who Cares About the White Working Class?* (London: Runnymede Trust).

Sachs, J. (2007) *The Home That We Build Together* (Continuum: London).

Sampson, R. and Sharkey, P. (2008) 'Neighborhood Selection and the Social Reproduction of Concentrated Racial Inequality' *Demography*, 45(1), 1–29.

Sandercock, L. (2004) 'Reconsidering Multiculturalism: Towards an Intercultural Project' in *Intercultural City Reader*. Wood, P., Ed. (Stroud: Comedia).

Sarkozy, N. (2011) Interviewed on *Paroles de Français* (TF1), 11 February 2011.

Searchlight Educational Trust (2011) *Fear and Hope Project Report* (London: SET).

Seldon, A. (2008) Speech given at Wellington College and reported in the *Daily Mail*. Available online at: www.dailymail.co.uk/news/article-508217/Private-schools-fuel-social-apartheid-saysheadmaster-25-620-year-Wellington-College.html#ixzz1OfjwuzgK.

Seko, K. (2004) 'Silent East: How Can We Give a Voice to Asian Theology?' in *Interculturalism: Exploring Critical Issues*. Powell, D. and Sze, F., Eds (Oxford: The Inter-Disciplinary Press).

Semyonov, M., Glikman, A. and Krysan, M. (2007) 'Europeans' Preference for Ethnic Residential Homogeneity: Cross-National Analysis of Response to Neighborhood Ethnic Composition' *Social Problems*, 54(4), 434–453.

Sen, A. (2006) *Identity and Violence: The Illusion of Destiny* (New York: W.W. Norton).

Shah, H. (2008) 'Solidarity in a Globalised Society – the Implications for Education Policy ' in *Citizenship, Cohesion and Solidarity*. Johnson, N., Ed. (London: Smith Institute).

Simpson, L. (2003) *Statistics of Racial Segregation: Measures, Evidence and Policy*, Occasional Paper No. 24 (Manchester: University of Manchester).

Simpson, L., Ahmed, S. and Phillips, D. (2007) *Oldham and Rochdale: Race, Housing and Community Cohesion* (Manchester: University of Manchester).

Slattery, B. (2003) 'Our Mongrel Selves: Pluralism, Identity and the Nation', in *Community of Right/Rights of the Community*. Gendreau, Ysolde, Ed. (Montreal: Editions Themis, 2003).

Smith, M. (2011) 'Foreword to' in *Inquiry Into Disability-Related Hate Crime* (London: EHRC).

Social Exclusion Unit (SEU) (2004) *Tackling Social Exclusion: Taking Stock and Looking to the Future* (London: ODPM).

Solomos, J., Back, L. (1996) *Racism and Society* (Hampshire: Macmillan Press Ltd).

Sondhi, R. (2008) *Foreword to 'Interculturalism: Theory and Policy'* (London: Baring Foundation).

Sondhi, R. (2009) Speech to the Awards for Bridging Cultures (ABCs) 1 December, London.

Soysal, Y.N. (2000) 'Citizenship and Identity: Living Diasporas in Post-War Europe' *Ethnic and Racial Studies*, 23(1), 1–15.

Stone, L. and Muir, R. (2007) *Who Are We? Identities in Britain, 2007* (London: Institute for Public Policy Research).

Think Global (2011) Available online at: http://www.think-global.org.uk/page.asp?p=3865.

Thomas, P. (2011) *Youth, Multiculturalism and Community Cohesion* (Basingstoke: Palgrave Macmillan).

The Times (2011) Leader on 'Future Disharmony' 28 October.

Tunstall, R. and Fenton, A. (2006) *In the Mix: A Review of Research Evidence on Mixed Income, Mixed Tenure and Mixed Communities* (London: The Housing Corporation).

United Nations (1945) Article 1 of The Charter of the United Nations, signed on 26 June 1945, in San Francisco.

United Nations (1948) The Universal Declaration of Human Rights, adopted by the UN General Assembly on 10 December 1948.

Varshney, A. (2002) *Ethnic Conflict and Civic Life: Hindus and Muslims in India* (New Haven & London: Yale University).

Weber, M. (1946) *From Max Weber: Essays in Sociology* (New York: Oxford University Press).

Weiner, E. Ed. (1998) 'Co-Existence Work; a New Profession' in *The Handbook of Interethnic Co-Existence* (New York: The Continuum Publishing Company).

Wildsmith, E., Gutmann, M.P. and Gratton, B. (2003) 'Assimilation and Intermarriage for U.S. Immigrant Groups, 1880–1990' *History of the Family*, 8, 563–584.

Winder, R. (2004) *Bloody Foreigners: The Story of Immigration to Britain* (Little, Brown: London).

Windsor, P. (2002) 'Cultural Dialogue in Human Rights'. in *Studies in International Relations: Essays by Philip Windsor*. Berdal, Mats, Ed. (Brighton: Sussex Academic Press).

Wolf, M. (2011) 'Living with limits: growth, resources and climate change'. The Grantham Institute for Climate Change Annual Lecture. London, 3 November.

Wolfe, A. (2002) 'The Costs of Citizenship: Assimilation and Multiculturalism in Modern Democracies' in *Cohesion, Community and Citizenship* Runnymede Trust (London: The Runnymede Trust).

Wood, P., Ed. (2004) *Intercultural City: Intercultural City Reader* (Stroud: Comedia).

Wood, P. and Landry, C. (2007) *The Intercultural City: Planning for Diversity Advantage* (London: Earthscan).

Wood, P., Landry, C. and Bloomfield, J. (2006) *The Intercultural City* (Stroud: Comedia).

Wood, P., Landry, C. and Bloomfield, J. (2006a) *Cultural Diversity in Britain: A Toolkit for Cross-Cultural Co-Operation* (York: Joseph Rowntree Foundation).

The World Bank (2010) Available online at: http://web.worldbank.org.

Younge, G. (2009) *The Guardian* 30 March.

Younge, G. (2010) *Who Are We – and Should It Matter in the 21st Century?* (Glasgow: Viking).

Index

Abrams, D., 145–6
academic deficit, 102
Action for Children, 205
active enmity, 87
Adler, R.D., 33
Adonis, A., 129
adoption, 41
Adorno, T.W., 165
affinities, 24–6
Afghanistan, 26
African communities, 48, 49, 188
age distribution in Britain, 13
Agg, C., 9–10
Ajegbo, Sir K., 209
Ali, S., 36, 39–41
Allport, G. W., 104, 145
'all of us' concept, 109
Anie, A., 128
An-Nisa Society, 44
anti-discrimination laws, 50
anti-diversity, 16
anti-globalisation, 4, 9
anti-migration, 12, 16, 63, 139
anti-Muslim organizations, 43
anti-racism, 39, 47–8
anti-terrorism programmes, 32, 45
Arab Spring, 35, 46, 171, 180, 205
Asian communities
    Christian communities in, 48
    collective identities of, 78
    country, importance of, 19
    in England, 59–60
    in mixed race communities, 22,
        59–60
    multiculturalism in, 5
    Muslim identities in, 49, 78
    parallel lives (with White
        communities) in, 113
    personal identities of, 19
    race riots and, 96
    school segregation of, 123
    stereotyping, 96

Asian identity, 37
assimilationism, 39, 88, 102, 112,
    153–4
asylum, 101
Auckland, New Zealand, 200
Australian communities, 34, 80
Australians identities, 21
Austrian Freedom Party, 85
authoritarian personality, 165
Awards for Bridging Cultures (ABCs),
    144, 156, 168

Back, L., 37
Bahrain, 8
Balderston, S., 148
Baldwin, C., 16
Balkans, 16
Bangkok, 34
banking crisis, 6
Barcelona, 34
Baring Foundation, 144, 156
barriers of entry, 164
Bartlett, J., 45, 99
BBC, 33, 101
Beck, U., 183
Belgium, 16, 25, 27, 81, 137
Bell, D., 7
belonging, 39, 108, 134
    interculturalism, fostering of, 155
    to local communities, 23
    sense of, 139, 205
Berger, P., 188
Berube, A., 126, 196
Beunderman, J., 148, 196,
    198–9
Bevan, Aneurin, 196
Bianchini, F., 156, 179
Biggs, M., 127, 132, 146, 165
bigotry, 167
bilateral accommodations, 32
Billig, M., 10, 27–8
binary Black/White opposites, 78

biological superiority, 48, 173
bi-polarity, 81
birth country, 19
Blackaby, B., 106
Black British identities, 11, 22
Black communities
    Black history month project for, 182
    Black-led housing associations
        for, 56
    bounded identities of, 41
    country, importance of, 19
    culture of, 36
    international identities of, 20
    mixed race communities of, 22, 38
    multiculturalism of, 5
    personal identities of, 19
    political consciousness of, 56
    political culture of, 37
    racism in, 79
    school segregation of, 123
    solidarity of, 78, 79
Black identities, 78–80
blackness, 78
Black on Black violence, 79
Black or Minority Ethnic (BME), 119
Bloomfield, J., 156, 179
Blunkett, D., 95
Bouchard, G., 35, 76, 80–1, 141,
    153–5, 202–4
Bouchard-Taylor Report, 154, 155
bounded identities, 31, 40–1
Brah, A., 22, 37–8
Brammen, Norway, 200
Brazil, 208
Brecknock, R., 209
bridge building, 147
Britain
    age distribution in, 13
    belonging campaigns in, 109–10
    Church of England in, 72
    dynamic societies in, 36
    ethnic diversity in, 31–2
    faiths in, 70–1
    integration in, 65
    intolerance in, 65
    Irish community in, 49
    migration in, 112
    minority communities in, 54
    mixed race communities in, 37

    multi-ethnic, 65
    Muslim communities in, 75
    national culture in, building of, 108
    national identities in, 28
    as nation-state, 24
    as one Nation, view of, 58
    racism in, 65
    school segregation in, 123
    segregation in, 112, 119–20
    social apartheid in, 130
    social divides in, 33
    workplace segregation in, 124
British-Chinese identities, 22
British Council (BC), 133, 150–1, 158,
    162
British Left, 108
British Muslim communities, 105
British Muslim identities, 11, 22
British National Party (BNP), 84–7,
    98, 101
Britishness, 22–3, 84, 108–9, 204
Brynin, M., 41
Buddhists, 184
Building Opportunity, Strengthening
    Society reports, 97
Burberry, 34
Burgess, S., 123
Burnett, J., 35, 95–6, 109
business, globalisation of, 6
business environment, 161

Cadbury, George, 196
Cameron, D., 32, 53, 68–9, 76, 109,
    116, 136–7, 185–6, 204
Canada
    English-speaking, 81
    ethno-cultural diversity in, 80
    French-speaking, 81
    integration in, 202–3
    interculturalism in, 141, 154
    middle class in, 33
    multiculturalism, adoption of, 63–4,
        154
    nation of, 24, 25
    school segregation in, 70
    segregation in, 118, 202–3
*Canadian Charter of Rights and
    Freedoms*, 203
Cantle Report, 94, 95

Cantle, T., 14–16, 23, 25, 36, 39, 41,
    48, 56, 59–60, 63, 66–8, 70, 73,
    76, 80, 91–2, 94–7, 100, 107, 109,
    112, 114, 117, 120, 122, 126, 128,
    130, 134–6, 138–9, 146, 165, 178,
    185–6, 190, 193–4, 201–2, 205
Cardiff University, 42–3
Carling, A., 121
Cashin, S., 118
Castells, M., 8–9, 10, 17–19, 24
Catalonia, 17
Catalonian nation, 25
Catholic communities, 25, 190
Catholic Education Service, 71
Cemlyn, S., 128
Central Bank, 170
Chatham House, 144
Cheesman, D., 20
Chek Wai, L. E., 78, 138
children, race of, 39
Chinese communities
    communications technology in, 8
    embourgeoisement in, 34
    employment in, 208
    international communications in,
        76
    middle class in, 33
    nationality-based diaspora identities
        in, 21
chosen identities, 30
Christian Aid, 13
Christian communities, 48, 72, 138,
    163, 184
Christian faiths, 70, 72, 184, 188
Church of England, 70, 72
church schools, 193
citizenship, 11
    active, 104
    common, 109
    concept of, 96
    easy access to, 161
    in England, 25
    functional segregation and
        integration and, 133, 134
    global, 187
    good, 150
    government support for, 76
    intercultural, 161
    multicultural, 161

national, 22
nationalities and, linking of, 25
nation-state, 19–20
rights-based concept of, 103
tests of, 25, 32, 138
Citizenship Surveys, 160
civilizations, 21, 42, 69, 137–8
civilized identities, 137
Civil society organisations, 177
civil spaces, 198
Clarke, T., 94
Clark, G., 31, 162, 207
clash of civilizations. 42, 69, 137–8
class, 33, 99
closed communities, 122, 167
clustered communities, 122
co-existence work, 104
cohesion. *See also* community
    cohesion
    low, 62
    nation-state, 25
    social, 20, 65, 207
cold identities, 36
Cole, I., 196
collective affiliation, 48
collective identities, 2, 5
    concept of, 143
    globalisation, impact on, 52
    of middle class, 34
    in mixed race communities, 60
    multiculturalism, impact on,
        14, 48
    post-war multiculturalism, threat to,
        48
    public realm of, 50
    of race, 30
    solidarity and, impact of, 18, 82
    within state, 10, 51
    super diversity, impact on, 52
    in United Kingdom, 28
    in Western societies, change of, 18
collective life, 15
collective memory, 155
colonialism, 167
Comedia Group, 155
comma-ed identities, 40
Commission for Integration and
    Cohesion (CIC), 68, 93, 108

Commission for Racial Equality, 60, 92, 96, 119, 147
commonality, 102, 108, 135
communication, 6, 8, 99. *See also* specific types of
global, 10–11, 21, 28, 62, 131
intercultural, 145
international, 6, 13, 76, 174
mass, 33
non-governmental organisations, important role of, 11
virtual, 131
communitarianism, 96
Communitarian Network, 67
communities, 18, 48–9, 65, 96, 114, 182. *See also* specific types of
community cohesion, 2, 14
academic appraisal of, 102
academic publications on, 95–6
birth of, 15
city-wide development of, 91–2
commitment to, 105–11
concept of, 91
conceptual development of, 92–102
contribution of, 91–111
cosmopolitan identities and, 35
defensive multiculturalism and, 57, 101
defining, 92–4, 105
development of, 92–102, 145
in England, 91, 107
ethnic diversity and impact on, 15–16
failure of, 148
formalization of, 94–5
guidance for, 106–7
impact of, 96
implementation of, 101
interaction and, 102–5
intercultural dialogue and, 145
interculturalism and, 88–90, 142
investments in, 16
at local level, 107–9
mainstreaming, 106
national review of, 149
positive vision for development of, 92
practical development of, 92–102
prejudices and impact on, 145

race and, 81–2, 98–9
reinforcement of, 106
school segregation and impact of, 70
separatism and, 70
solidarity and, 15–16
spin-off benefits of, 110
support for, 105–7
in United Kingdom, 22–3, 44, 91, 102–3, 105–6, 113
universal adoption of, 67
vision of, 94
Community Cohesion Unit (CCU), 94–5
community of communities, 65
competences, 157
conflicts, 16–19, 150, 172–3
identity, 30
interethnic, 79
intergenerational, 99
national, 29
sectarian, 80
contact theory, 14, 63, 104, 145
contextualized identities, 36
Coombes, A., 37–8
Copsey, N., 86, 101
cosmopolitan identities, 19, 20, 35, 182–3, 186
cosmopolitanism, 20, 24, 183–4
Council of Europe (CoE), 54, 68, 134, 139, 143, 153, 155, 169
crimes, 8, 100. *See also* hate crimes
criminality, 96
cross-border movements, 31
cross-cultural contacts, 127
cross-party political agreements, 178
Crystal, D., 21
cultural barriers, 210
cultural capital, 122
cultural distinctiveness, 67–8
cultural identities, 21, 85, 137
culturally distinctive communities, 65
cultural markers, 138
cultural navigation, 2
cultural networks, 116
cultural pluralism, 20

culture, 65
  barriers of, 34, 143
  of Black people, 36
  changes in, 155
  codes of, 18, 33
  concept of, 32–3, 37, 173–4, 204
  contextualized, 39
  cultural identities and, clash of, 137
  defining, 82
  describing, 36
  diversity within, 37
  dynamic, 39
  exchanges within, 7
  of faith, 33, 204
  idea of, 168
  intermixing of, 39
  of Jewish communities, 20
  language, differential marker of, 81
  literacy of, 209
  male occupational, 130–1
  Muslim, 36
  national, 108
  nature of, 167
  notion of, 67
  other, 39
  political, 37
  public, 208
  race and, 32–3, 36
  static, 39
  superiority within, 143
  White, 36
Cuperus, R., 5, 17, 120, 170, 182, 196
Curtice, J., 179

Dawkins, R., 187
decision-making process, 190
defensive multiculturalism, 47, 54–63,
    92
  blaming minorities for, 60
  community cohesion and, 57
  debates over, 53–4
  deprivation and, 61–3
  disagreement and, 58–9
  discrimination, protection from, 54
  equality and, 58
  ethnic segregation and, 60
  in France, 54
  in Germany, 54
  inequalities and, 63

  migration and, 55
  for minority communities, 54
  multiculturalism policies and, 53–4,
      56–8
  multicultural separateness and, 55
  in Muslim communities, 53–4
  notion of, 53
  objective reality of, 53
  poverty and, 61–3
  racism, protection from, 54
  right to be different and, 59
  secularism and, 59
  self-segregation and, 59–61
  separateness and, 57–8
  subjective reality and, 53
deferential worker, 33
Demirbag-Sten, D., 42, 75, 177
democracies
  in multifaith communities, 191–2
  Muslim communities, support for,
      46
  Western, 45–6, 76, 189–90
democratic deficit, 51, 135, 180
democratic politics, 10–11
democratization, 9, 18
Denham, J., 43, 92, 94–5, 204
Department of Communities and
    Local Government (DCLG), 93,
    94, 95, 103, 148
deprivation, 61–3, 74–5, 97
Diamond Jubilee, 138
diaspora identities, 5, 11, 20–1, 180
  faith-based, influences of, 50, 171
  influences of, 36, 180
  single, 138
  using social media to reaffirm, 6
differences, 62, 104
  community cohesion and, 99–100,
      165
  cultural identities and, 85
  fear of, 100, 128
  globalisation and, 78, 169–71
  hate crimes and, 165–6
  interculturalism and, 163–71
  minorities and, 82
  otherness and, 62
  of people, 101
  race, concept of, 163–5
  race and, 82

differences – *continued*
  racial, 77
  reaffirming, 181
  in United Kingdom, 166–7
Dinham, A., 50, 188
disabilities, 100, 128–9, 148
disagreement, 58–9
discrimination, 99, 101
  condemnation of, 66
  differences and, 141
  economic, 62
  multicultural policies of, 48, 56–7
  post-war, 56
  preventing, 135
  separatism, 69
  in United Kingdom, policies on, 112
  workplace, 124
diversity. *See also* specific types of
  changing patterns of, 32
  city openness and, 164
  within culture, 37
  in daily lives, exposure to, 14
  ethnic, 15–16, 31–2, 98
  ethno-cultural, 80–1
  in France, 189
  hyper (*See* super diversity)
  identity politics and, 14
  interculturalism, opportunities of,
    207–8
  within Muslim communities, 45
  negative effects of, 16
  in Northern Ireland, 166
  opportunities of, 207–8
  paradox of, 14, 27, 87–8, 160
  political, 172
  positive value of, 105
  social capital and, 15
  solidarity, impact on, 16
  in United Kingdom, 45, 98, 189
  within unity, 67
  values of, 158
  workplace, 196

Earth Summit (1992), 10
Eastern Europe, 16
economic changes, 18, 36
Eisenhower Foundation, 126
electronic global economy, 8
embourgeioisement, 34

employment, 124, 208–9
England
  affinities of, 24
  Asian communities in, 59–60
  Catholic Education Service for, 71
  citizenship in, 25
  community cohesion in, 91, 102,
    107
  ethnic diversity in, 98
  faith in, 70
  Far Right in, rise of, 43
  hate crimes in, 165
  migration in, 12
  mixed race communities in, 38
  nation of, 24
  non-White British in, 12
  race riots in, 81–2
  segregation in, 119
  spatial segregation in, 114–15
English Civil War, 23
English Defence League, 43, 86–7, 138
English, R., 186
English for Speakers of Overseas
    Languages (ESOL), 202
English identity, 86
English language, 21
English-speaking Canada, 81
equalities agenda, 196–7
equality, 58, 64, 135
Equality Act 2010, 50–1, 166–7
Equality and Human Rights
    Commission (EHRC), 13, 74, 100,
    101, 124, 166, 195
equal opportunities, 115–16, 135
essentialism, 58
Estonia, 81
ethnicity, 62
  classification of, 48–9
  coding of, 75
  conceptualization of, 37
  conflicts with, 16–19
  culture and, 32, 33
  differences in, 67
  faith and, 72–3
  functional segregation and
    integration and, 135–6
  hyphenating of, 21
  mixed race communities and, 40
  monitoring of, 48–9, 75, 135–6, 187

of Muslim communities, 45
Northern Ireland, classifications in, 145
perception of, 31–2
personal identities, important element of, 19
prejudices towards, 117
race and, 30, 51, 77–8, 98–9
segregation and, 101, 132
spatial segregation and integration and, 126–7
tensions and, 101
ethnicity box, 187
ethnocentrism, 121
Etzioni, A., 96
Eugenicist movement, 30
Euro, 17
Eurobarometer, 159–60
Europe
anti-migration in, 139
biological racism in, 82–3
democratic state of, 23
Extreme Far Right parties in, rise of, 14, 16
Far Right in, growth of, 82–5, 138
foreign-born population statistics in, 31
globalisation in, negative impact of, 4
integration policies in, 133
interculturalism in, 141
openness in, 159–60
peace in, 176
segregation in, 118, 130, 137
European Central Bank, 170
European Coal and Steel Community (ECSC), 170
European Commission (EC), 128, 143, 149
European Convention of Human Rights, 170
European Economic Community (EEC), 170
European Inclusion Index, 133
European Parliament, 84, 170
European Union, 9, 83, 149, 170
European Year of Intercultural Dialogue (EYICD), 143, 149
Eurozone countries, 9, 18, 170

Evans, G., 130
extremism, 43, 44, 86, 131

Facebook generation, 35
faith, 70–3, 174, 184–5, 188
coding of, 75
conceptualization of, 37
conflicts with, 16–18
cultures of, 33, 204
global communications and, 21
hyphenating of, 21
identities, 50, 52, 185–6
mixedness in, 38
mixed race communities of, 22
monitoring of, 75
in multifaith communities, 190–1
political salience of, 190–1
in public sphere, 189–91, 193
segregation and integration, responses to, 204
super diversity of, 40
in United Kingdom, 71–2, 77, 184–5, 190–1
in Western societies, 20–1
Fagiolo, G., 114, 194
Fanshawe, S., 16, 32, 39–40
Far East, 188
Farrell, D., 33
Far Right, 4, 6
cross-cultural contacts and, 127
differences and, 170–1
distinguishing types of, 85
diversity paradox of, 87–8
in England, rise of, 43
in Europe, growth of, 82–3, 138
globalisation, impact on, 83
growth of, 84–6
Hope and Fear report by, 86–7
migration, opposition to, 83, 85, 87, 133, 173
minority communities, opposition to, 63, 68, 83–4, 173
multiculturalism and, 82–8
Muslim communities, role in, 46, 49–50
no platform position of, 101
prejudicial views of, 165
race riots and, 96
racial debates of, 61, 87

Far Right – *continued*
  segregation and, 132
  support for, increasing, 46
  terrorism by, 131
  violence caused by, 46
  xenophobic populism, opposition
    to, 87
Far Right British National Party, 165
fear, 17, 86, 100, 128, 194, 207–8
Fear and HOPE report, 178
Fenton, A., 126
fifth column. *See* Muslim
    communities
financial capital, 6
financial crisis, 6, 8, 17, 51
Financial Times, 29
Finney, N., 59, 66, 121
fixed identities, 30
flagged identities, 135, 181
flagging, 29, 76
Forster Education Act, 71
France
  assimilation in, 112
  coercive powers in, 24
  cultural markers in, 138
  defensive multiculturalism in, 54
  diversity in, 189
  institutional separation in, 72
  segregation in, 137
  sovereignty in, 83
freedom, 164, 169
  of choice, 195
  of the city, 161
  diversity and, 54
  of rights, 184
  of speech, 205
Frenchness, 22–3, 85
French-speaking Canada, 81
Front National, 83, 85
Fukuyama, F., 24, 26–7
functional segregation and
    integration, 132–6
Future of Multi-Ethnic Britain, 58

Gale, R., 20
Gallagher, T., 71, 185
gateway leaders, 186
Germany, 33, 54, 112, 141, 157
ghetto, 117, 140, 174

Giddens, A., 8, 76
Gilroy, P., 78, 80, 82, 99
Glasman, M., 11
global brands, 6, 17, 33
global communities, 29
global economy, 26
global environment, 29
globalisation
  benefits of, 4, 14
  challenges of, 174–5, 207
  collective identities, impact on, 52
  dark side of, 8
  dimensions of, 6–12
  dynamics of, 135
  Far Right, impact on, 83
  future of, 11–12
  identity politics and, 183
  intercultural competences and,
    development of, 208
  interculturalism and, 90, 111
  minority communities, as cause of,
    6
  nationalism and, division between,
    83, 170–1
  navigational skills and,
    development of, 208
  negative impact of, 4–6
  origins of, 4
  personal identities, impact on, 52
  social impacts of, 11
  sovereignty and, 9
globalized identities, 17, 31, 171
global movements, 180–1
global village, 7, 27
Goodchild, B., 196
Goodhart, D., 109
good race relations, 56
Goodwin, M., 61, 77, 82–5, 87, 98,
    127, 133, 163, 204
Google, 8, 76
governance, 2
  faith, role in, 191
  global, 18, 29
  international, 26
  multiculturalism, impact on, 14
  in multifaith communities, system
    of, 188–94
  national identities, views of, 22
  nation-state, functions of, 26–7

segregation and integration,
    intervention in, 194
separatism, policies supporting,
    69–70
Greece, 141
Griffin, Nick, 101
Griffin, R., 85
Griffith, P., 133
guest workers, 112, 157, 178–9
Guidance on Community Cohesion,
    92
Gundara, J., 208–9
gypsies, 127–8

Habermas, J., 188
Hall, S., 36
Hammer, L., 67
harassment, 99, 100, 124–5
Harris, J., 12
Harris, M., 147
Harrison, H., 104
Harris, R., 123
Harvard University, 19
Hasan, R., 58–9
hate crimes, 65, 99–100, 103, 165–6
Heath, A., 62, 98
Held, D., 9, 183
Helsinki report, 199–201
heritage, 187
    global communications and, 21
    idea of, 168
    Italian, 21
    in minority communities,
        protection of, 47, 54
    multiculturalism policies on, 48
    multiple (*See* mixed race
        communities)
    nation and, protection of, 24
    using social media to reaffirm, 6
Hewstone, M., 63, 99, 104, 145, 165–6
Hickman, M., 124, 146
Hiebert, D., 115, 118, 194
Hillyard, P., 75
homogeneity, 20, 37, 80–1, 121
homogenous communities, 42
homophobic violence, 99
Hooson D., 17
Hope and Fear report, 86–7
horizontal identities, 34–5

hot identities, 36
House of Commons Communities, 45
House of Lords, 72, 190
Howard, A., 71, 193, 196
Huntingdon, S.P., 42, 137
Huntingdon's thesis, 42
Hussain, A., 65, 73
hybrid identities, 11, 32, 48, 49, 51, 52
hyphenated identities, 21, 22, 28, 40

Iceland, J., 118, 121
identities. *See also* specific types of
    changing patterns of, 22
    choice-based, 47–52
    choice of, 31
    components of, 36
    conceptualization of, 36–7
    dynamic, 47–52
    hot patterns of, 35
    interconnectedness of, 45
    of mixed races, 37–41
    multiculturalism policies and,
        relationship between, 47
    multiple, 47–52
    of Muslim communities, 42–6
    national, 22–3, 31–7, 171
    notion of, 21, 35, 52
    policies based on, 32
    political importance of, 85
    race and, linkage between, 36, 47–8,
        51
    reforming notion of, 30–52
    static concepts of, 36, 39
    universal conception of, 60
    vertical forms of, 5
identity politics, 2, 13, 87, 181–7
    barriers to, 184
    cosmopolitan identities and, 182–3
    cosmopolitanism and, 183–4
    development of, 28–9
    faith identities and, 185–6
    global communications and
        acceleration of, 28
    globalisation and, 183
    heritage and, 187
    mixed race and, omission from, 32
    multiculturalism policies and, 182
    national identity and, 181–2
    single-identity groups and, 186

identity politics – *continued*
  social identities and, 187
  state-sponsored community
    leadership and, 186
  sub-national identities and, 185–6
  supra-national identities and, 185–6
  in United Kingdom, 182
identity purity, 185
identity tribes, 87
imagined community, 27
immigration, 15, 86–7, 101
Independent Panel on Community
  Cohesion, 106–7
Index of Dissimilarity (ID), 119
India, 147, 208
indigenous Australians, 34
indignados, 9, 12, 205
inequalities, 63, 96–7, 99
Inglehart, R., 33, 50
Institute for Public Policy Research, 40
Institute of Community Cohesion
  (iCoCo), 84, 107, 144, 150–1
insular communities, 140
integration. *See also* interculturalism
  all or nothing, 47
  in Britain, 65
  conceptualizing, 114, 116
  defining, 113–14
  in Europe, policies on, 133
  identity and, importance of, 95
  interculturalism and, 154
  of Muslim communities, 69
  national identities and, 135
  segregation and, 112–40
  social, 64
  strategies for, 69–70
interaction, 5. *See also* interculturalism
  banal, 148–9
  competences of, 210
  interethnic, 147–8
  opportunity for, 149
interconnectedness, 9, 34. *See also*
  interculturalism
intercultural cities, 155–6, 179,
  198–200
intercultural competences,
  development of, 151, 206–12

intercultural dialogue (ICD), 143, 145
  breaking down barriers, 147
  British Council's investment in,
    150–1
  concept of, 143–4, 151–52
  interculturalism and, 143–52
  interethnic interaction and, 147–8
  prejudice and, 145–7
intercultural exchanges, 210
interculturalism, 1–3, 32, 82, 168
  choice of, 153
  community cohesion and, 88–90,
    142
  concept of, 68, 141–5, 155–6
  defining, 142, 143, 153, 156
  development of, 88
  differences and, 163–71
  elements of, 142
  entrenchment and, 142–43
  evolution of, 157–8
  foundational elements of, 142
  in Germany, 157
  global, 157
  globalisation and, 90, 111
  identity politics and, 142, 181–7
  integration and, 194–206
  in intercultural cities, 155–6
  intercultural competences and,
    206–12
  intercultural dialogue and, 143–52
  leadership and, 176–81
  in minority communities, 88
  models of, 49
  multiculturalism and, transitioning
    from, 88–90
  multicultural model of, 87–8
  multifaith communities and,
    188–94
  navigational skills and, 206–12
  notion of otherness and, 143
  openness and, 142, 158–63
  perspectives of, 152–8, 171–5
  policies for, 176–212
  practicing of, 176–212
  race and, 51, 142, 153
  secularism, component of, 188
  segregation and, 142, 194–206
  super diversity and, 90, 111
  vision of, 176–81

intercultural union, 37, 38. *See also* intermarriage
interdependence, 17, 22. *See also* interculturalism
interdependence of nation, 29
interdependent economies, 6
interethnic communities, 137
interethnic contacts, 117, 122
interfaith communities, 137
Inter Faith Network, 92
interfaith unions, 40
intermarriage, 22, 28, 36, 37, 69
International Criminal Court, 8
internationalism, 17, 168. *See also* interculturalism
International Monetary Fund, 8, 12
Ipsos MORI, 209
Irish communities, 21, 36, 49, 75

James, M., 141, 145, 149, 156
Jenkins, Roy, 65, 92
Jewish communities, 20, 184, 190
Johnstone, M., 10, 23
Johnston, R., 71, 115, 118–20, 123
Joseph Rowntree Foundation, 155, 196, 198
Jurado, E., 46, 71, 75, 181

Kaur-Stubbs, S., 147
Kenichi, O., 7
Khan, K., 44
Khanum, N., 20
Kharas, H., 33
Knauss, S., 127, 132, 146
Korten, D., 7
Kriemer, M., 130
Kundnani, A., 43, 93, 104
Kymlicka, W., 15, 70, 86, 109, 157, 185

laïcité, 72
Landry, C., 160
languages, 5, 21, 81, 201–2
Latchford, P., 79
Laurence, J., 62, 98
Law, B., 147
layered identities, 36, 207

leadership, 176–81
change and, vitality of, 179–80
city openness and, 179
community cohesion of, 106
global movements and, 180–1
grass roots form of, 179
at international level, 180
political class and, 181
state-sponsored community, 186
vision statement and, 179
Lederach, J.P., 104
Legrain, P., 15
Lentin, A., 66–7, 95
Leonard, M., 133
Le Pen, Marine., 83, 85, 170
Lesbian, Gay, Bi-Sexual, Transgender and Intersex (LGBTI) groups, 131–2, 167
Living Together, 54, 68
Local Government Association (LGA), 92
Local Government Select Committee, 45
local identities, 18–20, 109–10
Lockwood, D., 33
Logan, Australia, 200
London, 12
London Borough, 199
London Thames Gateway, 195–6
Lord Mandelson, 11
Lowndes, V., 50
Lownsbrough, H., 148, 196, 198–9
Lozells riots, 79
Luton in Harmony campaign, 180–1

Macklin, G., 86, 101
Malik, K., 188
Mansouri, F., 34, 183
Martell, L., 183
Mason, A., 135, 201
Mateos, P., 118
McGann, J., 10, 23
McGhee, D., 35–6, 96, 103–4, 108, 168, 182, 185
McLuhan, M., 7
Meer, N., 67, 141–2
Merkel, A., 54, 116, 137, 204
Messina, A., 85
Miah, R., 73

middle class, 33–4
Migrant Integration Policy Index
    (MIPEX), 133, 158–60
migration, 164
  in Britain, 112
  citizenship tests and, 25
  defensive multiculturalism and, 55
  Far Right, opposition to, 83, 85, 87,
      133, 173
  functional segregation and
      integration and, 133–4
  multiculturalism and, 12, 141, 173
  solidarity and, 15–16
  in United Kingdom, 35
  virtual connectedness and
      increased, 6–7
  in Wales, 12
Migration Policy Group, 133, 158
miniaturization of people, 21
minority communities
  beleaguered, 20
  in Britain, 54
  country, importance of, 19
  cultural changes within, 47
  cultural distinctiveness of, 67–8
  defensive multiculturalism for, 54
  Far Right, opposition to, 63, 68,
      83–4, 173
  globalisation, as cause of, 6
  heritage in, protection of, 47, 54
  identity conflicts within, 30
  interculturalism in, 88
  multiculturalism in, management
      of, 57–8
  racial harassment of, 124–5
  racism in, 88
  segregated, 122
  segregation and integration in, 195
  social changes within, 47
  spatial segregation and integration
      in, 124–6
Mirza, M., 49
mixed communities, 174, 196
mixed race communities, 21
  Asian communities in, 22, 59–60
  children dealing with notion of
      being, 39
  collective identities in, 60
  ethnicity and, 40

Far Right, opposition to, 56
  identity politics and, omission
      from, 32
  interfaith unions and, 40
  of natural families, 41
  personal identities in, 60
mixed race hybridity, 41
mixed race identities, 37–41
mixed race unions, 41
mixité, 81
Modood, T., 36, 59, 67, 78, 141–2, 188
monocultural identities, 32
monoculturalism, 14, 32, 39, 48, 49, 51
Moore, K., 42–3
Muir, R., 28, 34, 75–6, 108–10
multiculturalism, 1–2. *See also*
      multiculturalism policies; specific
      types of
  in Asians communities, 5
  assimilationist model of, 72
  of Black communities, 5
  blaming minorities for, 59, 60, 101
  British, 112
  British liberal, 56
  Canada's adoption of, 63–4, 154
  collective identity, impact on, 14
  concept of, 141
  critique of, 156
  debate over, 14
  defensive, 47, 54–63, 92
  description of, 53
  failure of, 14, 42, 53–90, 195
  faith and, component of, 72
  Far Right and, populist appeal of,
      82–8
  foundational elements of, 142
  global communications and, 62
  ideology of, 54
  language of, 67
  legacy of, 172
  in majority communities,
      management of, 57–8
  migration and, 12, 141, 173
  race and, 30, 51, 77–82, 141
  rebalancing of, 67
  rejection of, 153
  state, 68–76, 186
  super diversity and, 5, 12, 14, 62
  in White communities, 5

multiculturalism policies, 1, 32
  identity and, relationship
    between, 47
  identity politics and, 182
  intercultural model of, 52
  political processes in, 52
multicultural societies, 32
multicultural theory, 66
multi-ethnic Britain, 65
multiethnic communities, 72
multifaith communities, 72
  governance in, system of, 188–94
  secularism in, 188–94
Muslim communities
  Christians, relationship with, 138
  community cohesion in, 99
  cultural distinctiveness in, 204
  defensive multiculturalism in, 53–4
  demonization of, 136
  diaspora identities of, 20
  faith in, 72, 188
  faith in, privileging of, 71
  Far Right's role in, 46, 49–50
  as non-White minorities, 50
  separateness in, 137
Muslim identities, 46, 49, 75, 78, 204
Muslimness, 45

nation, 24–5, 27, 29, 30, 177
National Assembly, 203
national characteristics, 65
national communities, 83
national identities, 5, 19, 171, 208
  affinities and, 25
  constituting, 32
  distinctiveness of, 20
  downgrading, 179
  giving way to cultural identities, 27
  global communications, sustaining
    of, 21
  governmental views of, 22
  homogeneity of, 20
  identity politics and, 181–2
  integration and, 135
  local identities and, 109
  national conflict with, 29
  politics and, 76
  pre-eminence of, 27
  protecting, 138–9

  sensitizing, 30
  value-laden concepts of, 23
  weakening of, 20
nationalism, 20, 27–8, 208
  English, 186
  globalisation and, division between,
    83, 170–1
  linguistic, 104
  national conflict with, 29
  value-laden concepts of, 23
nationalities
  citizenship and, linking of, 25
  conceptualization of, 37
  country, components of, 19
  declining sense of, 18
  hyphenating of, 21
  mixedness in, 38
  mixed race communities of, 22
  of Muslim communities, 45
  race and, 51
nation building, 26
nation-state, 24
  end to, 7, 27
  interconnectednessn of, 9
  multiculturalism policies in, 53
NATO, 46
naturalization, 134
Nature of Prejudice, The, 145
navigational skills, development of,
  206–12
Netherlands, 67
Neville-Jones, (P) Baroness, 43
newcomers, 180
New Labour, 35, 95–6
9/11 terrorist attacks, 42, 77
no-go areas, 140, 174
non-governmental organizations
  (NGOs), 9–10, 205–6, 207
non-White British identities, 12
non-White minorities, 50
Norris, P., 19–20, 28
Northern Ireland
  bridge building in, 147
  diversity in, 166
  ethnic classifications in, 145
  faith in, 70
  hate crimes in, 165
  Irish communities in, 75
  sectarian conflict in, 80

Northern Ireland – *continued*
    spatial segregation in, 115
    spatial separation in, 127
Norway, 83–4

Obama, President, 38
Office of the Deputy Prime
    Minister, 92
OPENCites project, 162–3
openness
    city, 164
    interculturalism and, 142,
        158–63
    international, 133–4
    OPENCites project on, 162–3
    super diversity and, 162
    understanding degrees of, 161–2
Open Society Foundations, 137
Organization for Co-operation and
    Economic Development (OECD),
    169
Organization for European Economic
    Co-operation (OEEC), 169
Orwell, George, 27
Osler, A., 70
Oslo, Norway, 199–200
otherness, 21, 62, 143
others, 1
    community cohesion and, 110
    defining, 26
    demonization of, 14–15
    discrimination of, 49
    Far Right, threat of, 82
    fear of, 86, 194
    hate crime of, 103
    hostility of, 66, 86
    ignorance of, 88
    mistrust of, 88
    misunderstanding, 57
    Muslim communities as, 50, 84
    perception of, 15
    prejudices of, 117
    respect for, 139
    suspicion of, 66
O'Toole, T., 20
Our Shared Future, 68
'our shared future' concept, 109
Ouseley, H., 60, 86, 94
Ouseley Report, 94

out-groups, 117
Oxfam, 205

Pacific Islanders, 34
paradox of diversity, 14, 27, 87–8, 160
parallel lives, 15, 57
    in clustered communities, 122
    ethnicity and, 126
    segregation and, 132
    segregation and integration and,
        194
    spatial segregation and integration
        and, 127
    spatial separation and, 127
parallel societies, 15
Parekh, B., 58–9, 65, 188
Paris, 34
Park, A., 179
Party for Freedom (PVV), 85
peaceful co-existence, 156–7
Penninx, R., 118
personal identities, 207
    concept of, 143
    in mixed race communities, 60
    multiculturalism, impact on, 14
    nation and, protection of, 24
    state, establishment by, 10
Phillips, D., 122
Phillips, T., 119, 195
Place Survey, 79
Platt, L., 13, 38, 41, 184
Playing for Change, 206
Polish identities, 36
political correctness, 41, 57, 113, 120
political identities, 32, 36, 85
Pollard, S., 129
populism, xenophobic, 87
populist extremist parties (PEPs), 82–4
positive action, 75, 135
post-race society, 78
Poulsen, M., 117, 120
poverty, 61–3, 97–8
Powell, D., 21, 47, 55
prejudices, 14–15, 62, 99, 100–1, 103,
        104, 151, 167
    in closed communities, 167
    effects of, 146
    ethnicity and, 117
    of Far Right, 165

intercultural dialogue and, 145–7
intergroup, 145
manifestations of, 146
of others, 117
of out-groups, 117
psychological bases for, 145–6
reducing, 145–7
social solidarity, impact on, 145
Prevent Strategy, 42–6, 182
primordial distinctions, 30
primordial identities, 36
progressive multiculturalism, 47,
    63–8, 157
British approach to, 65
conception of, 67, 73
cultural distinctiveness of, 67–8
development of, 63–4
exclusion and, 66
inclusion and, 66
layers of separation in, 66
paradigm of, 68
scapegoating and, 66
segregation and, 66
Protestant communities, 25, 190
Public Interest Research Centre, 205
public spaces, 197–9
pure breeds, 22
pure identities, 48, 186
pure origins, 37, 38
Putnam, R.D., 15–16, 104, 197

Quebec, 16

race
binary Black/White opposites, 78
biological superiority of, 48, 173
Black identities, 79–80
children, importance to, 39
class and, tendencies of relationship
    between, 99
community cohesion and, 81–2,
    98–9
concept of, 37, 77
culture and, 32–3, 36
differences and, 82, 163–5
dual (*See* mixed race communities)
ethnic identities and, 49
ethnicity and, 30, 51, 77–8, 98–9
ethno-cultural diversity and, 80–1

faith and, 30, 51, 77
Far Right and, 101
Far Right's views on, 47
hybrid identities and, 49, 51
idea of, 30, 168
identities and, linkage between, 36,
    47–8, 51
intercultural conception of, 81
interculturalism and, 51, 142, 153
in minority communities, 88
mixed communities of, 196
multiculturalism and, 30, 51, 77–82,
    141
nationality and, 51
political superiority of, 173
pure, 52
salience of, 49–50
in segregated communities, 129
segregation and, 122, 132, 194
social context of, 168
static concepts of, 39
in United Kingdom, 79
in Western countries, 77
race (tick) box, 187
race relations acts, 77, 121–2
race riots, 81–2, 96
racial identities, 40, 48
racial purity, 22, 37, 39
racism, 47–8, 97, 99
biological, 82–3
in Black communities, 79
Black/White, 78
in Britain, 65
community cohesion and, 97–8
defensive multiculturalism,
    protection from, 54
defining, 82
ethnicity and, 62
in minority communities, 88
multiculturalism policies on, 48, 49,
    56–7
poverty and, 61–2
science of, 146
towards ethnic minorities, 127
in White communities, 79
Ratcliffe, P., 66, 188
regional identities, 5, 18–20
religious beliefs, 192–4
religious diaspora identities, 20

religious identities, 5, 21, 73, 101
religious schools, 185
Report of the Independent Review Team, 91
Rethinking Multiculturalism, 58
right(s), 93, 134
    equal, 168–9
    freedom of, 184
    functional segregation and integration and, 132–3
    inalienable, 169
    individual, 96, 170
    to openness, 158–9
    responsibilities and, 192, 201
    separate but equal, 158
Ritchie, D., 94
Ritzen, J., 178
Roebuck, E., 148
Roma communities, 74, 128
Romanian, 36
roots, idea of, 168
Runnymede Trust, 71, 193
Russia, 141

Sachs, J., 190
sameness, 36, 104
Sampson, R., 115, 121–2
Sandercock, L., 134, 139, 156, 167, 210
Sarkozy, N., 54, 116, 138, 204
Saxony, 23
Scotland, 17, 24
Searchlight Educational Trust, 18–19
secessionist movements, 16, 17
Second World War, 33, 176
sectarianism, 166
secularism, 188–94
    decision-making process and, 190
    defensive multiculturalism and, 59
    defining, 188
    faith in public realm, 188–90
    interculturalism, component of, 188
segregated communities, 129
segregation, 100
    in Belgium, 137
    in Britain, 112, 119–20
    in Canada, 118
    challenging, 132
    community cohesion and, 100–1

conceptualizing, 114
concerns about, 140
debates over, 122
de facto, 196
defining, 113–14
in England, 119
entrenchment and, 194
ethnicity and, 101
in Europe, 118, 130, 137
Far Right and, 132
fears of others, 194
in France, 137
globalisation and, 140
interculturalism and, 142
intervening in, 128
labour market, 130–1
layers of, 114
levels of, 117
in minority communities, 88, 121, 195
myth of, 121
natural phenomenon of, 194–5
nature of, 114–15, 122
parallel lives and, 132, 194
principal components of, 134
problematic forms of, 129
progressive multiculturalism and, 66
residential, 70–1, 117, 118, 120, 194
in Roma communities, 128
school, 70–1, 120, 123–4
spatial, 114–15
spatial segregation and integration and, 129
super diversity and, 140
in United Kingdom, 118, 120–1, 194
in United States, 115, 117, 118, 125–6, 194
virtuous circle of, 125
in White communities, 117–18
workplace, 124
segregation and integration, 112–40.
    See also specific types of
    in Canada, 202–3
    clustered communities, 122
    common languages in, 201–2
    common values in, 205
    of communities, 113
    conceptual definition of, 113–14
    core values of, 203–4

development of, 195–6
domains of, 113–16
entitlement to, 201
entrenchment and, 194
evaluation of, 197–8
faith and, 204
fears of others, 194
freedom of choice and, 195
functional, 132–6
government intervention in, 194
intercultural city report, 199–201
interculturalism and, 194–206
in minority communities, 195
in mixed communities, 194–7
national values and, 204
nature of, 114–15
non-governmental organizations
    role in, 205–6
parallel lives and, 194
physical, 114
promoting, 206
public spaces, 197–9
rights and responsibilities, 201
separate identities, 204–5
social and cultural, 129–32
spatial, 114, 116–29
understanding, 206
in United Kingdom, 112–13
values and, 136–40
Seko, K., 48
Seldon, A., 130
self-identity, 38
self-segregation, 59–61, 125
Semyonov, M., 97, 117–18, 121–2
Sen, A., 4, 14, 21, 32, 44–5, 48–9, 74
separate but equal development
    notion, 121
separate identities, 17, 27, 181–2,
    204–5
separateness, 55, 57–8, 137
separation
    of communities, 141
    doctrine of, 188
    institutional, 72
    interculturalism and, 153–4
    layers of, 39, 66, 114, 194
    spatial segregation and integration
        and, 128
separatism, 66, 69–70, 72

separatist ideologies, 14, 87
separatist movements, 16, 18, 27
sexual orientation, 50, 51, 62, 174
Shah, H., 183
shared political community,
    importance of, 134–5
shared society, 14, 88, 174
shared spaces, 148
Sharkey, P., 115, 121–2
Sikhs, 184, 189
Simpson, L., 59, 66, 120–1
Singh, Darra, 107
single diaspora identities, 138
single identities, 37, 40, 69–70, 73
single identity funding, 73, 136, 185,
    186, 193, 210–11
singular identities, 39–40, 48
Slattery, B., 22
Smith, M., 99, 100
social and cultural segregation and
    integration, 129–32
social apartheid, 129–30
social balance, 196
social capital, 15, 116, 122, 150, 197
    bonding, 130
    bridging, 130
social changes, 18, 33, 36, 47, 50–1
social class, 32–4, 196
social exclusivity, 130
social hierarchies, class-based, 33
social identities, 36, 187
social intermixing, 39
socialization, 31, 61
social media, 2, 6, 23, 35, 171
social mobility, 122–3
social networks, 116
social psychology, 145, 146
social solidarity, 15, 16, 23, 145
sociological theory, 146
solidarity, 2
    of Black communities, 78, 79
    collective identities and, 18, 82
    cosmopolitan identities and, 35
    of minority communities, 79
    multiculturalism and, 75
    national, 159, 171
    personal identities and, 82
Solomos, J., 37
Sondhi, R., 57–8, 61, 152, 156

sovereignty, 2
  erosion of, 22
  in France, 83
  globalisation and, 9
  international, erosion of, 9
  of nation-state, 7, 17, 27
  pretense of, 9
  state, 26–7
  states loss of, 19
Soviet Union, 24, 81
Soysal, Y.N., 190
Spain, 12, 25, 141
spatially distinctive communities, 65
spatial segregation, 114–15, 127
spatial segregation and integration,
      114, 116–29
  clarifying, 116
  clustered communities, 122
  in closed communities, debates
      over, 122
  concepts of, 116–17
  defensive multiculturalism and,
      121–2
  disabilities and, 128–9
  employment and, 124
  ethnicity and, 126–7
  growth of, 121
  gypsies and, 127–8
  harassment and, 124–5
  interventions in, 128
  locational factors for, 122–3
  in migrant communities, 118
  in minority communities, 124–6
  nature of, 118–19
  objectives of, 117–18
  parallel lives and, 127
  patterns of, 115
  school segregation and, 123–4
  segregation and, 129
  separation and, 128
  social contracts and, 123
  travelers and, 127–8
  in United Kingdom, 118–20, 122,
      126
  in United States, 118, 120–2
Sriskandarajah, D., 16, 32, 39, 40
state
  collective identities, establishment
      by, 10, 51

  common culture in, 32
  emotional attachment to, 25
  faith and, separation of, 72
  institutional framework for,
      development of, 25–6
  of interculturalism, 153
  national value system of, 26, 174
  personal identities, establishment
      by, 10
  super diversity in, 181
state multiculturalism, 32, 53–4, 64,
      68–76, 186
  concentrated reflexive monitoring,
      76
  concept of, 69–70
  culture and, 71
  definition of, 68
  deprivation and, 74–5
  disadvantages of, 74
  discrimination and, 74–5
  flagging of identity, 75
  identity politics and, 75–6
  intercultural model of, 76
  in migrant communities, 73–4
  positive action and, 75
  promotion of, 69
  separatism and, 69–72
  single identity and, 73
static identities, 40
statism, decline of, 19
steel bands and samosas' critique,
      147
stereotyping, 14–15, 96–8, 103, 128,
      150, 151, 167
Stone, L., 28, 34
Sudan, 16
super diversity, 4–29
  challenges of, 174–5, 207
  collective identities, impact on, 52
  differences and, 171
  era of, 31
  functional segregation and
      integration and, 136
  interculturalism and, 90, 111
  meaning of, 32
  multiculturalism and, 5, 12, 14, 62
  multiculturalism policies on, 49
  of nation-state, 32, 36

navigational skills and intercultural competences and, development of, 208
openness and, 162
personal identities, impact on, 52
segregation and, 140
supra-national agencies, 8–9, 11
supra-national claims, 27
supranational currency union, 18
supra-national identities, 185–6
swamping, 86
Syria, 8

Taylor, C., 154–5, 202
technological changes, 6, 8
telephony, 6
tensions, 14, 18, 101, 172–3
terrorism, 8, 42, 44, 46, 131
Think Global, 205
Thomas, P., 91, 96, 101–2, 104, 108, 146
tick boxes, 31, 40, 48
Tilley, J., 130
Times, The, 18
Titley, G., 66–7, 95
transitory identities, 30
transnational identities, 51
transnationalism, 12
travelers, 127–8
tribal communities, 30
tribal groups, 25–6, 29, 45
tribes. *See* identities
trust, 93, 150
Tunstall, R., 126
Turkish migrants, 34
two solitude's, 15
2001 reports, 94, 96–7, 101, 106

UK Independence Party (UKIP), 87
United Kingdom
Black history month project in, 182
British National Party in, 84, 86–7, 98
church schools in, 193
collective identities in, 28
community cohesion in, 22–3, 91, 102–3, 105–6, 113
Community Cohesion Unit in, 94–5
cross-party political agreements in, 178
cultural markers in, 138
differences in, 166–7
discrimination in, policies on, 112
diversity in, 189
employment in, 208
Equality Act 2010 of, 166–7
ethnic classifications in, 40, 145
ethnic monitoring in, 135
extremism in, 86
faith in, 71–2, 77, 184–5, 190–1
Far Right in, support for, 97–8, 105
foreign-born populations in, 16
gender, established basis of, 50
hate crimes in, 165
identity in, 86
identity politics in, 182
Institute of Community Cohesion in, 84
integration in, 112, 128
interaction in, 102–3
intercultural dialogue in, 144–5
interculturalism in, 141
Irish communities in, 75
Jewish communities in, 184, 190
Labour Party in, 11
language requirements in, 202
middle class in, 33
migration in, 35, 105
mixed race communities in, 38, 126
multiculturalism policies in, 56–7
Muslim communities in, 46, 69, 184
national identities in, 28
national league table in, 15
navigational skills and intercultural competences in, development of, 209–10
openness in, 160
personal identities in, 18–19
race in, 79, 81–2
race relations acts in, 77, 121–2
racial harassment in, 128
Roma community in, 49
school segregation in, 123–4, 209
segregation and integration in, 112–13
segregation in, 118, 120–1, 194

United Kingdom – *continued*
  social and cultural segregation and
    integration in, 130
  social exclusivity in, 130
  social segregation in, 122
  spatial segregation and integration
    in, 118–20
  super diversity in, 40
  terrorist prevention program
    (Prevent Strategy) in, 42–6, 182
  tourism to/from, 7
  UK Independence Party (UKIP), 87
  White host communities in, 79–80,
    84, 185–6
  workplace segregation in, 124
United Nations Charter, 168–9
United States
  bridge building in, 147
  Christians in, 72, 188
  ethnic racism in, 121
  faith in, 72, 188
  foreign-born population statistics
    in, 31
  integration policies in, 133
  Italian community in, 49
  middle class in, 33
  minority communities in, 118
  miscegenation in, 37
  physical segregation in, 137
  racism in, 121
  school segregation in, 114, 123–4,
    137
  segregation in, 115, 117, 118,
    125–6, 194
  social justice in, 56
  sorting of neighborhoods in, 122
  spatial segregation and integration
    in, 118, 120–2
  White communities in, 120–1
unity, diversity within, 67
universal Black identities, 78
Universal Declaration of Human
  Rights, 169
universalism, 47, 67

values, 47, 65
  added, 71
  common, 94, 108–9, 204, 205, 208
  concerns about, 140

core, 203–4
country-specific, 205
democratic, 64
differences in, 136
of diversity, 105, 158
extrinsic, 205
fundamental, 154
ideology and, fundamental
  differences between, 62
of interculturalism, 88
intrinsic, 205
living apart, 137
local identity and, 139
national, 139–40, 174, 204
national governments role in, 139
over-arching, 67
of segregation, 116
segregation and integration and,
  136–40
self-expression, 33
separate, 136
separateness, 137–8
shared, 114, 135, 136–7, 208
state role in, 138–9
universal, 47, 139–40, 205
virtual networks, growth of, 138
Western, 46
vanishing kingdoms, 23
Varshney, A., 147, 149, 197, 207
vertical identities, 34
virtual connectedness, 2, 6–7
vision, 94, 174, 176–81, 205
vision statement, 179
voluntary agencies, 210
voting, 177

Wales
  affinities of, 24
  Catholic Education Service for, 71
  hate crimes in, 165
  migration in, 12
  mixed race communities in, 38
  nation of, 24
  non-White British in, 12
'we,' 16, 26, 29
Weber, M., 24
Weiner, E., 104
Western democracies, 45–6, 76
Western identities, 42

Western societies, 18, 20–1
What Works in Community Cohesion, 104
White British identities, 41
White communities
    Black identities *vs.* differentiating, 80
    country, importance of, 19
    exclusionary nature of, 132
    mixed race communities of, 22
    multiculturalism and, 5
    openness in, 163
    parallel lives in, 113
    personal identities of, 19
    racial minorities in, 126
    racism in, 79
    segregation in, 117–18
    in United States, 120–1
White Flight, 60, 120, 121, 195
White host communities, 79–80, 84, 185–6
White identities, 79

White Irish identities, 79
White on White violence, 80
Wildsmith, E., 184
Winder, R., 55
Windsor, P., 144
Wolfe, A., 76
Wolf, M., 29
Women's Movement, 50
Wood, P., 155, 160–2, 183, 198
working class, 33
Workplace segregation, 124
World Bank, 12
World Trade Organization, 12
World Wildlife Fund, 205

xenophobia, 56–7
xenophobic populism, 87

Younge, G., 17, 45, 74, 85, 170–1
Young, P., 147
Yugoslavia, 147